ZION BEFORE ZIONISM

1838–1880

ARNOLD BLUMBERG

DEVORA PUBLISHING

JERUSALEM ◆ NEW YORK

Zion Before Zionism, 1838–1880.
Published by Devora Publishing Company
Text Copyright © 2007 by Arnold Blumberg

First edition published in 1985 by Syracuse University Press, Syracuse,
New York. All rights subsequently transferred to the author.

COVER DESIGN: David Yaphe
TYPESETTING: Jerusalem Typesetting
EDITORIAL AND PRODUCTION MANAGER: Daniella Barak
EDITOR: Sybil Ehrlich

Hard Cover ISBN: 978-1-932687-82-8
Includes index

E-mail: publisher@devorapublishing.com
Web Site: www.devorapublishing.com

Printed in Israel

To Raphael and Mona Blumberg
and Eva and Noam Livnat
who are my bridges to
Zion Before Zionism.

~ PREVIOUS PUBLICATIONS BY DR. ARNOLD BLUMBERG ~

Kovna, Two Street, and Jerusalem; Gem Printing, 2000.

The History of Israel; Greenwood Press, 1998.

Great Leaders, Great Tyrants? Contemporary Views of World Rulers Who Made History; Greenwood Press, 1995.

A Carefully Planned Accident, The Italian War of 1859; Associated University Presses, 1990.

A View from Jerusalem, 1849–1858: The Consular Diary of James and Elizabeth Anne Finn; Associated University Presses, 1980.

The Diplomacy of the Mexican Empire, 1863–1867; American Philosophical Society, 1971.

About the Author

Arnold Blumberg, *z"l*, was a history professor at Towson University for forty years and retired in 1998. He was described by the president of the University as a "rare breed" who had the ability to capture students' attention by his almost encyclopedic ability to add personal notes to the personalities and events that were part of the courses. He received his Ph.D. in modern European history at the University of Pennsylvania. During retirement, he and his wife, Thelma, lived in Israel where he passed away on July 10, 2006, at the age of 81. His six books include *A View from Jerusalem, 1849–1867* and *The History of Israel*.

Contents

Illustrations

Foreword

Arnold Blumberg, z"l Professor of History, Author, Lecturer

Arnold Blumberg, Professor of History at Towson University in Maryland for forty years, passed away in Jerusalem on July 10, 2006. He was born in Philadelphia in 1925, the son of Dr. and Mrs. Louis Blumberg. He served in the United States army during World War II, from ages 18 to 21. He was a scholar of mid-nineteenth century diplomatic European history and completed research in the archives of France, England, and Italy. In 1952 he earned his Ph.D. from the University of Pennsylvania.

Much respected by colleagues, and revered by students, he served as Professor of History at Towson University from 1958 to 1998. In 1995 he was winner of the Towson University President's award for distinguished service to the University. He was the author of seven books, with three of them relating to Palestine and Israel that were researched in the archives of Israel. Over fifty of his articles appeared in distinguished journals and his research was acclaimed by scholars world wide. During the '70s and '80s he wrote numerous perceptive articles in support of Israel, many of which appeared regularly in the Jewish Times of Baltimore.

Revealing with skill the challenges created by Israel's enemies, his constructive solutions were always upbeat.

An outstanding lecturer, he was a much sought-after speaker, nationwide, within the secular community, and at local schools and synagogues. His research was featured at a national conference of the combined Catholic and American Historical Societies, and he was invited frequently to read papers at universities. In the '70s, he was the first person known to be invited to debate an Egyptian diplomat on the Mid-East crisis.

Excerpts of comments by his son and daughter reveal:

My father was declared by Baltimore Magazine to be one of the 'ten smartest men in the City of Baltimore.' Certainly, through his writing, teaching and oratory, he had gained a reputation for brilliance. But at the end of the day, that God-given brilliance was not the main point. It was his character and true grit that stood out. He was an iconoclast. Like his namesake, Abraham Avinu, he was willing to hold opinions that were unpopular, without embarrassment, if he thought they were the truth. Thus, although he was raised in Philadelphia, a city that Jewishly was overwhelmingly headed towards assimilation, my father chose to readopt the Orthodoxy of his grandparents, at a time when almost no one else was headed in that direction.

Whenever Israel needed defending in the press, whenever a prominent anti-Semite said anything particularly spurious, my father would get numerous phone calls from people saying 'Dr. Blumberg, I hope you will be defending us!' and very often he did.

My father was known on the campus as a defender of Israel. Yet, an Arab student once approached him during Ramadan, when my father was scheduling a test at one o'clock in the afternoon. She explained that she would be fasting and the midday test would be hard for her. He immediately responded, "Come in at eight o'clock in the morning. I'll give you your test privately, before everyone else." The girl, who had apparently expected a different response, broke out in tears, and said, 'None of my other professors has shown a willingness to help me in this way.'

As a child growing up, his daughter recalls him baking challah (Sabbath bread) before every Sabbath, helping her with homework and passing on his love for Israel. In her words "He was the type of father who always had time for us".

In an article paying tribute to Dr. Blumberg, a colleague at Towson University, Dr. Evelyn Avery, has written of her memories and experiences, relating as follows:

As a new professor in 1974, I had inquired whether anyone on campus was involved with Jewish studies. Repeatedly Dr. Arnold Blumberg's name was mentioned as the one person with whom I should speak. When I first knocked on his office door he asked, 'and how can I help you, young lady?' Did he bow in a courtly way, or is it just my hazy recollection of this dignified gentleman? Quickly I learned that he had been having regular brown-bag lunches with students about Jewish history, culture, Israel, topics that they proposed. I volunteered to contribute my knowledge on literature and our partnership continued until we became advisors to the Jewish Student Association in the 1980s and acquired a cultural center on campus.

Meanwhile, one summer in the 1970s, I audited his very popular survey of Jewish History class. Sitting cross-legged on his desk, his eyes mischievously twinkling behind steel rimmed glasses, Professor Blumberg would mesmerize 30 or more lower classmen with a sweeping but thorough overview of Jewish history. From the Tanach (Bible) through Babylonian exile, Holocaust, and the State of Israel, he would move, armed with wall maps, facts and drama, his arm movement and facial expressions accompanying the process. Always scholarly but with a real passion for his subject, he was also interested in students' comments. I learned much more than Jewish history from auditing his class.

Following the memorial service for Dr. Blumberg held at the University, one colleague described the event in these terms:

It was my privilege to attend the awesome, beautiful tribute in loving memory of Dr. Arnold Blumberg. It was truly a memorable occasion. Each speaker eloquently described his qualities and characteristics: a scholar; a mentor; an author; a loving husband; a father and grandfather; a *mensch*; a teacher par excellence; a gifted, talented orator; an ardent Zionist; and a prince of a human being.

In Professor Blumberg's book, *Zion Before Zionism – 1838– 1880*, he employs the same talents that for thirty years he had employed to bring European History alive, and he now applies them to the Middle East, albeit with a largely European cast of characters. This work, within the context of the individual fascinating episodes that it describes, simultaneously documents how, in the larger scheme of things – even before the rise of the Zionism movement – thousands of Jews were already streaming to the Holy Land and Jerusalem was quickly becoming a city with a Jewish majority.

Contributed by colleagues and family

Preface

I originally intended to title this book, "Palestinians, Pashas, and Proconsuls, 1838–80." Earnest colleagues and friends dissuaded me, saying that however challenging such a title might be, it would seem far too mysterious to those who read historical works only for pleasure. Nevertheless, the three key words of the abandoned title describe, exactly, the thesis of the present work. Specifically, it examines the interplay between the native Palestinian population, the essentially foreign Turkish government imposed on them, and the aggressive ambitions of Christian nations represented by their consuls. The dates 1838–80 are also unique as delineations of a great historical watershed.

During the eighteenth century, Jerusalem had been the administrative center of a more or less stable sanjak. The first generations of the nineteenth century had witnessed its loss of status as a Pasha's seat. It had become a decayed town of fewer than 10,000 inhabitants. Foreign non-Moslems were absolutely denied the right of permanent residence in the Holy City.

Palestine was regarded as merely an appendage of Lebanon and Syria. The rebellious Viceroy of Egypt, Mehmet Ali, was about to throw the dice in his greatest gamble, attempting to tear all of

Syria, Palestine, and the Sinai Desert from the hands of his liege lord, the sultan of Turkey.

The Egyptian viceroy lost his gamble, but he fired a series of dynamite charges which changed the face of Palestine forever. In their aftermath the Turks gave serious attention to the local government of Palestine and Syria, dividing those territories into sanjaks, pashaliks, or provinces, each under its own governor. Jerusalem became the seat of a pasha who was subject to the *musheer* of Beirut, as the latter was subject to the wali of Damascus, the whole subject, of course, to the Sublime Porte at Constantinople. Jerusalem's isolation was ended. Foreign consuls and foreign churchmen pressed in upon the newly rediscovered city.

Most important of all, 1838 marks the first year in which the Turks recognized the right of foreign non-Moslems to lease property for permanent residence in a city sacred to Islam. It was to be another twelve years before the purchase of property by foreign infidels became possible at the Holy City. It was to be a full twenty years before the Turks codified a Land Registry Law in 1858. Nevertheless, the mere beginning of permanent residence at Jerusalem for foreign Jews and Christians makes 1838 a milestone year.

This book studies the interaction of the European, Turkish, and Palestinian natives for a forty-year period.

This work closes in 1880 because it is the last year before the great Jewish immigration began. Indeed, the Turks had begun the systematic colonization of non-Palestinian Moslems, notably Circassians and Algerians, in 1878. After 1880, the forces of nascent Jewish nationalism, foreign Moslem colonization sponsored by the Turks, and spontaneous Arab immigration prompted by the new prosperity of Palestine changed the demographic face of the land.

A great body of scholarly and popular literature has examined the history of the country since 1881. Israeli scholars have examined the condition of Palestinian Jewry before that date. Their work has reached a relatively narrow reading public because it is in Hebrew. Almost nothing, however, has been written in any language which attempts to describe the interaction between the Turkish masters of Palestine, the natives of the country, and the Europeans who entered the land before 1881.

It is, therefore, important for any study of what is today modern Israel to examine the years 1838–80. Those crucial forty-two years form the unique and essential incubative time period without which Zionism could never have prospered in Zion.

A Glossary may be found at the end of this work containing definitions of foreign words encountered in the text. Such words are in italics.

Acknowledgments

I n 1982, Towson State University offered me a research sabbatical leave which made this work possible. The university's Research Committee extended generous grants as a further encouragement. Thus, I was enabled to enlarge upon a research interest which I had developed during a previous sabbatical in 1975.

The greater part of my work, both in 1975 and in 1982, was completed at the Israel State Archives at Jerusalem. I am happy to have renewed a debt of gratitude to Dr. P.A. Alsberg, the State Archivist, who coupled his native courtesy with a flattering interest in my work. The entire staff of the State Archives did everything possible to enable me to make the most efficient use of my limited time. I am particularly appreciative of kindnesses shown me by Gilad Livneh, Research Consultant in the Reading Room of the Archives.

At the Central Archives for the History of the Jewish People, housed at the Hebrew University in Jerusalem, I am cognizant of the informal and friendly way in which I was offered assistance by Aryeh Segall, Assistant Director, and Rivka Gurvich, Librarian. Dr. Dov Schidorsky, the Director of the Israel National Library, shared his own research interests with me and was kind enough to offer me faculty privileges at the library.

In the many libraries in which I worked in the United States, I contracted special debts of gratitude to the staffs of the Cook Library and Media Services of Towson State University. I am most cognizant of the attention I received there from Debra Berlanstein, Eleanore Hofstetter, Helen Kaltenborn, Susan Mower, Michael O'Neill, Robert Shouse, and Carolyn Westbrook. The Reference Services of the United States Library of Congress also offered their usual prompt and courteous service.

Finally, I wish to thank those friends and colleagues who have prepared teaching schedules that make research possible, shared their own scholarly findings, or lent me their support in obtaining grants or in expediting the sabbatical leave that was essential to this work. At Towson State University these individuals included Professors Bette Bonder, Annette Chappell, Dean Esslinger, Jenny Jochens, Mary Catherine Kahl, Armin Mruck, Patricia Plante, Myron Scholnick, and Mark Whitman.

Those to whom I owe gratitude include distinguished colleagues at other institutions, notably Moses Aberbach and Robert O. Freedman, respectively Professor of History and Dean of the Graduate School at Baltimore Hebrew College, as well as Professors Lynn M. Case of the University of Pennsylvania, Moshe Davis of Hebrew University, David S. Landes and Bruce Kupelnick, both of Harvard University, Kenneth W. Stein of Emory University, Daniel Thomas of the University of Rhode Island, Bernard Wasserstein of Brandeis University, and Gedalia Yogev of Tel Aviv University.

Georges Dethan, Conservateur en Chef of the French Foreign Ministry Archives, provided detailed information on the careers of French consuls at Jerusalem. Similarly, His Excellency Mr. Alexander Philon, Chargé d'Affaires at the Embassy of Greece at Washington, provided me with the names and dates of service of Greek consuls at Jerusalem. Jose Lozano, Director of the Archivo General of the Spanish Ministry of Foreign Affairs, provided me with the same information concerning Spanish consuls at Jerusalem.

Jonah Wahrman, formerly a classroom teacher who is today one of Jerusalem's most scholarly tourist guides, was a walking encyclopedia of the city's traditions. The Reverend Arten Ashjian, Canon Sacrist of St. Vartan Cathedral of the Armenian Church of America at New York, and Father Constantine M. Monios, Dean of the Greek Orthodox Cathedral of the Annunciation at Baltimore, were very helpful in providing details about the history of their churches at Jerusalem.

I am grateful to Wayne Stoler, whose personal attention to the details of word processing ensured the technical success of this work. Mrs. Annette Klein, who typed the greater part of the manuscript, bore my illegible script stoically and encouraged me by demonstrating an enthusiasm for this book which went far beyond the call of duty. Mary Bowersox and Mrs. Barbara Sandaal, the very able secretaries of Towson's History Department, were, as always, the good right arms of those who count on them.

Finally, my wife Thelma has been content for more than thirty years to share me with my friends in the nineteenth century. Without her patient support, none of my work would be possible.

Notwithstanding everything I have stated, I assume full responsibility for anything committed to print in this book, unless specifically credited to some other translator or writer. Diffidently, I confide my work to the kind indulgence of its readers.

Arnold Blumberg
Baltimore, Maryland
January 1, 1985

CHAPTER ONE

The Land; Palestine in 1841

A visitor to Palestine in 1841 had to be driven by strong motivation to make such a journey. Most of those who came ashore intending a lengthy stay were on religious pilgrimage. Nothing else would have induced anyone with an instinct for self-preservation to visit a country effectively isolated from the centers of commerce and politics elsewhere in the Mediterranean world.[1]

There was not a single road in all of Palestine until 1867 when Jaffa and Jerusalem were linked along the natural line of the old pilgrim trail. A second, connecting Jerusalem and Nablus, was constructed in 1870.[2]

The master of a small, coastal, wind-propelled freighter might anchor at Gaza, Jaffa, Haifa, or Acre to sell goods or to pick up cargo. Unless he carried products specifically ordered by a Palestinian merchant, he was likely to stop in those ports only to fill an open space in his hold or to unload a bit of cargo unsold elsewhere.[3]

Coastal freighters regarded Alexandria, Beirut, or Constantinople as their home bases. Their arrival at the four principal Palestinian ports was rarely part of a long-scheduled voyage. The vicissitudes of tides or weather, the demands of merchants, or decisions made on impulse determined a Palestinian destination. A ship's captain might with equal certainty set out from Constantinople, Beirut, or Alexandria for Smyrna, the Antiochan coast, Latakia, Tripoli, Sidon, or Tyre. Vessels carrying merchandise could anchor at a dock in Gaza, Acre, or Haifa. Captains carrying pilgrims bound for Jerusalem, however, chose Jaffa in most cases, simply because it was the closest point on the seacoast to the principal trail leading to the Holy City. There was no possibility, however, of tying up at a dock for an uneventful disembarkation. The ancient harbor from which the Biblical Jonah had made his voyage was long forgotten. A graphic description by a United States consul captures the desolate scene.

Ships anchored off Jaffa, 1880. From Sir Charles Wilson,
Picturesque Palestine, Sinai and Egypt, *London, J.F. Virtue, 1884*

As there is no commercial intercourse between this Consular district and the United States, I have not deemed it necessary to send any report to the Department. There is no harbor at Jaffa; and the anchorage is unsafe, a great part of the time, between the months of November and May. The export trade of Jaffa is insignificant, consisting of a small quantity of grain, sesame, and oranges, carried principally in French and Austrian vessels.

There can be no profitable commerce with Palestine, until a safe harbor is made at Jaffa. The old harbor, to the north of the city, which existed in the time of Solomon, is now filled with sand, and covered with orchards of orange trees. These orchards are valuable, and it would be necessary to purchase them, before the old harbor could be excavated, which last could be easily done, but an expensive seawall would be necessary to protect the shipping from the South West winds which prevail with great violence during the six months above mentioned.

There is not the slightest prospect that this work will be undertaken by the Turkish Government.[4]

A small freighter, depending upon the roughness of the sea, would come as close to the shore as safety permitted, usually seeking the shelter of that ancient jetty called the Andromeda Rocks, and the passengers would make their way to the beach as best they could. Some leaped into the sea and walked ashore. Others hired small rowboats which ferried passengers and baggage for a price determined after much haggling. Individual Arabs distinguished for their strength sold their services carrying passengers piggyback over the waves. The very wealthy or delicate could even obtain the service of a palanquin, a covered litter carried through the surf by four men.[5]

The freighters' deck hands were Greeks, Arabs, African blacks, or occasionally Europeans of indeterminate nationality, the latter often wanted by the police in their homeland. The masters of coastal freighters were most often Greek, but a sprinkling of other Mediterranean ethnic stocks was represented.[6] The lingua franca of the Eastern Mediterranean continued to be a primitive Italian, as it had been since the days of Venetian and Genoese dominion on the eastern seas.[7] The merchants in the Palestinian ports were native Armenians, Jews, and native or foreign Greeks and Italians. Relatively few of the commercial houses in the Palestinian ports were owned by Moslem Arabs.[8]

The ties between Europe and the ports of the Levant were extremely tenuous before 1840. Steamboats made the voyage to Constantinople, but a traveler who counted on a schedule was usually disappointed. In 1840, however, the British Post Office signed a contract with the Peninsular and Oriental Steam Navigation Company to carry mail between Southampton, England, and Alexandria, Egypt. One round trip per month was to be completed. Actual sea travel time was to be fifteen days. With this modest beginning, it became relatively easy for western Europeans to reach Alexandria.[9] Once there, they could hire a native dragoman or interpreter who would haunt the waterfront until he found a wind-driven coastal freighter heading for a specific Palestinian port. The European traveler, once safely aboard such a vessel, was well advised to sleep on deck, preferably with a watchful companion at his side, his money strapped to his body. Fortunately, the run from Alexandria to Palestinian ports was short, but the prudent traveler timed his journey between April and October, the months when it was least likely that his night's sleep on the deck would be interrupted by rain.[10]

Once ashore, the stranger who came to Palestine as a pilgrim in 1841 was sharply reminded that he had better adjust to reality, or face the gravest danger. The newly arrived European, whether a pilgrim at Jaffa heading for Jerusalem or a merchant at Acre hoping to visit Nazareth or Safed, made it his first business to buy protection.

All of the principal towns of Ottoman Palestine were walled. The walls, manned by Turkish soldiers and by locally conscripted Arabs, were vital to the security of urban populations planted in the midst of an extremely dangerous countryside. The gates of the cities were locked at night, and no one entered or departed between sunset and dawn.

Protection for the traveler who ventured outside the walls

usually could be purchased from a number of sources, more or less trustworthy. The consuls of foreign powers were most dependable. Local merchants, who had learned the techniques required to ensure the safety of their own merchandise as it traveled inland, were almost as safe. Least dependable was the self-advertised dragoman, interpreter and guide, or cicerone. The latter was likely to be a thief who would strip the traveler of all he possessed and leave him to fate.

Protection, from whatever source it came, depended ultimately upon the ability of a non-Moslem city man to buy his way into the elaborate system of clan alliances prevailing in the territory to be traveled. A consul, merchant, or cicerone who wished to be sure of the safety of his protégés had to invite all the local Bedouin chiefs and village headmen to elaborate feasts. He had to receive the most solemn, formal assurances that anyone traveling under his protection would be treated as a guest of the Bedouin clan or the village through whose territory he passed.

Contemporary observers noted that under such protection a traveler, guided by a ten-year-old boy belonging to an allied Bedouin tribe, was offered hospitality and safety. The bold traveler who attempted to make a dash through the short sixty kilometers from Jaffa to Jerusalem without paying handsomely for protection faced almost certain robbery and very probable injury, without hope of redress.

It was this that made it profitable for the visitor to Jerusalem to wade through the surf at Jaffa rather than dock in comfort at Acre or Gaza. The much longer journey to Jerusalem from those places increased the danger and the expense in buying protection. Only a patron of truly diplomatic versatility could pretend to have dependable alliances with all the clans in a wider territory, many of them at war with one another.[11]

The traveler, whether his destination was Hebron, Jerusalem, Nablus, Safed, or Tiberias, would have to leave the narrow coastal plain and ascend the mountainous spine of Palestine. The trails, following the easiest pathways through the mountains, were worn smooth by centuries of the passage of camel, horse, and mule. On all sides, enemies could see the traveler from the heights without being seen. With a suddenness peculiar to Palestine, the traveler might ascend from sea level to a height of more than 1200 meters, then descend again in the valley of the Dead Sea to the lowest point on the face of the earth, 395 meters below sea level.[12] In the winter, rain and even snow might make the mountains impassable. In the summer, the debilitating dry heat of an unshaded trail might make travel at night the only tolerable means of making progress, provided that a bright moon gave light.

In the midst of so many other perils designed to deter casual tourist travel, pestilence stalked the land. An enormous infant mortality rate affected all elements of the population and prevented rapid population growth. Well into the twentieth century, western visitors expressed horror at the sight of children, their eyes covered with stinging insects, who made no effort to sweep away their tormenters. Trachoma made blindness common. North of the Sea of Galilee, a stagnant swamp in the Hula Valley provided a breeding ground for the anopheles mosquito, and made malaria endemic.[13]

At the heart of the land lay those fortified, walled cities, none of them more populous than a village in 1841. Jerusalem, the largest, had only 14,000 inhabitants. Even twenty years later when more exact counts became available, Hebron had only 5,000 – 10,000; Nablus had only 8,000; Jaffa, Safed, Bethlehem and Nazareth 3,000 each; and Gaza had risen to 15,000 – 16,000. Even at the end of the century, Haifa with its great natural seaport had only 6,000 inhabitants and was overshadowed by nearby Acre.[14] Nowhere else in the world were there cities so gigantic in their symbolic meaning for so much of humanity, yet so insignificant in purely physical terms.

On the trail from Jaffa to Jerusalem, at the heights near the Arab village of Abu Gosh, the pilgrim could catch the first mirage-like glimpse of Jerusalem.[15] For pilgrims, Jewish, Christian, or Moslem, the impact of the moment was enormous. The reality of the city's Jaffa Gate was likely to present a shocking contrast.

Chapter Two
The Sublime Porte and Its Pashas

In the years 1839–41, a series of coincidences gave rise to a complex of religious and national struggles which changed the face of all the Near East, and particularly of Palestine.

Since 1832 Mehmet Ali, the ambitious viceroy of Egypt, had ruled all of the Sinai Desert, the Palestinian area on both sides of the Jordan, Lebanon, and portions of Syria, and what would be Anatolian Turkey today. The ambitious son of an Albanian peasant plainly intended to expand his large fiefdom, torn by force from the hands of this theoretical suzerain, the sultan of Turkey. Pledging his loyalty to the Sublime Porte, Mehmet Ali was plainly biding his time, while he garnered political support abroad and strengthened his bases at home, preparatory to seizing either the Tigris-Euphrates valley or Constantinople itself.

Between 1832 and 1839, the rebellious vassal had been content to govern the Syrio-Palestinian realm as a viceroy, recognized by the sultan. So long as the greater part of his army was confined to Egypt, he posed no immediate threat to the survival of the Turkish Empire. In 1839, however, he began to mass his Egyptian forces in Syria under the command of his son, Ibrahim Pasha. In armed conflict with the Turkish army, he was victorious, and the only thing which prevented Mehmet Ali from completing his victory was the attitude of the great European powers. France was plainly in the Egyptian camp, encouraging Mehmet Ali's ambitions recklessly. Britain, after brief hesitation, determined that even a weak Turkey guarding the entry to the Black Sea and the mouth of the Danube was better than a Turkey shattered and partitioned. London was haunted by the grave danger that France might dominate the eastern Mediterranean or that Russia or Austria, still tranquil, might raise their claims to portions of the Turkish realm. Britain was moved not so much by a fear of Mehmet Ali, as by a fear that one or more of the great powers would so profit from the revised order of things that Britain would face new naval rivalries in the Mediterranean.[1]

Ibrahim Pasha's Egyptian army camped at Jaffa, 1841. From William Henry Bartlett, Walks in and about the City and Environs of Jerusalem, *London, G. Virtue, 1844.*

Lord Palmerston, Foreign Secretary of Great Britain 1830–41, devoted his considerable political skill to preventing the crisis from involving Austria and Russia and to checking French ambitions by containing Mehmet Ali's power. Palmerston's first, relatively modest goal had been an attempt to restore the status quo of 1838. He was even prepared to concede the Syrian-Palestinian area as a sphere of French influence if Mehmet Ali and Ibrahim Pasha would settle for the title "hereditary viceroy of Syria and Egypt" and cease their attempts to annex the Turkish-inhabited areas to the north. In the end the French gave Mehmet Ali an illusion that he could demand more and count on French aid. When it came to the brink of war between Britain and France, Palmerston's nerve proved to be sounder than that of Adolphe Thiers, the French chief minister. The British bombarded Beirut in 1840 and landed marines at Beirut and Acre. Facing the danger of having his Syrian army cut off from Egypt if the British expanded their beachheads, Mehmet Ali ordered a retreat. By trusting too long in French support, the Egyptians had lost Syria, Lebanon, Palestine, and the Sinai. At the London Conference of 1841, Mehmet Ali found himself in possession of a consolation prize. He and his heirs were declared "hereditary viceroys of Egypt." France remained, de facto, the premier European power whose voice was heard at Cairo. Nevertheless, it would be an exaggeration to say that Egypt became a French protectorate. Mehmet Ali's belated discovery that he could not count on France in a war crisis made him much more isolationist and less adventuresome until his death in 1849. What did develop at Cairo was a government, theoretically subject to the sultan at Constantinople, which began to assume more and more of the perquisites of independence.[2] Thenceforth, Mehmet Ali and his heirs named officials who were known as Ministers of Foreign Affairs. The foreign consuls at Alexandria and Cairo behaved more like ambassadors plenipotentiary, dealing with a sovereign state rather than a mere Turkish province.

Will it or not, the Turks inherited a regime in Palestine and Syria which had been created by Mehmet Ali, but which they could not easily scrap. The fact is that the viceroy of Egypt during his eight years in the north reformed the administration of those provinces so that tax collection and law enforcement were more efficient than they had ever been under the rule of the Turks. It is not so much that Mehmet Ali invented anything new as that he made it work better by creating a natural system under which he knew his appointees to office and played them effectively against one another.[3]

What the Turks inherited from Mehmet Ali in 1841 was a Palestine divided into three administrative divisions called sanjaks or pashaliks. Ultimately, the Turks themselves divided Palestine west of the Jordan River, and Lebanon, into seven pashaliks, governed from their chief cities, Jerusalem, Nablus, Acre, Beirut, Tripoli, Latakia, and the Mount Lebanon. The latter was governed as a separate district from Beirut. A pasha presided as governor over each sanjak or pashalik. In most matters of local civil and criminal justice he was supreme, though he might choose to associate himself with a *medjlis* or council composed of local notables. The seven sanjaks comprising western Palestine and Lebanon were subject to the musheer of Beirut, who presided over the *eyalet* of Beirut. The musheer served as an appellate judge in cases which had been tried in the pashas' courts. Each pasha was responsible for keeping order in his own pashalik, having the right to send the regular Turkish troops at his disposal into action. The expansion of the armed forces through the conscription of local inhabitants was carefully checked by the musheer. A pasha could, as needed, appoint a *mutsellin* or district governor for the principal towns in his pashalik.

In all matters touching changes in established practice, the greatest conservatism prevailed, and any substantive reform even in petty matters required an order from Constantinople issued by the grand vizier in the name of the sultan. A vizirial order, incorporated in an imperial decree or firman, was so difficult to obtain and so time-consuming in its gestation that only the most determined reformer could effect change. If Mehmet Ali had continued to hold Syria, Palestine, and the Sinai, it is probable that the process of change would have continued. As it was, the restored

Turkish regime, while retaining the structure which Mehmet Ali had used so effectively, pretty much froze it in place.[4]

Nevertheless, forces for change now existed which were beyond recall. The most important of these was the growing foreign presence in Turkish territory. The consuls of Europe had come to stay, and they were no longer content with the barely tolerated status granted to infidel foreigners before the age of Mehmet Ali.[5]

Chapter Three
The Consuls of the Three Horse Tails

The office of consul in the Levantine Mediterranean was scarcely an invention of the nineteenth century. Beginning in the twelfth century, the Italian city states which had important stakes in eastern trade encouraged their merchants to elect consuls in each major seaport. These consuls, having no official status, undertook to judge disputes between Italians subject to the same city state. In time, it followed naturally that consuls became the spokesmen for their voluntarily associated fellows, whether dealing with Byzantine, Turkish, or Arab authorities. When the great maritime Republic of Venice, acting in collusion with French Crusaders, destroyed the Byzantine Empire temporarily in 1204, the Queen of the Adriatic annexed Greek islands across the Aegean Sea. Genoa followed her rival closely, and shortly afterwards the Italians dominated both the Mediterranean and Black Seas. The Genoese ensign flew even in the distant Crimea.

Consuls, still not enjoying true diplomatic status in Turkish territory, were ultimately protected by treaty and came to be regarded as representing the dignity of their home republic. At a moment when Venice had the greatest navy in the world and a far-flung empire, the Turks were pragmatic enough to grant merchant consuls the honors and immunities of diplomats even without a formal treaty on the subject. By the end of the fifteenth century, the consuls had become the eyes and ears of their government, delivering regular written reports to the Venetian Senate.[1]

All of these developments, however, merely provided proto-types for the emergence of genuine consular power. The Byzantines had granted "capitulations" to the Venetians and Genoese to facilitate trade. The word originally had no nuance of surrender or submission in its definition. It merely referred to the capitula or chapters of the concession granted to foreign nationals.

Nor was it a humiliation for Suleiman the Magnificent, perhaps the greatest of the Turkish sultans, when he granted capitulations to France in 1535. French subjects living in Otto-man territories gained exemption from certain customs duties and local taxes and were granted judicial extraterritoriality. That is to say that court suits between Frenchmen could be tried by French consular courts under French law. France also became the defender of all foreign Roman Catholics living under Turk-ish rule.[2] It was only during the next three hundred years that France claimed, and usually gained, the more specious privilege of defending Ottoman subjects of Roman Catholic faith, and church property as well.[3]

It should be clear, however, that within the context of events in 1535 capitulations were merely a part of a balanced bargain struck between Suleiman the Magnificent and Francis I of France. Threatened by Habsburg power in Spain, the Holy Roman Em-pire, and England, it was France which played the suppliant, find-ing allies where they were available. At France's hour of greatest weakness, apparently beaten by the King – Emperor Charles V of Habsburg, the government at Paris had no qualms about alliances with Lutheran Protestants, the schismatic England of Henry VIII, and the Moslem Turk as well. It was with French assistance that Turkish war vessels entered the western Mediterranean to harass

Spain, even as the Turkish army marched to the very gates of Vienna. France might very well present herself as the defender of Roman Catholicism in the Turkish Empire, but it was French policy which made the solidification of Protestantism in northern Germany possible.[4]

It was not until 1580 that the English gained capitulatory rights in Turkey, though not pretending to the defense of any church in the east. Elizabeth I, building her own entente with France and Turkey and anticipating war with Spain, had no illusions that Turkey had been humbled because England and France both shared in a capitulatory system.[5]

The third great power to gain capitulatory rights, however, did so under very different circumstances, in 1774, having defeated Turkey in war, Catherine the Great of Russia forced the Turks to sign the Treaty of Kutchuk Kainardji. The Russians gained the rights for their subjects and consular courts conceded in the sixteenth century to France and England. Beyond that, however, a vaguely written clause in the treaty could be interpreted to mean that Russia was not merely the protector of the Greek and Russian Orthodox Churches, but the protector of all Orthodox Christians living in the Turkish Empire. Obviously, it was that latter pretension which would return repeatedly to provide Russia with pretexts for intervention in purely Turkish affairs.[6]

By the nineteenth century, however, each maritime power arriving newly on the scene could claim, as a matter of course, the special extraterritorial rights reserved for consuls.

The Turkish military aristocracy, drawing upon the proud traditions of warrior ancestors, were assigned horse tails as insignia of rank. A pasha or governor of the first rank was entitled to a standard bearing three horse tails. In a weakened Turkey, consuls sensing that they might exploit that weakness for the advantage of their own country ultimately asserted their right as representatives of their sovereigns to equality with the pashas.[7]

In 1838–39, while Mehmet Ali still ruled at Jerusalem, the first European consuls took up residence in the Holy City. No

European infidel had enjoyed the legal right of permanent residence there since the age of the Crusades.[8]

Testing the ground at every step, consuls and pashas circled one another cautiously to measure weaknesses. The Turks and the Egyptians had no illusions about their ability to defeat a first-rate European army or navy. Both Mehmet Ali and the sultan courted European support for their respective causes. However much the Egyptian and the Turk may have hated one another, they shared a mutual contempt for the infidel stranger, come as a trespasser to the House of Islam. The Moslem lords of the land, confident in the superiority of their completed faith, viewed these Christian parvenus as a temporary aberration in the normal scheme of life. They might not be able to defeat the European gunboat, but they had sublime faith in their capacity to outlast European intruders.[9]

The European, equally certain of the superiority of his civilization and his faith, viewed the corrupt entity called the Ottoman Empire as doomed. For the sake of his own country's interests, he may have wished to prolong its life or to profit from its hastened demise.

The first consuls who settled in rented quarters in Jerusalem 1838–39 aspired to a standard of three horse tails. For the moment, however, the armed Moslem *kawass* who escorted them as they walked the crowded markets of the city was a necessary companion. The kawass was more than a symbol of rank. For a despised stranger, he remained a guarantor of life.

Chapter Four
Palestinian Islam, 1841

No census was taken, but the best estimates point to a maximum of 300,000 inhabitants living within the sanjaks of historic Palestine in 1841.[1] The majority of that population were Sunni Moslem. In the far north there were concentrations of Shi'ite Moslems and Druse. Other major Druse settlements were near Haifa. In a land which never totally loses any of its historic ties, the presence of a small Samaritan remnant living among the Moslems at Nablus piqued the interest of observers. They lent additional color to the religious mosaic of the land. The four cities holy to Judaism in Palestine, Jerusalem, Hebron, Safed, and Tiberias, had substantial native Jewish populations. Small Jewish communities also subsisted in most of the larger towns and even in the villages of the Galilee. At Bethlehem and Nazareth, Christian Arabs constituted a majority of the inhabitants.[2]

In 1841, however, even in towns where non-Moslems were a majority, a plurality, or a significant minority, no one was allowed any doubt that Sunni Islam was dominant. Ethnic Turks constituted a tiny minority of the Sunni Moslem population. The pashas of sanjaks and most of the mutsellin in the larger towns, as well as the regular army units, were Turks, however. This meant, of course, that the land was governed by a series of officials rotated at irregular intervals, who came to their posts as strangers and who left as strangers. The Turkish official class and bureaucracy had remarkably little interaction with the Sunni Moslem Arab majority. Turkish was the language of official communication, though the pashas usually boasted a sufficient familiarity with French to communicate with Europeans. Precisely, however, because Palestine in 1841 was an underpopulated, impoverished, and primitive backwater of the Empire, the quality of pashas named to the sanjak of Jerusalem was inferior. At all levels of officialdom, bribery was normal, and the assumption persisted that a pasha ought to be richer at the end of his tenure than he had been at its beginning.

Precisely because the pashas in the Palestinian sanjaks were weak and incompetent, stronger rulers moved into the vacuum. The cadis of the Moslem religious courts, the head of the Moslem religious structure, the mufti, or coalitions between the mufti and an outstanding cadi might operate to exercise power behind the pasha's divan.

A strong pasha might oppose the overweening power of the religious establishment by resting heavily upon the medjlis or council, composed of representatives of the local population, including spokesmen for the Christian and Jewish communities. There were no strong pashas at Jerusalem, however, until 1855 when the exigencies of the Crimean War forced even the conservative government at Constantinople to send a competent man to Jerusalem. Throughout the years 1841–55, however, the Jerusalem medjlis was kept disunited and weak through collusion between the pashas who did not wish to see change and the cadis and successive muftis who wished to see Islam preserved as they had always known it.

Thus, the medjlis 1841–55 was composed of representatives of the great feudal, landholding, Arab effendi families. The Christian and Jewish representatives customarily were terrorized into silence, even in matters touching the essential needs of their own communities. Of course, the Turkish pashas did not trust the Arab

effendis any more than the Christians or Jews. To the Turkish official, all of the native population of Palestine were potential rebels
to be watched with suspicion.

Therefore, the effendis were allowed to use the medjlis for
debate, but no decision of substance was made there. The placement of ethnic Turks in positions of authority was one means
whereby the pashas avoided giving the Arab leadership any excuse for rebellion in the name of their jealousy of one another. The
Arab aristocrat could tolerate submission to a Turkish foreigner
much more readily than he could tolerate the preferment of the
scion of another Arab aristocrat whose blood line was no more
distinguished than his own. In the absence of real power, pride
in family tradition had to be the effendi's chief compensation. It
cost the Turkish pashas nothing to reaffirm the hereditary title
of the House of Darweesh as defenders of King David's Tomb on
Mount Zion.

Moslems, whether Turkish or Arab, were united in a determination to preserve the Islamic character of society, especially
in cities where Christians or Jews constituted large pluralities or
majorities.[3]

Under Koranic law, Jews and Christians were regarded as
"peoples of the Book" who had received authentic divine revelation,
but who had perversely rejected the ultimate revelation given to
humanity through Mohammed the Prophet. Infidels of that description were assured of toleration if they accepted inferior status
and paid a special head tax in lieu of military service. Since Islam
idealizes the soldier as a propagator of the faith, anyone denied
a soldier's career was necessarily humbled. Known as *Ahl Ud-
Dimma* or the "people of protection," they had an assured niche
in society, but labored under severe restrictions.[4] No church or
synagogue could have windows which looked down upon Moslem religious property. No church bells could be rung, nor could
Christian religious processions bear the crucifix or other Christian symbols through the public streets. At religious shrines sacred to two or more of the monotheistic faiths, priority was given

invariably to Moslem needs.[5] A mosque had been erected over the burial cave containing the remains of the biblical patriarchs and matriarchs, Abraham, Isaac, Jacob, Sarah, Rebecca, and Leah. Jews were permitted to climb only the first seven steps of the mosque leading to the shrine and suffered varying degrees of harassment even while submitting to that humiliating limitation.[6] Jews praying at the Western Wall at the Temple Mount, Judaism's holiest shrine, were prohibited from sounding the ram's horn or making any other noise which might offend Moslems. Jews could not erect a *mechitza* or barrier separating male and female worshippers at that wall, lest it be construed as a recognition of their right to build a true synagogue there.[7] Moslems freely threw garbage upon the heads of Jewish worshippers from the Temple Mount without interference by the authorities.[8] Only Moslems could climb the Temple Mount. Black Sudanese Takruri tribesmen enforced the exclusion of infidel trespassers. A few bold Christians are known to have dared the ascent, disguised as Moslems. The English artist F. Catherwood barely escaped lynching in 1833 when, in such a disguise, he climbed the Mount to sketch scenes in the plaza and gardens which surround the Mosque of the Dome of the Rock and the Mosque El Aqsa[9] which occupy the site of Israel's ancient temple. For Islam, El Aqsa on the Temple Mount had become the third holiest shrine, after Mecca and Medina, because post-Koranic tradition had designated that site as the place from which Mohammed had begun his mystic night journey to heaven.[10]

No new church or synagogue could be erected without a specific firman from the sultan, though old houses of worship could be repaired. Thus all sorts of subterfuge became the normal means whereby new non-Moslem houses of prayer were erected. In Jerusalem, for example, four separate synagogues pursued separate careers within the same four walls because the three newer ones had been built as mere "enlargements" of the oldest congregation.[11]

The purchase of property by foreign non-Moslems also required a special imperial firman. Since there was no Turkish land registry law until 1858,[12] each rare approval of land purchase by foreign Christians or Jews also required ratification by the local pasha. Both Christian and Jewish individuals and institutions were constantly engaged in litigation, attempting to prove legitimate inheritance of ancient land deeds.

The Turks, for their part, assumed an attitude of amused contempt as they surveyed the squabbling of the *rayah* or non-Moslem communities. They could afford to do so. Even in the walled cities containing Christian or Jewish majorities, virtually all property was in the hands of Moslem landlords who leased it on a long-term basis to tenants who were born, lived and died there with no expectation that they would own land.[13]

Although such modest commercial and political power as existed was concentrated in the walled towns, the bulk of the Moslem population lived in the unwalled villages and the nomadic encampments of rural Palestine. In a country having no rain through the late spring, summer, and early fall, most of Palestine was marginal desert. Farmers either depended upon the few fresh water springs or rivulets which flowed all year, or dug deep wells free of the infiltration of brine.

The village peasants were usually tenants, subsisting on a share-crop basis by contract with great effendi landlords.[14] The effendis, living in town houses within the walled cities, had only a casual contact with their tenants, entrusting day-to-day negotiations to resident stewards.[15]

Huddled on hilltops for security, peasant villages maintained farms on terraced lower slopes and in the valleys only by means of irrigation. The hardest working Arab peasant, however, knew that the fruits of his labor might be torn from him in an instant. Across all the land roved scattered bands of Bedouin tribes. Each band moved independently with its sheep, goats, horses, and camels, but stayed within an enlarged territorial range shared with a clan descended from a common ancestor.[16]

To the Bedouin, the Turkish sultan and his pashas were distant shadows having little relevance to life. The Bedouin viewed the world from the perspective of the friendships and enmities of his clan. Ancient blood feuds, whose origins could be traced through the centuries, were freshly etched on the communal memory and made endemic warfare part of nomadic life. Complex clan loyalties existed within an even larger matrix of blood loyalties, since almost the entire native Arab Moslem population, whether nomadic Bedouin or settled villagers, remembered that they were either Yeminis or Kais. The Yemenis recalled that their ancestors had been warriors from the southern Arabian peninsula. The Kais, whose residence in Palestine also was dated to the Moslem conquest of the land in the seventh century, traced their roots to tribes having hoary blood feuds with the Yemenis. Thus, for example, the great clan of Abu Gosh, whose village dominated the mountain heights through which ran the trail from Jaffa to Jerusalem, had to be paid handsomely to permit pilgrims to make the ascent. As Abu Gosh was Yemeni, however, adherents of the Kais could not even pay for transit across their lands, but had to make long detours.[17]

The Bedouin of kindred or allied clans, though respecting the grazing ranges of one another's flocks and herds, regarded springs, rivulets, and even wells as communal property. They resented any peasant villager who attempted to fence a water source. Their response was to destroy such walls and to seize any foodstuffs hoarded by villagers in defiance of the Bedouin's claim to free movement across all the land. Peasants, huddled on their hilltops, rarely had the will or the military skill to defend themselves.

A peasant, if he was to survive Bedouin depredations and the claims of hostile villagers, subsisted within a network of alliances, contracts and traditions governing the rights of farmers and shepherds to share the same water and land.

Thus, groves of citrus fruit and olives might subsist if the farmer was willing to buy their survival and to defend them by watchful guards. The Bedouin had long since destroyed the native forests which had once covered the land.[18] The hillsides, eroded to bedrock and deprived of top soil, were mute witnesses to a land subjected to man's rapine.

What the Bedouin did not take by force or by threat, Turkish soldiery took in the name of naked extortion.[19] Far worse than the regular Turkish troops, who were at least under some discipline, were the bashi-bazouk or *howari* irregular troops. These Arab conscripts, though springing from peasant villages themselves, had no scruples about seizing the poultry, cattle, or farm produce of a village belonging to strangers to whom they were unrelated by ties of blood or alliance.[20]

The year 1841 was almost the last in which a sketch of the old Palestine could be made. Just beyond the horizon lay forces which would change Moslem Palestine forever.

Chapter Five
Palestinian Judaism, 1841

Palestinian Jewry in 1841 looked back upon an unbroken history of residence in the "Land of Israel" dating to the remote beginnings of Jewish history. In those millennia of life in a country central to Judaism, the darkest hour had come during the Crusades, starting with the capture of Jerusalem in 1099. The triumphant Crusaders had massacred every Jew in Jerusalem and attempted, unsuccessfully, to extirpate Jewry in all of Palestine. Recovery began slowly when Saladin reconquered Jerusalem for Islam in 1189. A thirteenth century Mongol-Tartar invasion had dealt a new setback, but from then on the reconstitution of a viable Jewish presence in numerous Palestinian communities made steady progress. Oddly enough, Jerusalem's Jews lagged in that recovery, largely because the Moslem authorities there made the establishment of property title and the building of synagogues particularly difficult. Thus, it was in the Galilee that a Jewish population grew most rapidly. The Spanish and Portuguese persecutions of their Jews precipitated a steady emigration to the Holy Land, which accelerated when the Turkish sultan, Selim 1, tore Palestine from Egyptian Mameluke control in 1517. The Ottoman rule of Palestine for exactly four hundred years witnessed the expansion of Jewish communities at the holy cities of Jerusalem, Hebron, Tiberias, and Safed, and the establishment of smaller settlements throughout the land.

Sephardic Jewish family, Tiberias, sometime during the years 1875–80. From Dr. Louis Lortet, La Syrie d'au-jourd'hui; Voyages dans la Phènicie, Liban el Judée, 1875–1880, *Paris, Hachette, 1884. Courtesy of Towson State University Media Services.*

The Hebrew name for Spain is Sepharad. The Spanish and Portuguese Jews are collectively the Sephardim. Coming into Palestine in large numbers under Ottoman patronage, they inundated the native Jewish communities and absorbed them, so that Palestinian Jewry became Sephardic whether or not, in fact, descended from Spanish emigrants. Although necessarily obliged to communicate with their neighbors in Arabic and Turkish, among themselves the Jews spoke Ladino. In 1841 the bulk of the Palestinian Sephardim still spoke that dialect of antique Spanish, heavily laced with Turkish or Arabic words.[1]

Beginning in the seventeenth century, the Sephardim had begun to elect a Chief Rabbi bearing the title Rishon l'Zion or "First in Zion." It was not until 1842, in the aftermath of the Egyptian retreat, that the Turkish government gave official status to the Rishon l'Zion, recognizing him and the judges he appointed as the exclusive arbitrators of conflicts between Jews.[2] Alone among the rabbis, the Rishon l'Zion enjoyed the privilege of an escort by a kawass or armed Moslem guard.[3] The Chief Rabbi, solemnly elected and installed at Jerusalem's venerable Yohanan Ben Zakkai Synagogue, became a part of the official establishment at Jerusalem.[4] His dignity, which was shared by the humblest Sephardic Jew, gave him an entree at the pasha's seraglio, the medjlis, at the residences of the mufti and the cadis, and at the European consulates. The Chief Rabbi became the representative of the Jews in all relationships with the Christian sects, since the Turks placed his office at a par with the patriarchs and bishops of the various churches. This put the Chief Rabbi in the often embarrassing position of making and receiving visits to all the other members of the Jerusalem establishment on all major Moslem, Christian, and Jewish holidays. As the Rishon l'Zion could not, in delicacy, appear to be celebrating the festivals of Islam or Christianity, his visits were usually a day late or early for the event which was to be celebrated. His problem was understood and his behavior was reciprocated by the pashas, effendis, muftis, cadis, consuls, patriarchs, and bishops who formed the elite of Turkish Jerusalem.[5]

In a practical sense, the legal primacy of the Rishon l'Zion created peculiar and unanticipated problems for Jews who were not of Sephardic descent. For example, only the Chief Rabbi had the right to designate and license the slaughterers of kosher animals. All butchers were obliged to pay a tax for each animal slaughtered and sold. Quite unwittingly, the Turkish government, by tying tax collection to what was primarily a religious function of the Chief Rabbinate, made the processing and sale of meat in the Jewish community exclusively the province of Sephardim.[6] This problem, unimportant in 1841 when most of the Jews of Palestine were Sephardim, was to become a major source of conflict between the Jews as the second half of the nineteenth century saw Yiddish- and German-speaking Jews coming to dominate the old Ladino-speaking Sephardic community.[7] Similarly, the right of the Rishon l'Zion to control the fees charged by Jewish burial societies for the preparation and interment of the dead created endless, unseemly squabbles between the entrenched Sephardim and the newly arrived Ashkenazim from the German- and Yiddish-speaking communities of Europe.[8]

These problems, however, were not yet painfully evident in 1841. The Ashkenazim were still a minority of the Jewish community of Palestine. Indeed, the first permanent Yiddish-speaking settlement in Jerusalem took place in 1812 when a plague swept through the Galilee, driving some Lithuanian Jews to seek safety in the Holy City. These promptly adopted the oriental costume of the native Jews and became "honorary" Sephardim. To gain the protection of a recognized rayah community, they were prepared to acknowledge the authority of the Sephardic rabbinate. The only alternative was to become not merely stateless foreigners but a species of nonperson, not recognized as Jews or as anything else.[9]

In 1836 during the Egyptian occupation of Palestine and Syria by Mehmet Ali, Rabbi Abraham Shlomo Zalman Zoref, on behalf of the Ashkenazic Perushim Congregation, obtained permission to build a small synagogue to be called Menachem Zion, "Comfort for Zion," on a property to which Ashkenazim had held title since 1700.[10]

On January 1, 1837, a devastating earthquake struck the Galilee, ruining the two northern Jewish holy cities, Tiberias and Safed. Through death or flight, Safed lost 5,000 out of its previous population of 8,000–9,000. Tiberias lost almost its entire population of two thousand inhabitants, only a few hundred persons lingering in a place that was temporarily uninhabitable.[11] The Jewish refugees fled for the most part to Jerusalem, making Judaism the largest single religious denomination there. When in 1838 Druse clansmen had conquered the environs of Safed and seized the ruined city, still more Jews moved to Jerusalem.[12]

Dependable observers estimated that by 1846 there were four thousand Sephardim and three thousand Ashkenazim in Jerusalem for a total of seven thousand Jews, while Islam counted four thousand adherents[13] and the principal Christian denominations a total of thirty-five hundred.[14] It was not until the 1850s that the steady growth of Jewish numbers made Jews a permanent majority of Jerusalem's population.[15] Interestingly enough, the influx of European Jews produced a Jewish majority at Safed and Tiberias by the end of the 1840s while Jews were still only a plurality of Jerusalem's population.[16]

However, it was not earthquakes or Druse incursions alone which accounted for the sudden dramatic rise in Palestinian Jewish numbers. The new element was the arrival of large-scale Russian Jewish immigration.

Since 1825, Russia had been governed by Czar Nicholas I, a soldier-autocrat who demanded conformity. Determined to make Russian Orthodox Christians out of his Jewish subjects, the czar fluctuated between subtle and forceful methods. At the extreme of unsubtle technique, he drafted twelve-year-old boys into a form of premilitary training. When the prospective conscripts went into hiding, the czar resorted to bounty hunters, Jews willing to betray those who evaded service for a price. Ultimately the czar shifted his approach by constructing Crown Schools in which Jewish youth would be Russified subtly. As the czar's strategies failed, one by one, the Jews of Russia were united only by a common fear of a government which made Jew-hatred an unabashed policy. The masses of Russian Jews had no choice but to live out poverty-stricken lives within the Pale of Settlement, the portion of western Russia to which they had been confined since the days of Catherine the Great.[17]

Only a tiny fraction of the millions of Russian Jews unhappy with their lot chose escape to Palestine. In 1841, the steamboat made viable what had been only an impossible dream for previous generations. In the next thirty years the railroad made departure from Russia even easier. The telegraph carrying news of distant places to the most isolated Russian hamlets was the third great technological advance which was to make the years 1840–70 a crucial watershed for the Jews of Russia and of Palestine.[18]

Russian Jews moving to Palestine in a small but steady stream rarely came as family groups. A disproportionately large percentage were elderly people, who may have hoped to be joined ultimately by their children but who were dependent on monies sent them by their families in Russia. They had come to Palestine to live out their days in the four holy cities, devoting their lives to prayer and religious study.[19]

Although the native Palestinian Sephardim and the Russian Ashkenazim were both religiously orthodox in that they recognized rabbinic interpretation of Talmudic law, they accepted differing bodies of traditional custom that appeared superficial to non-Jews, but which assumed major importance in their own eyes. Wearing different costumes, speaking different vernacular tongues, and even pronouncing the Hebrew tongue, their common language of prayer, with distinctive accents, Sephardi and Ashkenazi found it hard to accept one another as equals.[20]

Most fundamentally the Sephardim, native to Palestine, were thoroughly acculturated to their inferior but assured role in Moslem society. They had their own rich and poor, their own benevolent charitable associations, and a basically self-supporting economy resting upon skilled craftsmen and small shopkeepers. Their family units were complete, and patriarchal dominance of the extended family made for an extremely stable social structure, buttressed by small children and aged grandparents under one roof.[21]

The Russians, however, flirted with constant starvation. Only a minority of those who had practiced a skilled craft in Russia attempted to pursue it in Palestine. Devoting their time to pious exercises, they lived on subventions sent them by their families in Europe and on funds known as *halukah*²² distributed by the *kollelim*. A kollel was a corporate body organized according to geographic place of origin which undertook to support all those who were devoted to full-time study and prayer from funds collected in the European homeland. The halukah was the share apportioned to each family head registered with the kollel.²³

Through the economic power of the kollelim, the European Ashkenazic rabbis exercised authority over their fellow countrymen. Nevertheless, so far as the Turkish government was concerned, only the Rishon l'Zion and his Sephardic rabbinate spoke for the Jews. Pragmatically, however, the Sephardic Chief Rabbi, while not willingly yielding his supremacy, found it prudent to deal with his Ashkenazic stepchildren through their rabbis and kollelim. Thus, while the East European Jews gradually became the majority of the Jewish community and while the Jews approached that moment in the 1850s when they became a clear majority of Jerusalem's population, the Rishon l'Zion maintained an uneasy truce with the unsettling newcomers.²⁴

In 1841, the Jews like their Arab Moslem neighbors had absolutely no sense of nationalist identity. It was the European, surveying the scene from the outside, who perceived nineteenth-century potentialities in a society which clung to prenationalist forms of self-identification.²⁵

Chapter Six
Palestinian Christianity, 1841

The roots of Christianity can be traced to origins in historic Judaism. Even after Christianity had broken with its Jewish origins and become a worldwide religion offering salvation to the Gentile, it continued to accord its Palestinian homeland a venerated place in its calendar of sanctity. After all, Jesus of Nazareth had lived all of his life in the turbulent Jewish society of a province chafing under Roman tyranny. Consequently, Christians associated Bethlehem, Jerusalem. Nazareth, and all the other scenes of his life with uniquely Christian emotional and religious meaning.

In the fourth century Christianity had become the state church of a Roman Empire, encompassing all the shores of the Mediterranean. In 451 at the Council of Chalcedon, the still united Roman world had recognized five patriarchates for the governance of the church. One of those was Jerusalem. Theoretically, the patriarchates of Alexandria, Antioch, Constantinople, Jerusalem, and Rome were equal. Historic developments and the theologians were ultimately to make Constantinople and Rome the great rivals for church leadership. There was no assumption of that sort of competition at Chalcedon, however.[1] The decline in the importance of Alexandria, Antioch, and Jerusalem for historic Christianity can be traced quite simply to the fact that Islam had seized all three cities within one generation of the death of Mohammed. Thereafter, those patriarchates were obliged to ensure their survival by submissive and circumspect behavior. In the year 637 when Jerusalem fell to Islam, distant Rome was hard pressed to ensure its own safety against pagan and heretical Christian attack. Only Constantinople, the center of a thriving Greek Byzantine Empire, survived as a Christian capital inheriting the religious and political claims of imperial Rome. It was only natural that all of the Greek Christians of the eastern Mediterranean should have looked to Constantinople for leadership and inspiration.[2]

Impression of a Jerusalem Christian family. From Count L.N.P. Auguste de Forbin, Voyage dans le Levant, en 1817 et 1818, *Paris, Imprimerie Royale, 1819. Courtesy of Towson State University Media Services.*

The claims of the patriarch of Rome, or the pope, to be the heir of St. Peter and the vicar of his church enjoyed only sporadic recognition in the Greek east. With the exception of a brief re-union in the eleventh century, the Roman Catholic Church with its Latin liturgy and the Greek Church centered at Constantinople condemned one another as schismatics.[3]

In 1099, however, when the triumphant Roman Catholic Crusaders from the West seized Jerusalem, they erected a chain of kingdoms, principalities, and counties which recognized the pope at Rome as the leader of the church universal. Thus, the Greek and Latin churches were brought into a collision course. The successive popes named Latin patriarchs of Jerusalem who stood as rivals to the Greek patriarchs recognized by Constantinople. When Islam recaptured Jerusalem in 1187, the Latin patriarch retreated to Acre. When Christendom lost its last base in Palestine in 1291, the Latin patriarchate suspended its functions, abandoning the field to its Greek rival who functioned under Moslem rule. Thereafter, the Latin patriarchs of Jerusalem were usually Italian prelates who held the title but did not venture out of Italy or attempt to rebuild Roman Catholicism in Palestine. During the following centuries, Roman Catholic churches survived in Palestine and Syria which recognized the pope as supreme spiritual head, though they may have celebrated the mass in Arabic or Greek, if not in Latin. Roman Catholic interests were vested in the Franciscan Order under a Custodian of the Terra Santa. As noted previously, in the sixteenth century King Francis I of France undertook to represent Catholic interests in Palestine and to assert the right of French consuls to protect all Roman Catholic clergy and property there.[4]

Thenceforth, the Turkish government found itself forced to act as arbiter between the more numerous Greek Orthodox Christians led by a resident patriarch of Jerusalem, and the small and splintered Roman Catholic community defended by Turkey's most important European ally. Since Roman Catholics and Greek Orthodox Christians venerated the same shrines and worshipped in the same churches, the Turks found themselves engaged in settling such puerile quarrels as which church had the right to repair a leaking roof, which could replace a fallen ornament, or which priest could officiate at what hour at the same altar. Over the centuries, Turkish arbitration finally resulted in certain Moslem families gaining the hereditary right to hold the keys to specific rooms in disputed churches and to lock themselves in, and contesting rivals out, at night.[5]

The triumph of Catherine the Great over the Turks in 1774 ensured that Greek Orthodoxy, with its greater numbers and its resident patriarch in Palestine, would enjoy precedence. A host of smaller Christian denominations jostled one another for survival in the spiritual marketplace, as Armenian, Jacobite, Syriac, Coptic, and Abyssinian churches advanced their conflicting claims. Annually, the advent of Holy Fire Day on the morrow of Good Friday threatened riots in the Church of the Holy Sepulchre as the faithful laity of the Greek, Armenian, and sometimes the Latin communions pressed forward to light tapers from flames ignited by supernatural provenance. That Turkish soldiery had to be summoned into the church to prevent bloodshed was a source of embarrassment for Christians who did not share the beliefs of the rioters.[6]

The earliest fairly reliable figures for the Christian population of Jerusalem refer to the year 1850, but the size of that community was probably only slightly larger in 1850 than it had been in 1841. Those figures report a total Jerusalemite Christian population of 3,500, of whom 2,000 were Greek Orthodox, 1,000 Roman Catholic, and the remainder divided among other Christian sects, the Armenians dominating that group.[7] As stated earlier, there were clear Christian majorities divided neatly between the Greeks and the Latins in such towns as Bethlehem, Nazareth, and some smaller villages.[8]

The Protestant churches, however, had almost no membership among the native Palestinian population subject to the sultan. Ever since the late seventeenth century, however, there had been plans afoot by Protestant missionaries to win souls for their diverse churches. The English were at the forefront of the effort, followed closely by Germans, Scandinavians, and ultimately by Americans. The goal of establishing a Protestant mission anywhere in Palestine presupposed a central headquarters in Jerusalem. There were, however, two seemingly insuperable obstacles to be overcome. The first was that until Mehmet Ali's rebellion in the 1830s, no "Frank," as all Europeans were called, could establish permanent residence in the Holy City. Foreigners were permitted to make short visits for religious or commercial purposes, but it was necessary to resort to subterfuge if a longer stay was contemplated. Secondly, Turkish law absolutely refused to tolerate Christian proselytization among Moslems.[9] The latter prohibition, while offensive to the intended Protestant missionaries, did not dampen their ardor because they regarded all the native eastern Christian denominations as hopelessly primitive and superstitious, crying out for purified faith.[10] Rather naively, the missionaries also regarded the native Jewish population of Jerusalem, the largest single denomination in the city, as ripe for mass conversion. For the Protestant missionaries, the first obstacle seemed open to elimination when the struggle between Mehmet Ali and the Sublime Porte made both the Egyptians and Turks seem anxious to buy British support by concessions. As a consequence, the first British consulate in Jerusalem was opened in 1838. William Young, the first occupant of a singularly sensitive post, was designated a mere vice consul, though his efforts were shortly rewarded by promotion to full consular rank.[11]

At that moment on September 19, 1838 when British Foreign Secretary Lord Palmerston sent his first instructions to Vice Consul Young, Mehmet Ali had not yet become a military threat to the sultan. The pretense could be maintained that the Egyptian was merely a loyal viceroy serving the Sublime Porte. Thus Mehmet Ali could make a concession to the Franks, painful to Moslem sensibilities, in order to court British support. The sultan could give his consent to a concession in Palestine since he did not actually control that country anyhow.[12]

However much the missionaries may have been the principal

promoters of the idea of planting a permanently resident British consul in Jerusalem, Palmerston was more conscious than they of the need to proceed cautiously and to avoid giving offense to Islam. Young arrived safely in Jerusalem in October 1838, and true to his orders, kept himself aloof from the Protestant missionaries already present in Palestine.[13]

In London, however, two extremely well-supported and aggressive missionary groups were active in seeking British consular support for an expanded Protestant presence in Palestine. The first was the Society for Promoting Christianity Among the Jews, usually called the London Jews Society. The other was the Church Missionary Society, some of whose members had the naive idea that they might convert Moslems, though their main thrust was necessarily devoted to making Protestants out of the native Christian denominations of Palestine.

The two missionary societies had the good fortune to have the support of Lord Ashley. The future Earl of Shaftesbury was able, aggressive, and idealistic. This aristocratic evangelical had married the niece of Prime Minister Lord Melbourne. His mother-in-law was shortly to marry her second husband, Foreign Secretary Lord Palmerston. It was Ashley, more than anyone else, who used his family connections to the Whig-Liberal leadership and his own political career in Parliament and Cabinet to advance the notion that a British consulate at Jerusalem must necessarily give the most active support to missionary activity. Ashley was thus equally the patron of both the London Jews Society's program for massive conversion of Palestinian Jews, encouraging them to farm the land as a fulfillment of prophecy, and the Church Missionary Society's concept of creating an Anglican Bishopric of Jerusalem.[14]

It is hardly surprising, then, that new instructions were sent to Young from the Foreign Office dated January 31, 1839. John Bidwell, superintendent of the Foreign Office's consular service, ordered Young "to afford protection to the Jews generally" and to report upon the state of the Palestinian Jews as soon as possible."[15]

That Young fully understood Palmerston's definition of the word "protection" is revealed in a report written to the Foreign Secretary on March 14, 1839.

> There are, My Lord, two parties to be noticed who will doubtless consider themselves entitled to some voice in the future disposition of affairs here: The one is the Jew unto whom God originally gave this land for a possession, and the other the Protestant Christian, his legitimate offspring. Of both Great Britain seems…the natural guardian….[16]

Young also took the occasion to urge, ardently, the need for a Protestant church at Jerusalem and suggested to his chief that permission be obtained both from the Sublime Porte and from Mehmet Ali. Here, Young abandoned the abstractions of religious expression and urged the move as a check against the French who supported Roman Catholicism and the Russians who supported Greek Orthodoxy in Palestine.

The use of the church as an element in the great powers' rivalry was an argument which the cynical Lord Palmerston understood much better than saving souls.[17] Palmerston was fully aware of the strength of that part of the British public which regarded the restoration of the Jews to Zion and their conversion to Protestantism as a fulfillment of biblical prophesy and a part of the messianic plan. For his own part, Palmerston viewed the establishment of the Jews in Palestine under British protection as an element of strength in the Near East for Britain, and as a block to the further ambitions of Mehmet Ali, and hence a source of strength for Turkey.[18]

As early as 1833, Patrick Campbell, the British Consul General at Alexandria, Egypt, had attempted to persuade Mehmet Ali to allow the construction of a Protestant church at Jerusalem.[19] Lord Ponsonby, British ambassador at Constantinople, had attempted to obtain consent of the Turkish government to the same end. Although conciliatory replies were received from the two parties contending for control of Palestine, actual authorization to build a church was harder to obtain. Mehmet Ali, though caring little about the authority of the sultan, was happy to refer the matter to the Sublime Porte. The Turkish Government, in this case, was able to blame Mehmet Ali for any difficulties. In fact, neither party was anxious to cooperate in establishing a Protestant church at Jerusalem, but neither was willing to offend Britain by an outright refusal.[20]

While the slow minuet of diplomatic correspondence proceeded, one of the missionaries of the London Jews Society at Jerusalem forced the issue without legal authorization from either the British, Egyptian, or Turkish governments. John Nicolayson, a Dane who had been an illegal but permanent resident of Jerusalem since 1823,[21] first rented a house in which he held clandestine Protestant services in 1838. In 1839, he bought two plots of land through an intermediary, one Hohanes, whose name suggests that he was an Armenian rayah. Finally, he transferred all the property to the London Jews Society, without obtaining the consent of either the Turkish or Egyptian government for the entire illegal transaction. Of course, the London Jews Society, which knew all about Nicolayson's activities, paid £800 for his land purchases and expenses. Evidently the missionaries assumed that they might do as they pleased at Jerusalem, despite the fury of the local Moslems, because both Mehmet Ali and the Turkish government courted British support as the Egyptians made an open break with the sultan in 1839. With an audacity which was foolhardy, Nicolayson built a fence around his property, expropriating part of a public path which he had not bought, and began to dig the foundations for the intended church. An English surveyor architect was sent out from London, but the work was done by local labor. Predictably, the fury of the Jerusalemite population prevented the work from moving rapidly. It came to a complete halt when Consul Young and all the Anglican missionaries were expelled from Jerusalem after it was clear that Britain would support Turkey against Mehmet Ali.[22]

The enforced retreat of Mehmet Ali and the restoration of Turkish authority in Syria and Palestine were accomplished almost entirely by British firmness. Nevertheless, the Turks, if they felt gratitude, were not sufficiently moved to approve the completion of a Protestant church at Jerusalem. Thus, what was already called Christ Church remained a large forty-foot-deep hole in the ground, rendered the more conspicuous by the fact that it was located just within the Jaffa Gate under the walls of the Turkish citadel. It is sufficient to say that it was not to be until September 1845 that the church was finally authorized by an imperial firman obtained by the firmest pressure on the sultan's government. Even then, the Turkish authorities at Jerusalem and the local Moslem population laid every obstacle in the path of the building. Sir Stratford Canning, shortly to be Lord Stratford de Redcliffe, the British ambassador at Constantinople, scored the first of his many future victories by forcing the Porte to enforce its own decree. It was not until January 21, 1849, however, that the church itself was completed and formally consecrated.[23]

The goal of establishing an Anglican bishopric at Jerusalem was only slightly less difficult than building a church in a city sacred to Islam. The physical construction of a church symbolized the missionary impetus of European Protestantism, for there were scarcely enough native Protestants in Palestine in 1849 to justify all the money and effort spent on the construction of Christ Church. The creation of a bishopric, however, represented the political aspirations of the Protestant powers in Palestine. By the creation of a bishopric, Great Britain and Prussia underlined their support for the missionary effort to create a native Protestant population which would look to them for protection as Roman Catholic rayahs looked to France, and Greek Orthodox rayahs looked to Russia.

The original impetus for the bishopric seems to have come from Berlin rather than London. King Frederick William IV had ascended the throne in 1840. The King of Prussia had been impatient, from his earliest youth, with the fine and even gross differences between Protestant churches. He dreamed of an ecumenical union of Protestant Christendom through the installation of a bishop of Jerusalem who would be above narrow theological disputes. The king, rather naively, imagined that there would be no great difficulty about obtaining Turkish recognition of the bishopric, in view of the fact that the European great powers had just restored Palestine and Syria to the Sublime Porte, pushing Mehmet Ali back beyond the Sinai Desert.

On June 19, 1841, Chevalier Christian Charles Bunsen arrived in London as Prussian special envoy. Bunsen was a classicist and a student of oriental languages who had entered Prussian diplomatic service. The son of a Dutch father, he was married to a pious Anglican of English birth. The future Baron Bunsen was the ideal agent for the creation of an ecumenical bishopric of Jerusalem.

An Anglo-Prussian agreement emerged after a surprisingly short three weeks of negotiation. That pact provided that the Bishop of Jerusalem was to be an Anglican, nominated alternately by the Crowns of Britain and Prussia, subject to his being approved by the Archbishop of Canterbury and submitted to his metropolitan authority. The nomination of the first bishop was to be awarded to the British. All Lutheran clergy resident in Palestine who had already subscribed to the Confession of Augsburg were then to be ordained as Anglican clergy.

Anglican Vicar John Henry Newman, then the most outstanding intellect in the Oxford Movement's attempt to revitalize England's State Church, alleged later in his life that it had been the Jerusalem bishopric which had moved him to accept Roman Catholic conversion. Though he never stated it bluntly, he regarded the Anglo-Prussian agreement as a cynical abandonment of important religious principles for the sake of political gain.

Lord Ashley, an equally sincere Christian, saw no objection to an ecumenical bishopric if it would advance the cause of the two missionary organizations in which he had interested himself. Precisely because it was agreed that the main reservoir of potential Protestant converts were to come from the Jewish population of

Palestine, the missionary spokesmen argued that the new bishop ought to be a Jew converted to Christianity.

It was difficult to find such a person possessing the intellectual qualities which a bishop ought to own. The candidate shortly chosen was a former Prussian Polish Jew named Wolf, who had become a naturalized British subject and an Anglican convert. While changing his nationality and religion, he had also adopted the name Michael Solomon Alexander. The new Bishop Alexander was consecrated by the Archbishop of Canterbury at Lambeth Palace on November 7, 1841. Thanks to the influence of Lord Ashley, he was conveyed to Palestine with his wife and six children aboard HMS *Devastation*. The bishop had declined to travel on a frigate bearing the name HMS *Infernal*.

The bishop and his party, accompanied by the British consul general for Syria and Palestine, Colonel Hugh Rose, reached Jerusalem on the afternoon of January 21, 1842. The guns of the citadel at the Jaffa Gate were firing a salute in honor of the eve of the Moslem festival of Corban Beiram. The Turkish garrison band was playing marching music. The naive bishop assumed that all of this was intended to honor him.

He was very shortly to be awakened from his illusions. The Turkish government had protested vigorously against the dispatch of a new Christian prelate to a city which was already well supplied with hostile clergy. The Jews, who were supposed to be the principal objects of Bishop Alexander's solicitude, shunned him as a renegade apostate. Until his premature death in 1845, the Anglican bishop of Jerusalem did not even have a completed church building in which he could worship.[24]

Nevertheless, the assertion of Protestant rights at Jerusalem, side by side with the claims to primacy of so many other churches, set the stage for that great political struggle between the European powers which lay just ahead.

Chapter Seven

The Tanzimat and the Palestinian Consuls, 1839–50

His Imperial Majesty, Abdul Medjid Khan, ascended the throne in 1839 at age sixteen. This gentle and humane sultan has been described as full of good intentions, but lacking the energy or will to save his realm by carrying out necessary reform. As the heir to Ottoman power, he was potentially one of the great powers of the world, suzerain of lands in Asia, Europe, and Africa. As *Caliph ul-Islam*, the Commander of the Faithful, he laid claim to being the supreme protector of Moslem interests everywhere. Ideally, he was to preserve the integrity of the Turkish state and a great universal monotheistic faith by governing both under the law of the Koran. Actually, Abdul Medjid's personal life was such that he could be neither an orthodox Moslem nor an effective statesman. The sultan was beguiled by the joys of his harem and the release offered by alcohol, and his reign is actually a study in the power rivalries of those around him. The Ottoman Empire did not suffer major losses in territory during his reign. However, that result was due far more to the chance conflicts of the major powers than to the sultan's skill at statecraft. The Ottoman

Empire had become the passive object of the successes and failures of men and nations, contemptuous of Turkey's claim to be an equal among equals.[1]

Willy-nilly, the survival of Turkey was bought by concessions to the Christian monarchies which produced the ironic result of earning Abdul Medjid's reign the historic title of an age of reform. The *Tanzimat* or reform movement might have saved Turkey if there had been a sultan capable of maintaining its continuity and of supporting ministers like Grand Vizier Reshid Pasha, who pressed for it.[2] Instead, the hesitant reforms of the reign of Abdul Medjid served only to alienate conservative Moslem opinion, without winning the wholehearted respect of Europe's great powers.[3]

It was in Palestine where the *Tanzimat* was to have some of its most important results. The Palestinian sanjaks on both banks of the Jordan River were ill prepared to absorb change. Nowhere else in the Turkish Empire were the vital interests of Islam, Christianity, and Judaism more directly in conflict. Precisely for that reason, the consuls stationed throughout Palestine played a greater role than "mere" consuls played elsewhere.

It must be remembered that the telegraph did not connect Palestine to Europe until 1864. Indeed, the European telegraph did not reach Constantinople until 1855.[4] Therefore, even with the best of luck, steamboat connections between the Palestinian seaports and western European capital cities made it impossible for a consular dispatch to reach its destination in less than three weeks.[5] Even if an immediate reply was sent, attended by the same fortunate, speedy, three-week journey, a consul was quite isolated if urgent decisions had to be made. He could not expect to hear from his superiors before the passage of one and a half to three months from the date of the original request for instructions. The consul at Jerusalem might transfer responsibility for truly risky decisions by sending his request for instructions both to his superiors at home and his country's ambassador at Constantinople. The fastest that he might hope to get a reply from Constantinople, however, was about three weeks. Even a request for authoritative instructions from his superior, the consul-general at Beirut, Alexandria, or Cairo, was unlikely to elicit an answer in less than two weeks. Thus, consuls stationed in an outpost as isolated as Jerusalem behaved pretty much like ambassadors, exercising plenipotentiary powers. Wars, riots, threats of religious massacre, and insults to consular dignity did not allow for long-delayed answers to pressing questions.[6]

It is, therefore, not surprising that the earliest consuls behaved cautiously and avoided making demands of the local authorities, who scarcely disguised the fact that these Franks were unwelcome intruders in the Home of Islam. As the first European Christians to gain the privilege of legal residence in Jerusalem, the consuls rented their living quarters from Moslem landlords.[7] William Tanner Young, named British vice consul in 1838 and promoted to full consular rank in 1841,[8] was joined by a Prussian consul, Dr. E. Gustav Schultz,[9] and a French consul, Count de Lantivy,[10] both in 1843, and Austrian consul Count J. de Pizzamano in 1849.[11] The first Spanish consul, Pío de Andrés García, did not arrive until 1854.[12]

The Russians contented themselves until 1856 with a consular agent at Jaffa and a consul general at Beirut, both of whom made frequent visits to Jerusalem.[13] For a brief period, 1843–49, the Italian Kingdom of Sardinia-Piedmont,[14] and for a short period beginning in 1851, Greece stationed consuls in Jerusalem.[15] In the first decade and more of consular residence at Jerusalem, maritime states such as the United States or Belgium satisfied themselves with resident vice consuls or consular agents, usually Turkish subjects, who served at Jaffa, visiting Jerusalem only as necessary.[16] Indeed, the United States did not name a resident consul[17] in Jerusalem until 1857.[18] The first independent Asian power to name a resident consular agent in Jerusalem was Persia in 1857.[19] Maritime states such as Sweden and the Netherlands, which had very modest commercial interests in Palestine and which did not even find it worthwhile to support a consul at Beirut, entrusted the protection of their nationals to one of the governments having a consul at Jerusalem. Such individuals, during their residence in Palestine or Syria, were treated as bona fide subjects of the state to whose care they had been confided.[20] Precisely because one of the most important functions of a Palestinian consul was the administration of justice for his compatriots, it was sometimes a mixed blessing for a Netherlands subject to find himself claimed simultaneously as a protégé by the Prussian consul general at Beirut and the British consul at Jerusalem.[21]

From 1838 until the outbreak of the Crimean War, the foreign consuls experienced only a grudging admission to the seraglio or official household of the Turkish pashas. Consuls could not fly their flags at Jerusalem, nor did the Turkish governors willingly agree to special honors on the birthdays, saints' days, or national holidays of Christian sovereigns. The Turks did not celebrate their sultan's birthday as the Europeans made holidays of their kings' birthdays. Turks reserved public celebration for Moslem religious holidays, such as Corban Beiram or Mohammed's birthday. The pasha was thus able to fire cannon salutes from the walls of the citadel at the Jaffa Gate without doing the same for European royal birthdays.[22] The pasha would tender a reception in honor of Corban Beiram, to which the consuls and all the local notables, including the Christian and Jewish religious leaders, were invited. If, for example, the British consul was squeamish about appearing to join the celebration of a Moslem religious holiday, he might either decline the pasha's invitation altogether or pay a formal visit to the seraglio a day or two late. The pasha, the mufti, the cadis, and the local Arab effendi aristocracy would reciprocate in kind, when invited to a reception honoring Queen Victoria's birthday. Sometimes, both parties in an affront to national honor would boycott one another's social invitations completely.[23]

However much the small European consular community was obliged to mirror accurately the hostilities and friendships of the world balance of power, it presented a common front to the overtly contemptuous Turks. It was as though the Europeans represented an enclave of civilization surrounded by a backwater of barbarism. The Turks did not advance their own cause very much, preferring to maintain a similarly closed society, convinced of its superiority. An inordinately large amount of ink and stationery was expended by consuls informing their colleagues that court uniforms and ceremonial swords, or that modest civilian dress was *de rigueur* at a given royal birthday celebration or reception. Pride in rank and in precedence became substitutes for real influence with the pashas of Jerusalem during that first difficult decade, and even later.[24]

For example, when Prince Albert of Prussia, brother of King Frederick William IV, decided to visit Jerusalem in the spring of 1843, he stirred a hornet's nest. At the highest levels the Prussian embassy at Constantinople inquired as to the sort of reception he might expect in Palestine. The embassy was told that he would be held in quarantine like any ordinary traveler at the port of entry. The Turks told the startled Prussian ambassador that passengers aboard merchant vessels were held to a fifteen-day quarantine and that seamen aboard warships were held to a twelve-day quarantine, but that as a special favor the prince would only have to accept confinement at Jaffa for nine days. The Prussians regarded that as a very inadequate concession to a Hohenzollern prince of the blood. To avoid the embarrassment of being refused such royal perquisites as cannon salutes and honor guards, it was decided that Prince Albert would travel incognito. Nevertheless, the Prussian embassy took every precaution to avoid humiliation for their prince. A blizzard of documents fluttered down from Constantinople to every possible place where accident or design might carry the prince. An imperial firman bearing the sultan's seal warned the authorities in Egypt, Syria, Palestine, and Smyrna that the prince was coming. The grand vizier was induced to write letters supporting the prince's visit to the viceroy of Egypt and the musheers of Syria and Lebanon. Letters of recommendation were sent to the Turkish sanitary officers at Gaza, Jaffa, Jerusalem, Beirut, and Smyrna.[25]

Everyone breathed more easily when the prince disembarked uneventfully at Jaffa. Without having promised anything to the Prussians which might set a more relaxed precedent for future European tourists, the Turkish sanitary officer at Jaffa dispensed with quarantine altogether. It may have been just as well that the only Prussian representative who met Prince Albert at the Jaffa beach was Jacob Serafin Murad, an astute Armenian rayah who served as Prussia's consular agent at the city. Very probably, Mr. Murad had mastered the fine art of easing his way past Turkish bureaucratic regulations. It was Murad who escorted the prince to Jerusalem via Ramla with his own armed kawassin. The distinguished traveler may have had the illusion that he had received an honor guard, though the Turks made no gesture in that direction.[26] In any event, a year later Prince Albert was still writing letters of gratitude to Murad, so it may be assumed that the pilgrimage to Jerusalem passed satisfactorily. There had been no substantive concessions by the Turks, though Prince Albert's pioneer journey did test the willingness of the Sublime Porte to look the other way while its own rules were bypassed.[27]

During the crucial period 1838–50, the consular corps at Jerusalem laid a firm foundation upon which future generations might build, after the Turks had become reconciled to the permanent presence of the hated foreign infidels. In proportion to the wealth of each nation having a consul at Jerusalem, an elaborate service structure was created. Wealthy great powers such as Great Britain and France would empower their consuls at Jerusalem to employ vice consuls at a small salary in the principal ports. Vice consuls might be bona fide subjects of the country they served or they might be rayah merchants, competent to write in French or Italian if not in the native language of their consular chief. Vice consuls might be merchants earning the greater part of their living from commerce, content to accept as their only salary the fees they received for fixing the consular seal to legal documents.[28] There was, in addition, the advantage which a rayah could claim as a consular employee in evading certain Turkish taxes normally laid upon infidel subjects of the sultan.[29]

In towns where there was too little business to warrant the appointment of a vice consul, the consul at Jerusalem would name a respectable local inhabitant as consular agent, who performed the same functions as a vice consul, but received only consular fees as income for limited services. The more literate and respectable Christian and Jewish merchants avidly coveted the right to be a consular agent, not for the sake of the small income it brought but because such association with a European power enhanced their own security.[30]

Consuls also increased their own usefulness by naming dependable local religious or business leaders as "correspondents." Such correspondents received no salary and transacted no official business, but were requested to write regularly to the consul at Jerusalem, reporting on all matters of interest. Thus, for example, a German physician who ran a small hospital at Hebron wrote regularly to the Prussian consul,[31] and rabbis representing both the Sephardic and Ashkenazic Jews wrote to the British consul from Safed, Tiberias, and Hebron.[32] Roman Catholic clergy at all levels were protégés of the French consul.[33] Being a consular correspondent lent the individual prestige in his own community, special access to protection, and the occasional possibility of gaining the privileges of a naturalized foreigner with the right to travel abroad carrying a European passport.[34]

Consuls having a large number of correspondents gained, at almost no financial cost to themselves, a network of observers throughout the country, permitting them to know everything which transpired without the danger and inconvenience of travel. An aggressive and courageous consul could reserve his energy for unannounced visits to towns where the interests of his country were in jeopardy, surprising his foes by his sudden and unexpected appearance in their midst.[35]

As a slowly increasing stream of pilgrims and other tourists began to visit Palestine during the decade of the 1840s, consuls began to vie with one another for control of the tourist trade. As noted earlier, this involved offering generous feasts to the Bedouin sheiks and village headmen and drawing up elaborate contracts with dependable guides, specifying the exact payment to be demanded for each person escorted to the Jordan River, to Petra, to Es Salt or to the other exotic sites east of the sanjak of Jerusalem which grew steadily more attractive to Europeans. Because foreigners in Palestine were in grave danger unless they traveled under some sort of protection, consuls were in a uniquely advantageous position to build their own influence by winning the allegiance of all the local notables through whose territories tourists would have to travel. By assuring selected tourist guides that they alone would be recommended to tourists, the consuls ensured the growth of a body of loyal men who knew the country and its people intimately, and who could be counted upon for the service of the consulate.[36]

Once the consul had made it plain to the Bedouin sheiks and village headmen along the principal pilgrim trails that it was profitable to be a consul's friend, all sorts of other possibilities opened. A traveler who had suffered theft might have his property restored if the consul could contrive the collective punishment of an entire village until the villagers themselves ferreted out and surrendered the thief. As time passed, increasingly aggressive consuls learned how to threaten the pashas themselves with foreign intervention unless they jailed the entire family of a suspected thief, pending the confession of the real culprit.[37]

Because consuls personally enjoyed diplomatic immunity which included exemptions from Turkish customs duties, they were enabled to import goods under consular seal which were not intended for their personal use.

In the fall of the year, grapes were imported from Europe on special consignment to the consuls so that the non-Moslem population of the land could make their own wine. A modest native viniculture produced table grapes, and already the grapes of the

Hebron Mountains had a reputation for superiority. The Moslem peasantry, prohibited by the Koran from drinking alcoholic beverages, had neither the knowledge nor the motivation to experiment with wine grapes.

In a land denuded of native forests, the annual importation of European charcoal was a major trade item at the onset of winter. Any interruption of trade with Europe represented a crisis for people utterly dependent on foreign charcoal as the only defense against winter's dampness and frost. Whether for grapes or for charcoal, an increasing clientele found themselves dependent on a consul's good will.[38]

Palestine produced little which could not be purchased elsewhere in the eastern Mediterranean. A few unique items such as the glassware of Hebron had an attraction for merchants, but no ship's captain was likely to put in at Gaza only for the sake of such fragile exotica.

The presence of European consuls, however, meant that ships' masters were willing to visit Palestinian ports more often.

Trade became self-generating. As consuls demonstrated that they could offer effective service to their own nationals, an increasing volume of European steamship trade began to visit Palestinian seaports.[39] Consuls were given adequate opportunity to demonstrate that they had the kind of influence with the Turkish authorities which would hasten the arrest of a seaman who deserted his ship.[40] Equally, an able consul could save European seamen, merchants, and travelers from the vagaries of Turkish justice. In 1841, the only alternative in Palestine to a consular court was a Moslem religious court presided over by a cadi, if any Moslems were parties to a legal suit. In such courts, non-Moslems could not serve as sworn witnesses. Thus, each European power included in its treaty rights a consul's right to be present if a European was to receive a cadi's justice.

Obviously, each European consul strove by every technique of cajolery and threat to keep his nationals out of the cadi's jurisdiction. Emboldened by success, consuls within the decade of the forties began to claim consular jurisdiction in cases wherein both plaintiff and defendant were Turkish subjects, but where European property rights were involved. The juridical tug-of-war between pasha, cadi, and consul often became tests of personality and will.[41]

In the consular house of cards, however, much rested upon extending the right of legal resort to as large a body of protégés as possible. Consular effectiveness was by no means uniform, and the real power exercised by a consul rested upon his mastery of the techniques of persuasion and coercion more than upon formal treaty right.

At each consulate, a staff of interpreters had to be employed. The word dragoman implies only an interpreter. In the Ottoman Empire generally, and in Palestine particularly, the dragoman was indispensable. In Palestine it was necessary, at an absolute minimum, for a consul to have immediate access to someone capable of translating Turkish, Arabic, Hebrew, Yiddish, Greek, Ladino, French, and Italian. The dragoman not only had to be fluent in essential languages, but he had to be intelligent enough to carry on delicate negotiations with people whose support the consul needed, but who would otherwise have been strangers to him because of a language barrier. It was a rare dragoman who spoke and wrote all the required languages. Thus, each consulate employed a corps of translators as large as its budget permitted. An intelligent and ambitious dragoman could make himself indispensable to a consul with important interests at stake and secrets which he wished to keep. If a consul were careless, a dragoman might enrich himself illegally, using his privileged position to victimize those who were willing to pay for favors.[42]

Frequently, the same men served simultaneously as consular agents or even as consuls for two or more nations. Thus, no one raised an eyebrow when a rayah named Hanna Mitri, who had once served as a consular agent for Russia at Jaffa, left Palestine briefly and returned as vice consul for Belgium.[43] Nor was it considered unusual that Constantine Avierino, a British subject born in the Ionian Islands, was simultaneously a consular agent for Russia and Greece at Haifa.[44] The entire confusing kaleidoscope of double and even triple loyalties could be traced to one simple fact: there was a severe shortage of multilingual, economically secure, highly intelligent men capable of threading their way through the complexities of Turkish bureaucratic regulations, yet able to conform to the needs of western nations.

Perhaps one example of the species will suffice to cover them all. Jasper Chasseaud was a prosperous Beirut merchant of mixed ethnic origins who described himself as a native of Macedonian Thessaly, hence a Turkish subject.[45] For almost twenty years, until his sudden dismissal in 1850, Chasseaud was United States consul in Beirut with jurisdiction covering the coast of the eastern Mediterranean. He was authorized to name unpaid consular agents at Aleppo, Latakia, Tripoli, Saida, Tyre, Acre, and Haifa, as well as Jaffa. All of the agents in his service were Arab, Armenian, Greek, or Jewish rayahs.[46] For at least four years, 1843–47, Chasseaud was simultaneously the consul of Prussia at Beirut.[47] In 1847, the Prussian consul at Jerusalem advanced the interests of another Beirut rayah, Y.B. Catafago, by giving him specific duties at Beirut. Chasseaud, apparently thinking that he was indispensable, offered his resignation as Prussian consul. To his evident surprise, it was accepted and Catafago was named in his place.[48]

During this entire brouhaha, the United States kept Chasseaud in its service even though he was flying two flags. Perhaps he was valued at Washington because he had continued calmly at his post, rendering useful service to United States citizens even during the violent events which rocked Beirut from 1839 to 1841.[49] It does not seem to have mattered to his American patrons that his regular reports revealed him to be an ignorant and provincial obscurantist, totally out of touch with the nineteenth century. In 1840, when the Jews of Damascus were collectively accused of having murdered a Roman Catholic friar and to have used his blood to make unleavened bread for Passover, Chasseaud supported those absurd charges uncritically. Chasseaud was perfectly prepared to defend the torture and massacre of numerous Jews, solemnly enclosing translations of spurious documents allegedly taken from Jewish scriptures, justifying blood-ritual murder.[50] Secretary of State John Forsyth certainly did not share Chasseaud's superstitious bigotry, and indeed he exerted the modest influence of the United States at Cairo and Constantinople to effect the rescue of those Jews awaiting death in Damascus prisons.[51] Perhaps Forsyth did not even read the outrageous reports of Consul Chasseaud. In any event, he continued in his office without rebuke.

In 1850, however, the United States began a policy of reserving all consular posts for United States citizens. Consular posts had come to be regarded as excellent patronage plums to be dispensed as political rewards. Nothing could describe more eloquently the virtues and the vices of the consular system in Syria and Palestine than the pathetic letter written by Chasseaud to Secretary of State John M. Clayton, begging for the restoration of his consular post. It is worth reading in its original form, grammatical errors included:

> Allow me the honor, I beg respectfully, to state how painful has been to my feelings the report which I hear that I am going to be changed from my office after twenty years of faithful services to your country, and this for no other motive but because unfortunately I am not a Citizen myself of the U.S. and that a born Citizen has asked for it.
>
> It is natural, Sir, that a Citizen may claim a preference over a foreigner to hold the office of Consul, abroad, but in all Countries and nations there are exceptions, I believe. I was in hopes that my long services might have been taken into consideration. Though I have not the honor of being a Citizen, yet I flatter myself that I have served Honourably and faithfully your Country to the full satisfaction of all my superiors, as well as that of all the Officers of the Navy, Missionaries, travellers, and no one of them has ever had motives of discontent.

This was the title which made me hope to pass the rest of my few years in serving the U.S. and to die Honorably under the Stars and Stripes.

The U.S. Citizens occasionally insulted have *all* obtained full satisfaction; Those who have been robbed, I procured them back their stolen property. The sick have received all the attention and care; The distressed found always assistance; The travellers a cordial reception and hospitality; and the U.S. flag in my hands was respected and saluted always on the 4th of July.

To protect the rights of the Citizens of your country. Sir, as of course in duty bound, often times I had to quarrel with the other Consuls my colleagues and particularly with the one under whose jurisdiction and vengeance I must now, in my advanced age fall as soon as the Flag is removed from my house.[52] How mortifying it is to me, that after all the consideration, liberty, and Independence which I have enjoyed for so many years as your Consul, to have to fall now under Slavery and the Caprice of others. It is not, Sir, for any reason of pecuniary interest that I make these observations and show my grief. I have never charged a single Cent to any Citizen of the U.S. for fees of my office. I have lost severely last Summer, perhaps more than all my Consular pay together has amounted, hitherto, in opening a new branch of trade between the U.S. and Syria, and I would even have renounced my salary of the $200 which your Government was pleased to allow me, for the Honor only of continuing in my Office.

It has pleased your Government to honor me with the Consulate. I am thankful and grateful for it, and trust I have discharged my duty honorably. It is now pleased to remove me; the pleasure again is theirs. Had my friends in America been sincere to me, this perhaps would not have been the case, but it seems that while on the one hand they were flattering me with promises and hopes, on the other hand they were working for themselves. Of course, I can demand nothing for myself, but I am still in hopes that your Government will be pleased to take my case into consideration and do something for the advancement of my Sons, the eldest of them, Augustus, aged 17 years who knows the English, French, Italian, and Arabic languages. The second, George Washington, 14 years old, who equally knows those four languages, and the third Edwin yet an infant of 4 years, all of whom born under the flag of the U.S., and Washington baptized on board the Frigate Constitution, Comre Elliot having served as Godfather to him.[53]

Jasper Chasseaud's pleas did him no good, and he was replaced early in 1851 by J. Hosford Smith, an authentic United States citizen.[54] For all of the consuls in Palestine and Syria, the decade of the fifties would prove to be a watershed era. The great maritime powers, conscious of Turkish weakness, made their consuls the hard-cutting edge of their expanded interest in the Near East.

Chapter Eight
Palestine and the Crimean War

Religion has often provided a respectable pretext for the most disreputable Machiavellian behavior. No better example of this can be found than the Crimean War, 1853–56. The spark which set off that mad and futile conflict was the debate whether the Roman Catholic Church, defended by France, or the Orthodox Church, defended by Russia, would enjoy dominance in the Palestinian holy places sacred to Christendom. The Turks, from the moment that that ancient quarrel was revived in 1850, saw the peril to their own interests implicit in this "battle of the keys." The Turks took the sensible view that the tree which bends in stormy winds is least likely to be broken. They therefore yielded as much as possible as French and Russian diplomats revived centuries-old claims to the rights of their respective churchmen to hold the keys to the doors of Christian shrines at Jerusalem, Bethlehem, or Nazareth. The sultan's government was perfectly willing to transfer keys back and forth between the Latin and Greek patriarchs, pretending that all the fuss was a strictly Christian family squabble to which Islam was entirely foreign and in which Turkey was perfectly neutral.[1] At any one of a number of points in the years from 1850 to 1853, Turkey might have ended up with a totally different set of allies and enemies than she was eventually assigned by fate.[2] Indeed, through most of that interim period no one foretold the coming of war at all. At the beginning of the quarrel in 1850, as the world was seen from St. Petersburg, it seemed likely that Britain would actively collaborate with Russia if it came to a partition of the property of the Turkish "sick man of Europe."[3] Czar Nicholas I, a soldier rather than a diplomat by training, also had the utterly naive notion that there was a place in the diplomatic dictionary for the word "gratitude." Inasmuch as Russia had crushed the Hungarian revolt of 1849 and handed the kingdom of Hungary back to Emperor Franz Josef of Austria, the czar imagined that Austria would support Russia in any war that the czar might launch against the Turk. The czar had no reason to fear opposition from Prussia, which at the Olmütz Conference of 1850 had agreed to renounce all aspirations to displace Austria as the dominant German power. Czar Nicholas, therefore, felt perfectly free to pursue a strong anti-French policy, confident that Louis Napoleon Bonaparte, president of the Second French Republic, would not risk war against Russia without a major ally.[4]

Correspondence in which Count Pizzamano bemoans the hardships of life at Jerusalem and begs Austrian Chancellor Count Buol to make him consul at Genoa (1855). Copy of document supplied by Austrian Haus-Hof und Staatsarchiv, Vienna.

Numerous studies have explored the unpredictable chain of events which produced a diplomatic revolution. At the end of that revolution, it was Russia which went to war against Turkey without a single ally. Turkey, against all probability, was to fight the Crimean War as the ally of Great Britain, France, and Sardinia-Piedmont. Austria maintained a neutrality which was so openly benign to Britain and France that it was injurious to Russia. Only Prussia lent benign support to Russia, though Berlin guarded its official neutrality.[5]

For the purposes of this study, no attention will be given to the central theatre of developments, as the original focus of events in Palestine was shuffled aside and the war was actually fought in the Black and Baltic Seas. Notwithstanding the apparent insignificance of Palestine in the realpolitik of the powers, the Crimean War had a tremendous effect upon the relations between Europeans and Turks in the Holy Land. Most studies of the Crimean War dismiss Palestine as having little part in the Treaty of Paris which ended the struggle in 1856. This study will devote its examination of the war years to the dramatic and permanent changes wrought in Palestinian history by the events of a struggle fought far from Jerusalem.

During the long centuries in which Palestine had been a dusty and neglected provincial appendage of Ottoman Syria, Jerusalem had become little more than a large, walled village. With travel perilously difficult, the Holy City was abandoned even by those religious leaders whose titles derived from the See of Jerusalem. Since 1291, the Latin patriarchs of Jerusalem had lived abroad, usually in Italy.[6] Even the Greek Orthodox patriarch, leader of the largest single Christian communion in Palestine, spent most of his time in Constantinople, where his presence might be politically useful to his church. It must be added, however, that the Greek patriarch always had resided for part of each year at Jerusalem.[7]

In the aftermath of Mehmet Ali's rebellion, 1839–41, however, the arrival of the first consuls was accompanied by the newly granted right of European Christians to take up permanent residence in Jerusalem. As noted previously, the brief tenure of Michael Solomon Alexander as first Anglican bishop of Jerusalem, 1842–45, became symbolic of Christendom's renewed interest in the city of its birth. The fact that King Frederick William IV immediately asserted his prerogative to name a second Anglican bishop, Samuel Gobat, underlined the newly revived Christian missionary interest in Jerusalem. The new bishop during the years of his episcopate from 1846 to 1879 reversed the policy of Bishop Alexander. The original exponents of an Anglican bishopric at Jerusalem had been the London Jews Society. That missionary organization had dreamed of building a Protestant community in Palestine by a large-scale conversion of Jews. The virtually complete failure of that effort resulted in Bishop Gobat changing the direction of his mission. A French-speaking Swiss, the new bishop had been raised in the Calvinist tradition, but was ultimately ordained both as a Lutheran and as an Anglican. He felt much more comfortable with the goals of the Church Missionary Society than with those of the London Jews Society.[8] He expressed it years later:

> I knew that it was not the object of those who had appointed and sent me to Jerusalem that I should restrict myself to the work of an ordinary local pastor or missionary to the Jews…. I was a debtor not only to the Jews, but also to the ignorant Greeks, Romanists, Armenians, Turks, etc….[9]

Although the bishop made an effort to be civil to the local, resident, native Christian prelates of other churches, his essentially arrogant view of the rest of the world put everyone on guard. Gobat's dream was to establish Anglican hostels and schools throughout Palestine on both sides of the Jordan, to win Christian Arabs of other denominations to his church.[10]

It is entirely a coincidence, of course, but three of the most important native Christian churches received new leaders within a year of Gobat's arrival and his challenge to his fellow Christians. In 1845, a new Greek Orthodox patriarch of Jerusalem was invested as Cyril II. This aggressive prelate, who lived until 1872, offered firm resistance to Gobat while maintaining the amenities of civility on a social level. As though to underline his view of Jerusalem's importance, he began to spend increasing portions of each year in the city, visiting Constantinople only as he viewed such visits as politically helpful.[11]

In 1846, the Armenian Church had elected Kyriakus I as patriarch of Jerusalem, but he died in 1850. The Armenians were fully awake to the threat which missionary activity posed to their church and promptly chose a new patriarch, Hovhanness of Smyrna, who reigned from 1850 to 1860.[12] Both patriarchs, Kyriakus and Hovhanness, rallied the close knit and intensely self-conscious Armenian community against the Protestant interloper. The entire situation was rendered potentially embarrassing when James Finn became the second British consul at Jerusalem in 1846, the same year as the arrival of Bishop Gobat. Both Finn and his iron-willed and aggressive wife, Elizabeth Anne Finn, remained convinced that their life's work was the conversion of Jews, side by side with training them to be farmers and manual laborers and settling them on the land. Thus, while Finn and Gobat developed an increasingly abrasive personal relationship, the British missionaries at Jerusalem contrived to frighten, challenge, or to offend the Jewish and native Christian population of Palestine.[13]

It is certainly no coincidence that in the midst of such confrontation between all the non-Moslem sects of Palestine, the Roman Catholic Church also strengthened its position. In 1846, Pope Pius IX ascended the throne of St. Peter. Almost immediately he took the unusual step of deposing the last of the purely titular Italian patriarchs of Jerusalem.[14] In his place in 1847, he named Monsignor Joseph Valerga. The new patriarch arrived at Jaffa on January 13, 1848, aboard a French warship. He was met by representatives of all the Catholic powers having consular agents in Palestine.[15] It must be underlined that Valerga enjoyed an extremely strong title to influence. French governments under King Louis Philippe, the Second French Republic, and Napoleon III's

Second French Empire reasserted French primacy as the protector of Roman Catholic interests in Palestine.[16] In addition, the patriarch was the personal representative of the pope who was not merely a spiritual leader, but a sovereign prince. Thus, in a sense, the rank of Monsignor Valerga was that of a papal nuncio, far outranking the consuls of Jerusalem. Immediately, the Roman Catholic Church in Palestine became the spearhead of French influence as French-speaking nuns and priests established first-rate schools and hospitals, ministering to the needs of native Arab Roman Catholics and aggressively opening missions for the rest of the non-Moslem population.[17]

It was in this atmosphere of increasingly vitriolic relations between the Palestinian Christian communities that Russia opened its attempt to obtain possession of the keys to the Palestinian churches for Greek Orthodox Patriarch Cyril II. Confident that France and the Latin Church were isolated, Russia moved with foolhardy ruthlessness to assert the primacy of the Orthodox churches. Over the centuries, the Turks as arbiters of Christian quarrels had carefully divided the control of the shrines between the contending churches. The Orthodox already possessed the edge in all such honors, both because they constituted the largest single Christian denomination in Palestine[18] and because the Orthodox patriarch could claim predecessors who had resided almost continuously in Jerusalem ever since the Council of Chalcedon in 451.[19] Had the Russians succeeded in gaining full custody of the keys for Patriarch Cyril, all the other churches would have had to acknowledge that they worshipped at Greek Orthodox altars as guests of a church protected by Russia.[20]

In view of the crisis which came to a head at this point, it is unfortunate that the governor of Jerusalem, 1851–54, Hafiz Ahmed Pasha, was a sickly old man past eighty years of age.[21] Caught between the pressures of France and Russia to grant concessions to their respective churches, the sultan and his pasha at Jerusalem played for time.

In the vain hope of ending this puerile but dangerous battle of the keys, the sultan sent Afif Bek, a member of the Imperial Council of State, to Jerusalem, bearing a firman clearly setting forth the rights of the contending Christian religious communities. At his arrival on September 14, 1852, the Greek and Armenian patriarchs rode out to meet him.[22] Why the Latin patriarch failed to pay him a similar conspicuous honor is open to speculation. Monsignor Valerga may not have wanted to act in concert with his rivals, thereby admitting that they were his equals. He may also have felt constrained as a foreigner to avoid showing the forms of reverence which Turkish subjects tendered to the bearer of a sultan's firman; both the Greek and Armenian patriarchs were rayah. Certainly, however, the Latin patriarch was conspicuous by his absence when even the aged pasha honored his guest by meeting him outside the city walls at the Meidan, the army parade ground near the Damascus Gate. For reasons unknown to the writer, Afif Bek did not read the firman to the pasha and the assembled consuls until October 26, more than a month after his arrival. He may have been awaiting further instructions from Constantinople, or he may have been spinning out the delay as long as possible, just to gain time. In any event, a neutral observer analyzed the firman as disappointing to all parties because it made modest concessions to the Latins, but essentially preserved the preferences always hitherto shown to the Greeks.[23] The extreme detail of the firman makes an extensive quotation of its language worthwhile. The Hatti-Sherif of 1852 states in part:

> Although a key to the main door of the Bethlehem Church had been given to the Latins,…the [unique] right has not been given to them to officiate there, nor to possess it in common with the Greeks. Furthermore, permission has not been accorded to Latins to alter, in any manner whatsoever, the present state of this church…, and in a word, it is not permitted to them to change what has been practiced at all times…in what concerns passage through the church to the Grotto…. Though the gatekeeper of the Bethlehem Church…

has been for a long time a Greek priest subject to the Sublime Porte, that gatekeeper has no right to refuse passage to the nations which have enjoyed the right of passage....

The Star which has just been placed in the Grotto of the Bethlehem Church as a public reminder of my Imperial gift to this Christian nation, and to put an end to all contest, and which is made on the model of the star which used to be in the Grotto and disappeared in 1847; no new right is accorded to any Christian nation....

The Christian nations which have the right to visit the Tomb of the Holy Virgin and to celebrate their religion there, will officiate there daily. In this Tomb, the Greeks will officiate first, at the beginning of sunrise, on the condition of not opposing themselves to the other nations also performing the ceremonies of their religion. After the Greeks will come the Armenians, and after the latter, the Latins, each in turn will officiate for an hour and a half....

The two gardens situated in the village of Bethlehem and which are contiguous to the Franciscan Monastery, will be administered by the Greeks and Latins as in the past, without one or the other having any right of preeminence....

With the exception of that which is in question, here, there is no concession which has newly been put into force by consequence of an official order in favor of any nation, whatsoever. All will be confirmed in the present state.[24]

Afif Bek's mission and the Hatti-Sherif of 1852 failed completely to halt the slide toward war. In March 1853, two months before the final break in relations between Russia and Turkey, the sultan sent a copy of his firman of 1852 to each consul at Jerusalem and the pasha of that sanjak. Each person receiving such a copy also received a copy of an additional firman in which the sultan promised to repair the cupola and other parts of the Church of the Holy Sepulchre at Jerusalem, and giving the Greek Orthodox patriarch the right to approve all plans for such repairs.[25]

Such concessions, if they had been made in 1850 when the Battle of the Keys had been launched by Czar Nicholas, would have been classed as a clear Russian victory. As it is, the concession to the Greeks came only when the Russians had raised their demands to new heights.[26] Prince Alexander Menshikov's mission to Constantinople from February to May 1853 demanded not only the keys to the Palestinian holy places, but a reaffirmation of the most extreme interpretation of the Peace of Kutchuk Kainardji of 1774. That interpretation gave Russia the title to protect all Orthodox Christians in the Turkish Empire. Plainly no nation could recognize such a pretension without losing its sovereignty. It had become apparent by May 1853 that the Russians had raised their gambling stakes so high that they must either win all or lose all. No compromise was possible. Colonel von Wildenbruck, the Prussian ambassador at Constantinople, wrote to his good personal friend, Dr. Georg Rosen, the consul at Jerusalem, "…you can be assured that a Russian grenade produced at Jerusalem is going to explode." Wildenbruck, who made his prediction in February 1853 when Menshikov had just arrived in Constantinople with his ultimata, proved to be a prophet.[27]

The role of the British ambassador to the Sublime Porte in encouraging the Turks to refuse Russia's demands is still debated.[28] There is little doubt, however, that during his long tenure of the embassy in Constantinople Stratford Canning, who became Lord Stratford de Redcliffe in 1852, was a diplomat almost unique for his influence. By sheer force of personality, he was able to dominate the weak sultan and his ministers. It may also be speculated that Lord Stratford, who was briefly in England in 1852–53, may have helped to draw up his own instructions at the Foreign Office before proceeding to Constantinople again. He was thus a diplomat in the rare position of having created the policy which he alone was uniquely fitted to implement.[29]

At the repulse of Menshikov's demands for a Russian protectorate over all the Orthodox Christian subjects of the sultan, the Russians withdrew their embassy staff. The break took place on May 19, 1853. Neutral observers still noted with optimism that the commercial section of the Russian embassy remained open.[30] Hope was dimmed for a peaceful solution when on July 2 the Russian army invaded Turkish Wallachia.[31] The resultant Turkish declaration of war on Russia did not occur until October 4. It was not until October 22 that the British and French fleets were given the order to pass the Dardanelles. Their ultimatum to the Russians to quit Turkish territory was not sent off until February 27, 1854. An actual alliance between Britain and France was not consummated until March 12. Britain and France declared war on Russia only on March 28. The fact that the Russians had destroyed the Turkish fleet at Sinope on November 30, 1853, and that the British and French began the systematic destruction of the Russian fleet in January 1854, seemed almost incidental to the reality that a major war was beginning for which no one was really prepared. That the Austrians offered armed mediation to the belligerents and forced the Russians to abandon Moldavia and Wallachia would seem to reasonable observers to have ended the danger of war. The entry of Austrian troops into these two principalities to stand as mediatory referees between the combatants offered an illusory hope that the danger of war had ended by eliminating the only land area in which large-scale military maneuver was possible. No one thought seriously of a large-scale war in the Caucasus Mountains.[32] Only the feverish imaginations of some of the consuls stationed in Jerusalem conceived of an actual Russian invasion of Palestine.[33] It is the crudest kind of irony which ultimately led the belligerent powers to redeem their honor, once first blood had been shed, by launching an attack upon the Russian Crimea to capture the naval base at Sebastopol. The Russian naval forces, once stationed there, had already been decimated.[34] The sober statesmen of Europe were behaving like adolescent German university students, anxious to earn a livid scar on their faces to prove their manhood. During all of this blood-stained burlesque, the Russians continued to sell government bonds on the British and French stock markets and faithfully paid interest and principal on debts owed to their enemies.[35]

For Palestine the war remained far away, all of its events transpiring as distorted rumors, confirmed, denied, or revised weeks after they had happened. Obviously, Ottoman Turkey could not be at war, however, without profound effects in the most isolated provinces of the empire.[36]

Because of their distance from the center of action, the Russians in Palestine seemed to have no notion that their country was about to go to war. As late as June 3–6, British Consul Finn at Jerusalem was surprised to receive purely social calls from Count Nostitz, Commander of a Russian war ship anchored off Jaffa. The Russian naval officer had failed to receive word that Menshikov had quit Constantinople.[37]

When hostilities actually opened, Russia gave custody of all her property in Palestine to the Austrians. This included the duty of protecting Russian nationals trapped on Turkish soil and unable to leave.[38] Obviously, the Russians were as surprised as anyone by Austria's diplomatic betrayal and her transformation, de facto, into a neutral power tending toward hostility.

The most important immediate consequence for Palestine of the outbreak of war was the withdrawal of almost all regular Turkish soldiery for service in the war zone. On September 19, 1853, the Turkish battalion which guarded Jerusalem held a last review on the Meidan parade ground and began its march to Jaffa. The surrounding countryside was denuded of horses, camels, and mules to carry the battalion's baggage. About a company of Turkish artillery remained at the Jaffa Gate to overawe the hostile countryside. From then on the maintenance of order rested upon an octogenarian governor, a few artillerists, and some hundreds of hastily conscripted Arab peasant boys impressed into service as howari or bashi-bazouk irregular soldiers. Less than a militia, the bashi-bazouk, undisciplined and predatory, terrified those whom they were supposed to protect.[39] Actually, for a year preceding the official departure of the regular Jerusalem garrison, the Turks had been engaged in stripping Jerusalem of men and weapons potentially needed elsewhere. Consequently, Hafiz Ahmed Pasha lost control of the countryside long before the dramatic departure of the garrison had advertised the weakness of the governor of Jerusalem.[40] In July 1853, brushfire wars had broken out all over the Palestinian area. The dreaded Taamri Bedouin, whose range normally lay between the shores of the Dead Sea and the outskirts of Bethlehem, sent armed men to the walls of Jerusalem itself. The great clan of Abu Gosh, which held the mountain passes between Jaffa and Jerusalem, struck an alliance with kindred clans to seize the village of Ein Kerem, west of Jerusalem, the battle spreading south of Jerusalem to Beit Safafa. Even the hilltop village of Silwan, next to the Mount of Olives east of Jerusalem, opened a blood feud with the village of Beit Sahhur.[41] In the Galilee, the great Sheik Aqili Aga was already well launched into a thirty-year career as the true master of all the north, prepared to support the Turks against the Druse and Kurds or to rebel against the Turks as his own interests dictated.[42]

Under the circumstances, even if Hafiz Pasha had been a competent governor, he would have been obliged to be circumspect. The Turkish government did not wish to give any European power a pretext for intervention in Palestine, with the Russians already on their backs. The consequence was that for the first time since the days of Mehmet Ali, the Turks seemed anxious to consult closely with the European representatives on Turkish soil. Suddenly, consuls were shown a deference they had never known before at Jerusalem. The British consul, James Finn, was more fully prepared than anyone else for the opportunity when it came.

The French consul, Paul Emile Botta, a distinguished archeologist who is remembered for his excavations at ancient Nineveh, was a bitterly unhappy man. He was at that point awaiting transfer to a better post, having come to regard Palestine as a dead end for his career. He did not obtain transfer until 1855, but contented himself with defending French and Roman Catholic interests without taking lively initiatives.[43] Inasmuch as Britain and France were allies of Turkey, Botta did allow himself to be associated in a limited way with Finn's aggressive activities.[44]

The Austrian consul, Count J. de Pizzamano, was a Venetian Italian aristocrat married to a Viennese wife.[45] It was Pizzamano's bad fortune to have been born too early or too late for a clear definition of his self-identity. In a decade when most Italians had become passionately nationalist and anti-Austrian, Pizzamano remained a self-conscious anachronism devoted to the Habsburg dynasty and eschewing Italian national sentiment.[46] When he came face to face with the celebrated Italian nationalist Princess Cristina Trivulzio Belgiojoso, who had raised a troop of cavalry at her own expense to fight Austria in 1848–49, he studiously avoided greeting her.[47] It is a kind of commentary on Pizzamano that he wrote all of his reports to Vienna either in German Gothic script or, more rarely, in Italian. Most men in his position would have chosen the perfectly acceptable nineteenth-century escape of using French.

The Prussian consul, Dr. Georg Rosen, was a native of Lippe-Detmold near Hanover who had served in the Prussian embassy in Constantinople as an interpreter. Rosen, an attorney by training, was an authority on oriental languages. Still a bachelor in his early thirties, he returned briefly to Europe in 1853 to marry and to bring his bride back to Jerusalem in 1854. Mrs. Rosen, a daughter of the great pianist Ignaz Moschelles, was a valuable addition to the literary and musical circle formed by the consuls at Jerusalem.[48] Under ordinary circumstances, Dr. Rosen, representing a Protestant power, would have been a natural ally of James Finn. However, inasmuch as Prussia was the only great power whose sympathies tended to support Russia, Rosen found himself, quite innocently, involved in a major battle with Finn which came close to embroiling their superiors at London and Berlin in a potentially dangerous clash.[49]

For one reason or another, James Finn found himself the only consul at Jerusalem able to exert maximum leverage to break the xenophobic exclusivity of the Turkish government at Jerusalem.

Finn seems to have mastered the Arabic dialect spoken in Palestine, a remarkable feat since he had been ignorant of the language before coming to the country in 1846.[50] He therefore undertook to make himself a peacemaking mediator between the warring Bedouin clans and the villagers near Jerusalem. Fond of camping in tents during the long dry season, Finn undertook to hold a series of conferences with all the Arabs at war with one another. A man of extraordinary personal courage, he was prepared to enter battle zones, confident that both sides knew and respected him. He had spent the years since 1846 well and had a large network of correspondents, missionary employees, consular agents, and other clients in every corner of the country who regularly reported to him. More than that, he had ruthlessly made himself the patron of tourist guides, all of whom had useful family ties to sheiks and village headmen, or to religious factions on both sides of the Jordan.[51]

Building on such a foundation, Finn was able by raw nerve and sheer sense of theater to control men who hated one another. The British consul made himself useful to local Arab notables threatened with deportation because Hafiz Pasha suspected them of treason. The best that Finn could usually accomplish was to obtain a deferment of such deportations. Nevertheless, by winning the gratitude of effendi notables of the Jerusalemite aristocracy, such as the houses of Wafa, Darweesh, Nakeeb, and Afif, the British consul earned credits to be cashed in later years.[52]

With allowances for wifely exaggeration, Elizabeth Anne Finn's memoirs describe the "wholesome dread" in which her husband was held. Somewhat ingenuously, she entered a typical note for the year 1854: "Mr. Finn had to go off again in December to quell some of the popular disturbances. He really was the Turkish Government at that time, for there was no one else to represent law and order." In the same vein, she frequently noted the superstitious dread with which malefactors of all stripes were afflicted whenever Finn appeared with his ubiquitous notebook. The entry of a name in the notebook was supposed to be accompanied by inexorable punishment.[53]

However, even with their preoccupation with the theater of war, the Turkish government could not ignore the rapid slide of Palestine toward anarchy. Unable to spare fresh troops, Constantinople belatedly decided to retire the ineffective pasha of Jerusalem. Hafiz Ahmed Pasha was so old and sickly that when he left Jerusalem for the last time on December 17, 1853, he had to be carried in a palanquin all the way to Jaffa. In firing a sixteen-gun salute to the retiring pasha, an inept Turkish artilleryman had his arm shot off. Upon reaching Jaffa, the pasha died on January 14, 1854.[54] The misfortunes of the old man were like mournful harbingers of the grief of the entire country.

Until a new governor could be named, the government of the sanjak of Jerusalem devolved upon the cadi who presided over the Makhkameh, or Moslem Supreme Court at Jerusalem.[55] Hafiz Pasha's successor did not arrive until March 16.[56] The new governor had undoubtedly been chosen because he was the scion of one of the empire's noblest families. Having the rank of musheer, he was theoretically the equal of his administrative superior, the musheer of Beirut, who governed all the sanjaks of Palestine and the Lebanon. Unfortunately, however, Yakoob Pasha Kara Osman Oglu was eighty-four years old. In him, the lassitude of age was accompanied by a passion for bribery that made him outstanding even in a society where gifts to officials were normal. His sudden death on October 20, 1854, ended his little more than seven months as governor without having moved Palestine an inch closer to stability.[57]

It was not until February 15, 1855 that the third and final Crimean War pasha of Jerusalem arrived at his post.[58] Fortunately, Kiamal Pasha was a truly superior administrator and an extraordinarily adept diplomat. At the time of his appointment, still in his early twenties, he was liberal, well-educated, and a fervent Anglophile. During his long life, he was destined to serve four times as grand vizier. To the very end, he maintained his pro-British attitudes. Indeed, at the outbreak of World War I, when it was plain that the sultan was committed to Germany, he took refuge in Cyprus and died there under British protection in 1916.[59]

It was Kiamal Pasha who opened Jerusalem to Europeans as it had never been opened before. Although his first term as pasha lasted only until 1857 or twenty-six months, Palestine and its attitudes would never be the same again. Kiamal Pasha's openness to foreigners, absolutely unprecedented at Jerusalem, was undoubtedly approved at the highest levels in Constantinople. Still, the young governor dramatized his friendship for westerners and his gratitude for the Crimean alliance against Russia in ways which went far beyond the sort of latitude allowed him by the Sublime Porte.

On January 6, 1856, before the signing of the Treaty of Paris which ended the Crimean War, Kiamal Pasha electrified the conservative Moslem society of Jerusalem by publicly attending Anglican church services at the newly opened Christ Church. Kiamal Pasha also commissioned an artist to construct a miniature duplicate of the Church of the Holy Sepulchre to be sent as his personal gift to Queen Victoria. It made its way, ultimately, to the South Kensington Museum at London.[60]

Even more dramatically, the governor relaxed the old proscriptions against honors to visiting foreigners. Cannon salutes were now routinely fired from the Jerusalem citadel on the national holidays of all the nations represented by consuls at Jerusalem. The pasha, cadis, mufti, and the members of the medjlis began to pay formal visits to consuls in honor of the birthdays of Queen Victoria, Emperor Napoleon III, King Frederick William IV, Emperor Franz Josef, or Queen Isabella II.[61] In return, consuls had to swallow their prejudices and visit the Moslem notables on major religious holidays in Islam.[62]

Nothing underlines the reforms of Kiamal Pasha more completely, however, than his courageous decision to open the Temple

Mount and the mosques of El Aqsa and Al Haram to non-Moslems.

The first test of the new program came when the heirs to the throne of Belgium, the Duke and Duchess of Brabant, made a pilgrimage to Jerusalem, arriving on March 30, 1855. A royal salute was fired at the Jaffa Gate. With a great deal of nervousness, plans were made for the royal couple's ascent to the Temple Mount on Friday, April 6. The duke, the older son of King Leopold I, had taken the precaution of obtaining the sultan's firman for a visit to the Temple Mount and mosques previously barred to non-Moslems. Even Kiamal Pasha, however, could not vouch for the safety of foreign Christians bold enough to enter the forbidden mosques on the Moslem sabbath which happened also to coincide with Good Friday. To achieve basic safety for his guests, the pasha used almost all of the small Turkish garrison at Jerusalem to temporarily arrest and confine the fierce Sudanese Takruri tribesmen who traditionally served as guards against foreign intrusion in the mosques. Indeed, such a large concourse of consuls, their families, and ordinary European tourists decided to take advantage of the unprecedented opportunity to visit the Temple Mount that the arrival of the Duke and Duchess of Brabant delayed the recitation of the regular Friday afternoon prayers at the mosques. Certainly the visit of the future King Leopold II of Belgium provided a striking contrast to that of Prince Albert of Prussia back in 1843.[63]

The only person at Jerusalem who was outspoken about his unhappiness with the Belgian royal visit was the long-suffering Count Pizzamano. Belgium had no consul at Jerusalem. Therefore, by default, the honor of entertaining the duke and duchess fell to the Austrian consul, since the Duchess of Brabant was a Habsburg. Countess Pizzamano, on very short notice, had had to prepare her modest home for the very important visitors suddenly thrust upon her. No other accommodations were available. The Roman Catholic pilgrim hospice, the Casa Nuova, was described as vermin-ridden. The European-owned hotels within the walled city were almost as bad. Pizzamano kept a careful record of his expenses and sent the bill to the Austrian foreign ministry for the expensive honor thrust upon him.[64]

It was to be a financially exhausting but socially triumphant year for the Pizzamanos. The next very important guest to enter Jerusalem was Archduke Ferdinand Maximilian von Habsburg, younger brother of Emperor Franz Josef of Austria and heir pre-sumptive to his throne. The future tragic Emperor Maximilian of Mexico was then aged 23, but held the rank of an Austrian Vice Admiral. As he was accompanied by his fellow naval officers and a prince of the kingdom of Württemberg, as well, Kiamal Pasha raised no difficulty about cannon salutes and honor guards. For-tunately for the expense account and the nerves of the Count and Countess Pizzamano, the archducal party's visit was short. Arriving at Jerusalem on Saturday, June 30, they ascended the Temple Mount and visited the mosques on Sunday, July 1. It was not necessary to arrest the Takruri guards who were apparently reconciled to the once shocking spectacle of infidels entering the third holiest shrine in the Islamic world. On July 2, after a visit to Bethlehem, the archduke returned to Jaffa. On the day of his ar-rival, the archduke had erected another milestone in the history of religious tolerance at Jerusalem. For the first time, a Turkish pasha had given his consent to a Catholic religious procession, carrying a crucifix through the streets of Jerusalem.[65]

The next test of Kiamal Pasha's tolerance came with the ar-rival of the distinguished Anglo-Jewish philanthropist, Sir Moses Montefiore. Sir Moses was on the fourth of his seven pilgrimages to Palestine, and as usual traveled in a semi-official capacity with the support of letters of introduction from the British Foreign Office, as well as a firman from the sultan authorizing the nu-merous charitable works he proposed to undertake. On July 20, 1855, when the Montefiore party approached Jerusalem, Kiamal Pasha asked the Chief Rabbi, Chaim Nissim Abulafia, whether he thought that Sir Moses would expect a mounted honor guard to escort him into the city. The rabbi, scarcely accustomed to such deference from Turkish governors, referred Kiamal Pasha to the British consul. Finn's reply was that a half dozen bashi-bazouk soldiers would suffice. Kiamal Pasha ended by following his own generous instincts and sent a mounted honor guard of regular Turkish cavalry to welcome Sir Moses Montefiore in style. On an even more generous and decidedly risky level, it was decided that the Montefiore party and the British consul and his wife were to visit the mosques on the Temple Mount. If the Takruri had any hostile impulses at this new intrusion by infidels, they were converted to ecumenical tolerance by the cash gifts Sir Moses distributed to them.[66]

As the Crimean War wound to its close, the numbers of foreign visitors increased tremendously. Numerous officers on their way home from the war took advantage of their presence in the Near East to visit Jerusalem. By 1856, visits to the Temple Mount had ceased to be novel, but were part of the expectations of ordinary tourists. In a certain sense, Kiamal Pasha was so generous that he embarrassed himself trying to show dramatic honors to visitors of moderate prominence. When Colonel F. Walpole, commander of Britain's new Land Transport Corps, came to Jerusalem in January 1856, he was escorted by fifty Turkish cavalrymen carrying lances decorated with ostrich plumes and horse tails. As the latter was the ensign of a pasha, Walpole's entry at the Jaffa Gate was the most impressive ever given to a foreign commoner to that date.[67]

It must be understood, however, that all of this liberal change rested upon the determination of the young governor to break through the thickly encrusted prejudices of a very insulated Moslem society. He could impose his will where he was personally present, but he could not be everywhere at once.

When in the first rosy glow of victory at the end of the Crimean War, the sultan issued the firman of Hatti Humayun, it expressed the pious intention of recognizing full religious liberty for all the sultan's subjects.[68]

Anglican Bishop Gobat, with more enthusiasm than good sense, interpreted the firman to mean that churches could erect and ring bells. As church bells had been previously prohibited, the bishop would have been well advised to test Moslem tolerance in a secure setting before taking foolish risks. Instead, he hastily installed church bells at an Anglican chapel at Nablus, a largely Moslem town with minuscule Christian, Jewish, and Samaritan populations. The ringing of the church bells created an extremely tense atmosphere in Nablus.[69] Before calm could be restored, news arrived in Palestine that a son had been born to Emperor Napoleon III and Empress Eugénie. The birth of an heir to the French throne was naturally an occasion for celebration by the French consul and all the Crimean allies. At Jerusalem, all consulates raised their national flags as the cannons at the Jaffa Gate fired a salute on March 31, 1856. The raising of flags was another innovation approved by Kiamal Pasha.[70] At Nablus, however, when the French and British flags were raised, an angry mob still embittered by the affront of Christian church bells tore the flags from their staffs. By unfortunate coincidence, a British scholar, the Reverend S. Lyde, a fellow of Jesus College, Cambridge, happened to arrive at Nablus two days after the riot. Accosted by a beggar who appeared to raise his hand in a threatening way. Lyde shot and killed the man. The result was a renewed riot, a general assault on all foreigners, the sacking of the Protestant mission, and the destruction of the offensive church bells. One elderly native Christian was killed. Lyde barely escaped with his life and, after a tumultuous trial, had to be escorted back to England, hopelessly psychotic.[71]

Crimean victory and Kiamal Pasha notwithstanding, much remained to be done to make Palestine a land open to genuine toleration of foreigners and infidels.

Chapter Nine
The Hebron Affair

Although the great chancellories of Europe had abandoned Palestine as the central fulcrum for their national rivalries, the consuls at Jerusalem continued to behave as though their activities materially affected change in the world balance of power. On the greater international stage, Austria, while remaining neutral, had assumed a benevolent attitude toward the French and British effort against Russia. Austria's leading German rival, Prussia, had also remained neutral, but assumed a pro-Russian posture.

Thus, in the limited setting of the Palestinian microcosm, the Prussian and British consuls, who had for so long been the joint defenders of Protestantism, developed an icy social hostility to one another. The social problems of two ill-informed consuls, working in a political vacuum, would have been of no consequence had their hostilities not led to serious attempts by both of them to involve London, Berlin, and Paris in what the two consuls undoubtedly regarded as an aspect of the greater European struggle. That they did not succeed in changing a teapot tempest into an international crisis was due far more to the conclusion of the Crimean War than to the restraint and good sense of any of the parties involved.

Abu Gosh, the village dominating the mountain route from Jaffa to Jerusalem. From Count L.N.P. *Auguste de Forbin,* Voyage dans le Levant, en 1817 et 1818, *Paris, Imprimerie Royale, 1819. Courtesy of Towson State University Media Services.*

Deprived of an effective force of professional soldiers, even a competent governor such as Kiamal Pasha was hard-pressed to maintain order. At Hebron, the nearest significant town, a series of brigand chieftains succeeded in wrenching virtually all of the southern part of the pashalik from Turkish control. As it was estimated that the Turks could not reconquer rebellious Hebron, the consuls at Jerusalem were forced into the politically and physically dangerous position of having to negotiate directly with the local sheiks and with the sometime ruler of the rebels at Hebron, mixing cajolery and bribes with threats of armed intervention by foreign troops. The most tenacious and effective of the Hebron rebels, Abderrahman el Amir, was an Arab effendi with substantial landed wealth, who managed to hold Hebron and its environs free of Turkish control, 1852–55. It is unlikely that he ever commanded more than eight hundred armed men. Once war had begun in Europe, however, it is doubtful that the pasha of Jerusalem was able to count on an equal force, his possession of artillery giving him no advantage against an enemy supported by the local villagers and operating in mountainous terrain.

Thus, Abderrahman el Amir found himself in the enviable position of a man able to dispense favors to the foreign consuls to keep them quiet while defying with impunity the legitimate government of the country. All of the consuls were forced, in order to protect their nationals, to deal directly with overt rebels against Turkish authority. Thus, all were equally guilty of offering aid and recognition to a seditious movement aimed against the power of the Sublime Porte. Everyone, including the pasha of Jerusalem, seemed to have regarded this irregular relationship with Abderrahman as a pragmatic necessity. The Turks did not protest against it, nor did the consuls complain about one another, since all were equally involved.[1]

In June 1855, however, Abderrahman finally overstepped the limits which the consuls were prepared to tolerate. In a particularly vicious series of attacks and robberies, he had taken numerous lives and destroyed considerable property claimed by foreign nationals.

After informal conferences with his colleagues, the other consuls at Jerusalem, Dr. Georg Rosen, the Prussian consul, requested Kiamal Pasha to convene a formal meeting of the Austrian, British, French, Prussian and Spanish consuls to plan joint action against Abderrahman.

The extraordinary consular conference met on June 12 at the Jerusalem residence of the Turkish governor. Kiamal Pasha opened the meeting by warning his guests that the large European population of Hebron, many of them elderly Jews unfamiliar with the use of weapons even in self-defense, ran considerable risk if the town became a battleground or if the Turkish forces suffered defeat. He stated frankly that he would not run such a risk unless the consuls supported him and absolved him from blame. He added, however, that there no longer seemed to be any alternative, since Abderrahman had abandoned restraint and ignored all attempts to negotiate for his submission to Ottoman rule.

On a more positive note, the pasha revealed that he had received orders from Constantinople to seize Abderrahman, dead or alive. He had already received authorization from the Jerusalem medjlis to recruit two hundred horsemen and as many infantrymen as the loyal village headmen could conscript for him. He expressed the view that the Arab troops might sufficiently supplement the undermanned regular Turkish forces at his disposal to crush Abderrahman. Kiamal Pasha then invited questions and advice.

James Finn, British consul, was most aggressive in his questioning and his advice. As dean of the consular corps and as a long-time resident of Palestine, who regularly traveled with his own armed guard throughout the pashalik, he expressed himself authoritatively. It was Finn who emphasized his role as the representative of a country allied in the present war to the Turkish Empire. Having spoken first and having urged the strongest possible military measures against Abderrahman, Finn undoubtedly helped to set the tone for the others. The consul of France, who could claim equally well that his country was Turkey's ally, was much less emphatic about it than Finn had been. Paul Emile Botta was merely recorded in the official *Procès Verbal* of the meeting as simply seconding the Englishman's opinion and urging its implementation "rigorously, by all the means of which we dispose."[2]

Count de Pizzamano, the Austrian consul, straddled a fence. He agreed that further attempts to negotiate with Abderrahman would get nowhere. At the same time, he urged the pasha to be cautious unless he was sure that he possessed military superiority. Dr. Rosen of Prussia who, it will be recalled, had initiated the meeting in the first place, urged the pasha to use his limited military strength merely to secure Hebron without attempting to destroy Abderrahman unless Turkish troops were clearly able to do so.

Spanish Consul Pío de Andrés García took the most cautious tack of all, urging deferment of the military option and one last attempt to negotiate the submission of Abderrahman el Amir. The meeting was closed by a formal resolution offering the support of all the consuls to the pasha, whatever his course might be.[3]

From Kiamal Pasha's point of view, the meeting had produced one valuable result. It had exculpated him from any blame which might attach to the sufferings of Europeans caught in the middle of the proposed battleground. It was vital for Turkish sovereignty in Palestine to avoid giving any European power a pretext for intervention on the grounds that Turkish troops had been used irresponsibly against rebels entrenched in the midst of a mass of European civilians.[4]

It was not until the evening of July 27 that the pasha, his Turkish regulars, and his new conscripts were able to begin the thirty-five kilometer march to Hebron.[5] In order to commit each of the consulates more firmly to his cause and to ensure that the needs of the Europeans caught in the battle would be quickly considered, Kiamal Pasha requested each consul to send a member of his staff to be attached to the pasha's service until the Hebron campaign had ended. Each consulate complied.[6]

As a consequence of intensive action, August 3–6, 1855, the pasha managed to destroy or scatter the forces of Abderrahman el Amir. Although the rebel chieftain himself escaped the siege of Idna, his stronghold, he was no longer an effective challenge to the Turks.[7] At last, Turkish sovereignty had been restored in the entire pashalik of Jerusalem.[8]

All of the consular representatives who had accompanied Kiamal Pasha to Hebron made themselves available to Europeans under their protection. The Austrian, Prussian, and Spanish officials had then taken leave of the pasha and returned to Jerusalem. As a gesture of good will and solidarity, the British vice-consul, Mr. Rogers, and the French consulate's chancellor, Mr. Legueux, had remained with the pasha as a sort of symbol of the union of the Crimean allies. It is important to note that neither Kiamal Pasha nor anyone else who had witnessed the Hebron-Idna campaign regarded the departure of the consular representatives of the non-belligerent European powers as offering any sort of affront to the Turkish government.[9]

Beginning on August 20, however, James Finn began a series of dispatches to the British Foreign Office in which he accused the Prussian and Austrian consuls at Jerusalem of complicity in a plot to support Abderrahman and to overthrow Turkish authority in Palestine. Allegedly, they had prevented Kiamal Pasha from acting vigorously against the Hebron rebels and had been actively in contact with those sheiks who were in the rebel camp.[10] His accusations were based entirely on rumor and circumstantial evidence. For example, he placed great weight upon the fact that the Prussian physician in charge of the hospital at Hebron was known to be a supporter of Abderrahman and a friend of Georg Rosen. He did not adduce any proof that would necessarily make Rosen a partisan of the rebels, but simply allowed the innuendo to work its own mischief.[11] If the telegraph had been extended to Jerusalem, London could have gotten the facts about Finn's entirely fantastic and irresponsible charges and demolished them immediately. Instead, the British government had to take the charges seriously. A dispatch traveling from London to Jerusalem might take as long as two months to reach its addressee, and a three-month passage merely aroused mild concern. As the Crimean War was still in progress at the moment of Finn's accusations against Rosen and as Prussia was regarded as pro-Russian,[12] the British Foreign Office could not overlook any suggestion that Prussia was engaged in weakening the Turks by stirring rebellion in Palestine, the original theater of the Russo-Turkish quarrel.

As bad luck would have it, Finn's irresponsible dispatches reached London in only a month. The British Foreign Secretary. the Earl of Clarendon, immediately instructed the British *chargé d'affaires* at Berlin to make an official inquiry into the matter.

Baron Manteuffel, the Minister-President of the Prussian Council of State, was deeply distressed and embarrassed by the receipt of a formal British request for clarifications. Prussia would have been reluctant to go to war in support of Russia even if Austria had attacked that empire. It, therefore, came as a decided shock to be accused of entering a Machiavellian conspiracy to seduce Austria into shifting allegiances while weakening Ottoman power in the Near East.

Consequently, Manteuffel fired off a stiffly worded set of instructions to Rosen, demanding the facts. It was made quite clear to Rosen that his consular career was at stake, as well as the international position of his country. Of course, Manteuffel assured the British, as best he could, that the Berlin Cabinet was totally foreign to any plot to subvert Turkish authority in Palestine.[13]

Dr. Rosen, however, did not receive Manteuffel's frostily worded dispatch until early November.[14] No one had mentioned Consul Finn as the source of the accusations against Rosen. Nevertheless, the Prussian Consul deduced that the sort of accusations made by Lord Clarendon could have originated only in the British Consulate at Jerusalem.

Placed in such a dilemma, Dr. Rosen penned an official note to Finn asking him if he had indeed accused him and the Austrian Pizzamano of having prevented Kiamal Pasha from acting energetically against the rebels. He made every effort to maintain a friendly tone, to avoid accusing Finn, and to remind the English consul of their years of collaboration as the defenders of Protestant interests in Palestine.[15]

Finn's reply the next day was a masterpiece of obfuscations. He did not deny having attacked Rosen in dispatches to London. Neither did he specifically admit having done so. He merely took refuge in his diplomatic privilege of refusing to discuss any matter touching his official correspondence without the consent of his superiors. He pretended that he had to ask for instructions before discussing the matter with Rosen.[16] The Prussian replied on the same day, openly expressing his anger and resentment. His note closed with the pointed comment that he was proud to serve a government which did not require him to seek permission before telling the truth.[17]

Finn's response attempted to minimize the imbroglio by asking if he and Mrs. Finn could pay a social call to Dr. and Mrs. Rosen the next morning, in order to maintain their personal friendship however much politics might temporarily separate them.[18] It can only be supposed that it cost Rosen all of his urbanity to reply in the same tone, particularly inviting Mrs. Finn to entertain them on the piano newly installed in the Rosens' handsome salon.[19]

Dr. Rosen did not spend all of November 9 appreciating Mrs. Finn's musical accomplishments. Instead, he sent off almost identically worded notes to Kiamal Pasha and the consuls of Austria, France, and Spain. Before doing so, he had personally conferred with Count Pizzamano, the Austrian consul, who had also been the object of Finn's insinuations. Having assured himself that Pizzamano would raise no objections to the airing of the entire affair, Rosen requested the Turkish governor and his consular colleagues to send him letters of support, Specifically, he asked each one to attest to the truth of his claims to have avoided giving any support to the rebels, to have always been a firm supporter of Ottoman sovereignty, and to have been, indeed, the initiator of the consular conference of June 12, 1855.[20]

It was now Finn's turn to be surprised that others were plotting behind his back. The British consul learned of Rosen's solicitations of affidavits only when he paid a sick call on the French consul, Edmond de Barrère, who had just replaced Paul Emile Botta. The new arrival was convalescing from an injury suffered while horseback riding. Finn noted in the diary which he kept faithfully that his charges against Rosen had indeed been erroneous.[21] It is that admission of error in his diary which makes it so hard to understand why Finn could not make an apology to the Prussian. Such an admission might have been personally awkward for Finn, but it would have averted the tempest which Rosen was about to stir at Berlin, London, Constantinople, and Jerusalem.

The replies received by Rosen exceeded anything for which he could have hoped. The Turkish governor offered Rosen a completely positive reply on all the matters for which support was sought.[22] The Spanish and French consuls sent not only their own impressions of Rosen's good behavior in the Hebron affair, but the accounts of their consular officers who had accompanied Kiamal Pasha to Hebron. In the case of France, the latter was Mr. Legueux, who had also been acting consul prior to de Barrère's arrival and subsequent to Botta's departure.[23]

The value of the French testimony was heightened by the fact that Finn had held the behavior of the British and French to be exemplary, while accusing Prussia and Austria of sedition and ignoring Spain. Quite understandably, Count Pizzamano, who had shared the obloquy of Finn's accusations, indulged in a little personal recrimination by way of revenge. He pointed out several occasions on which Finn had been guilty of making false accusations which he had had to retract. With understandable malice, Pizzamano stated that Finn was worthy of respect when constrained to mind his own business.[24]

With his thick file of affidavits in hand, Rosen was able to send the originals off to his government at Berlin on November 17.[25] The next day he wrote a fuller vindication of his own position in a private letter to Baron Manteuffel.[26] Just for safety's sake, he also approached Samuel Gobat, the Anglican bishop of Jerusalem, and received a warm letter of support from that prelate as well.[27]

With his defense well in hand, Rosen then turned to his self-vindication. In an official note to Finn, Rosen offered the British consul a chance to admit his error, in writing, assuring him that Baron Manteuffel would then drop the matter and desist from seeking any sort of additional disciplinary action from Lord Clarendon.[28]

Finn replied, falling back on the same lame excuse he had

used when first caught in his error – the incapacity to discuss his correspondence with his superiors without their authorization. He merely promised to send Rosen's latest note on to Lord Clarendon for the record.[29]

Perceiving that Finn had no intention of seeking the escape which had been offered him, Rosen then sent a review of the entire affair to Colonel von Wildenbruck, the Prussian ambassador at Constantinople, in order that his superior might be aware of all the facts if Lord Stratford de Redcliffe, the redoubtable British ambassador to the Sublime Porte, should ask for explanations.[30] Since Finn was in the habit of writing the most severe criticisms of Kiamal Pasha to the British ambassador and to the Turkish authorities,[31] Rosen's precaution was a wise one.

Although at Jerusalem the crisis was approaching fever heat, at Berlin and London the affair was being thrust out of sight as an embarrassment to both parties. The Crimean War was drawing to a close.[32] Neither side could draw any profit from the blunders of James Finn.

At Jerusalem, however, a month removed from factual reality and separated from one another by an abyss of misunderstanding, Finn and Rosen continued their war of words. In an unconsciously comic note, Finn admitted that Lord Clarendon had sent him authorization to reveal the contents of his correspondence on December 6, 1855, but that he had waited until January 29, 1856, expecting that Clarendon might have a change of mind. What he now submitted to Rosen was a large sheet of paper, folded double to make what he called a notebook, on which he had copied all of the attacks he had made on Rosen and Rosen's associates and which had led to the potentially dangerous Anglo-Prussian misunderstanding.[33]

On February 5, 1856, even at Jerusalem the news of a ceasefire in the Crimea was known.[34] On the next day, Rosen sent a circular note to the consuls of Austria, France, and Spain informing them of his vindication by his own government. He added that Lord Clarendon had admitted that Finn's accusations had been rendered absurd by the support given Rosen by the Jerusalem consuls, Kiamal Pasha, and Bishop Gobat.[35] Albert, Count Bernstorff, the Prussian ambassador at London, had offered copies of all the affidavits to Lord Clarendon, the British Foreign Secretary. To avoid having to reply in writing, he had not accepted copies but had examined them unofficially[36] and offered a veiled apology to the Prussian government and to Consul Rosen.[37]

Dr. Rosen, good lawyer that he was, then sent copies of the dispatches from Bernstorff and Manteuffel to Finn, adding the veiled threat that he had not sent all of Finn's correspondence to his superiors, but that he had a complete file on the matter in his consulate and would send it on to Berlin if the matter were raised again.[38] Finn's reply was frigid but correct. He could not bring himself to confess an error or to ask pardon.[39] Rosen also protected himself from any future puerile maliciousness at Finn's hands by sending a full account of the case for the records to Colonel Wildenbruck, his old friend and present superior at Constantinople.[40] As Finn had not apologized and as word of the continuing hostility between the two consuls continued to reach Berlin, the Prussians once again approached Lord Clarendon. This time they asked him, as a favor, to exercise coercion on his own man at Jerusalem. Clarendon complied with a terse note to Finn:

> I have been informed by the Prussian Government that without entering into a detailed examination of the differences which unfortunately have arisen between yourself and the Prussian Consul, which seem moreover to be involved in much obscurity, they will send instructions to this Consul which they expect, will allay angry feelings on his part and restore harmony between you…. I concur entirely in the view taken by the Prussian government of this matter and I have to instruct you to act in a spirit of conciliation toward your Prussian Colleague and to endeavor to bring to a close the disputes in which you have heretofore been engaged with him.[41]

Manteuffel did, indeed, write to Rosen urging magnanimity, inasmuch as the British government had offered a veiled apology since Finn would not.[42] The strange ending of this quarrel succeeded in reconciling no one, however.

Both Britain and Prussia persisted in keeping the quarreling consuls at their Jerusalem posts in spite of the fact that they remained openly inimical to one another and that they continued to be unable to communicate except at an official level, thenceforth.[43] Although Prussia had escaped involvement in the Crimean War, the Hebron affair temporarily ended the formerly cordial unity of the great Protestant powers in Near Eastern religious policy.

Chapter Ten

Palestine and the Firman of Hatti-Humayun

On January 9, 1856, before the Congress of Paris had convened to draw up a treaty ending the Crimean War, the first of a series of conferences took place at Constantinople. Grand Vizier Ali Pasha presided, assisted by Turkish Foreign Minister Fuad Pasha. Present at all the meetings were Lord Stratford de Redcliffe, British ambassador, Edouard Thouvenel, French ambassador, and Anton, Baron von Prokesch-Osten, newly appointed Austrian ambassador, who had just arrived at his post on December 17. A total of four very confidential talks took place on January 9, 16, 19, and 29. Britain and France participated as military partners in the late war, and Austria was invited to contribute to the discussions as a neutral power which had been benevolent to the Crimean allies. The purpose of the conferences was to negotiate the terms and language of a firman to be issued by the sultan, guaranteeing his non-Moslem subjects civil and religious rights.

From the beginning the Turks found it easy to refuse the sort of meaningful concessions which would have provided for genuine religious equality between Moslem, Christian, and Jew.

Lord Stratford and Edouard Thouvenel regularly undercut one another by secret approaches to Ali Pasha which permitted the grand vizier to play one against the other.

Notwithstanding the public camaraderie and the private disloyalty of the Crimean allies, the sultan's firman could have become a major milestone on Turkey's road to reform in the spirit of the *Tanzimat* of 1839. In the long run, the document became a nullity because it remained an expression of the sultan's good wishes toward his rayah subjects, but was in no case a commitment having the force of law. Because Hatti-Humayun was not enforceable as part of the Treaty of Paris, it left the sultan perfectly free to abrogate it in full sovereign freedom.

The firman was issued on February 18, 1856. A hasty reading of its text would make it appear to be a kind of Turkish Bill of Rights, consonant with the best traditions of nineteenth-century liberalism.[1] In view of what has been said in previous chapters of this study, the following quotations would create the illusion that Hatti-Humayun had effected a peaceful revolution:

> Every distinction or designation tending to make any class whatever of the subjects of my Empire inferior to another class, on account of their religion, language, or race, shall be forever effaced from the Administrative Protocol. The laws shall be put in force against the use of any injurious or offensive term, either among private individuals or on the part of the authorities…. All commercial, correctional, and criminal suits between Mussulmans and Christian or other non-Mussulman subjects, or between Christians or other non-Mussulmans of different sects, shall be referred to mixed tribunals.
>
> The proceedings of these tribunals shall be public: the parties shall be confronted, and shall produce their witnesses, whose testimony shall be received, without distinction, upon an oath taken according to the religious law of each sect.[2]

Military service was to be opened to non-Moslems, and the old shameful head-tax in lieu of military service for such subjects was eliminated.[3]

Lord Stratford wanted the firman to include a specific statement that it was no longer a capital crime for a Moslem to accept conversion to another faith. Ali Pasha, supported by Thouvenel, was able to evade that issue neatly. He averred that the sultan as Caliph ul-Islam, the head and protector of the Moslem faith, could not possibly admit the right of Moslems to apostasize. The compromise text which avoided that issue states:

> As all forms of religion are and shall be freely professed, in my dominions, no subject of my Empire shall be hindered in the exercise of the religion that he professes, nor shall be in any way annoyed on this account. No one shall be compelled to change their religion.[4]

Another thorny issue involved the right of foreigners to buy property in Turkey. A compromise text preserved the freedom of the Turks to maintain the old restraints by making the privilege of property ownership by foreigners a matter of bilateral treaties. The compromise text read:

> As the laws regulating the purchase, sale, and disposal of real property are common to all the subjects of my Empire, it shall be lawful for foreigners to possess landed property in my dominions, conforming themselves to the laws and policy regulations, and bearing the same charges as the native inhabitants, and after arrangements have been come to with Foreign Powers.[5]

If there were any doubt about Turkey's determination to retain complete freedom of action, it vanished when Article ix of the Treaty of Paris stated:

His Imperial Majesty the Sultan, in his constant solicitude for the well being of his subjects, having issued a firman which, while improving their future without distinction as to either religion or race, dedicates his generous intentions toward the Christian populations of his Empire, and desiring to give a new expression of his sentiments in that regard, has resolved to communicate to the contracting Powers said firman spontaneously emanating from his sovereign will. The contracting Powers verify the high value of that communication. It is quite understood that it may not, in any case, give the right to the said Powers, to intervene either collectively or separately, in the relations of His Majesty the Sultan with his subjects, nor in the internal administration of his Empire.[6]

Lord Stratford de Redcliffe, who was forced into retirement at the age of seventy-one, a year after the signing of the Treaty of Paris, regarded Article ix as the ruination of everything he had fought to achieve. He believed that Turkey could be saved, in spite of herself, only if the great Powers forced her to reform. From his own point of view, Lord Stratford was a sincere friend of Turkey since he desired to save the Ottoman Empire from dissolution. From the viewpoint of the Turkish conservatives, however, Lord Stratford was simply the hated Christian foreigner attempting to end Moslem superiority in the House of Islam. From their perspective, Lord Stratford proposed to save the Turkish body while destroying the Turkish soul. They wanted no part of his friendship at such a price.[7]

In distant Palestine, word of the Hatti-Humayun of February 18 was received on March 3.[8] Kiamal Pasha delayed until April 6 the necessary public reading of the firman at his seraglio.[9] All of the resident consuls, the prelates of the churches, the representatives of the rabbinate, and the sanjak's notables were present. The members of the consular corps wore dress uniforms, but rather theatrically, British Consul Finn chose the ostentatious simplicity of civil costume in order not to appear to gloat over the humbling of Islam.[10]

If Kiamal Pasha felt that any humiliation had been heaped upon his sovereign or his religion by the concessions contained in Hatti-Humayun, he did not show it. Indeed, the happiest relationship between the Turks and the consuls had subsisted during the war itself. Every one of Kiamal Pasha's concessions had been made prior to Hatti-Humayun and the Treaty of Paris. Once the war ended and the dependence of Turkey upon Britain and France was over, a perceptible chill could be felt, even at the seraglio of the liberal Kiamal Pasha. It will be recalled from the previous chapter, however, that the Nablus riots occurred in the context of grass-roots Moslem fears that Hatti-Humayun had granted religious equality to rayahs.

In July 1856, the governor attempted to get control of the political patronage inherent in the distribution of the tourist trade. Kiamel Pasha had apparently learned quickly the means whereby he might build a power base by assuming the exclusive right to license tourist guides. Consul Finn, who had the largest corps of tourist guides under contract, sent a stiff note to the governor. It stated that the British consulate would assume no responsibility for the consequences if any traveler journeyed to the Jordan or Dead Sea under a contract negotiated between the pasha and a tourist guide, in contravention of the consul's previous agreement with tourist guides, Bedouin sheiks or village headmen en route. The consul's note was a subtle way of reminding the governor that if he valued order in the country he would be unwise to tamper with the delicate balance of alliances painfully worked out by the consuls and local notables.[11]

Kiamal Pasha understood the message and made no further attempt to control tourist guides, but the handwriting was on the wall and future governors found it easier to circumvent consular power by getting control of the important tourist guides' contracts early in their tenure of office.[12]

On March 14, 1857, word reached Jerusalem that the governor was to be transferred to a new post. Five days later, Kiamal Pasha began to refuse entry to the Temple Mount for foreign non-Moslem visitors. Kiamal Pasha gave, as excuse for his new coldness, the fact that he was about to leave and could not compromise the freedom of action of his successor. The fact is that he relented occasionally prior to his actual departure from Jerusalem in early April, but the pasha's frigid manner was a harbinger for the future.[13]

On March 23, the Jerusalem Turkish garrison was restored to its prewar strength. The battalion returned to parade across the Meidan in triumph as the cannon at the Jaffa Gate fired a welcoming salute.[14] The conditions of chaos in which consular influence had thrived had ended.

On April 13, the new pasha was known to have arrived at Jaffa. Suraya Pasha delayed his entry into Jerusalem until May 2.[15] Although Elizabeth Anne Finn described him as "a man of very gentlemanly manners and courtly speech," everyone shortly discovered him to be very different from Kiamal Pasha. Mrs. Finn recalled in her memoirs, written more than sixty years later, that Suraya Pasha was strongly anti-British. She alleged that "in an unguarded moment [he] let slip the words that he had been sent to Jerusalem to break the power of the English Consulate and to destroy British influence in Palestine."[16] Suffice it to say that the British, triumphant in the Crimean War, were spurned now that the Turks felt that the issue of the Palestinian Holy Places was settled. Russia, which had lost the Crimean War, was to enjoy a signal triumph in the new Palestine. On the very Meidan itself the Russian compound would rise, its churches and hostels etching a new profile against the ancient walls of Jerusalem.[17]

Chatpter Eleven
Land Purchase and the Expansion
of European Influence in Palestine

The greater part of Turkish Palestine was held directly by the government as the Sultan's crown lands, by great effendis, or by the Wakf or Moslem religious establishment. The fellah or simple peasant as a landowner, was almost extinct. The danger posed by the Bedouin, the tax collection system, and competition by large landowners in a country where the possession of water sources was the key to agricultural survival, had combined to wipe out small peasant holdings.[1]

Until 1867, Turkish law made land purchase impossible for foreign non-Moslems without specific permission embodied in a firman from the sultan.[2] Thus, rival religious sects such as the Coptic and Abyssinian churches clung to ancient land deeds, tracing the genealogy of claims to property or even to portions of buildings to the remotest times. Cemeteries, often located at holy places such as Mount Zion, became the scenes of frantic quarrels as Greek fought Latin or Protestant for a few disputed meters of earth in which to bury the dead.[3]

The first European to succeed in purchasing land near

Jerusalem as purely private property was British Consul James
Finn in 1850. The second European to do so was Sir Moses Mon-
teflore in 1855. Both purchases were obtained by a specific imperial firman from the sultan and were registered with the pasha of
Jerusalem.[4] It will be recalled that there was no Turkish land registration law until 1858.[5] Both the Finn and Montefiore properties
were adjacent on the slopes of the Talibiyeh, outside the walls of
Jerusalem facing Mount Zion. Interestingly enough, the Finns
had first attempted to purchase the land in Mrs. Finn's name since,
as Mrs. Finn described it in her memoirs, "under Turkish Law, a
woman is a nobody."[6] When it was made plain that the Turks
would not tolerate such subterfuge, the British embassy at Constantinople had obtained the necessary firman through the good
offices of Lord Stratford de Redcliffe.[7]

*View of Haifa and Mount Carmel by a Dutch Navy Cartographer in 1851.
From Lieutenant Carel Van de Velde,* Narrative of a Journey through
Syria and Palestine, in 1851 through 1852, *Edinburgh, Blackwood,
1853. Courtesy of Towson State University Media Services.*

In 1852, Mrs. Finn had again taken the lead in purchasing a farm approximately one mile northwest of Jerusalem's Damascus Gate in the area known then, and still called today, Abraham's Vineyard or Kerem Avraham. A house which they constructed still stands there, off what is now Ovadia Street. After 1857, that property was transferred to the London Jews Society for the purpose of training potential Jewish converts to Anglicanism in the skills of farming and stonemasonry. In 1856, the Finns purchased a large, well-watered farm at Artas near Bethlehem.[8] Shortly thereafter, they purchased another farm at Taghoor, about one hour's horseback ride from Artas. Neither the Artas nor the Taghoor properties were bought with the aid of the embassy or with the approval of a firman. Their title was decidedly shaky, and they were ultimately lost when the Finns were declared bankrupt for their Palestinian properties in 1863.[9]

Other foreign Christians who attempted to acquire property without the support of consular influence had less success. In February 1853, Dr. James Thomas Barclay, an American medical missionary better remembered today as an archeologist,[10] attempted to buy land. There was, as yet, no United States consul at Jerusalem, so Dr. Barclay approached Moosa Tannoos, the Christian Arab dragoman of the British consulate. As it was Barclay's intention to use his land as a training farm for Jewish converts to Protestantism, he imagined that he shared identical goals with James Finn. Tannoos informed Barclay that he could buy land at Wadi Ferra near Jerusalem at a lower cost than could Barclay, because he was a native of the area and knew the local landlords. As a consequence, Barclay gave Tannoos 17,000 Turkish piasters and signed an agreement naming him as his agent for the purchase.

When Barclay and his son went to the site to inspect their intended purchase, they indiscreetly informed the local peasants that they were to be the new landlords.

The infuriated fellahin attacked the Americans, who barely escaped with their lives. When Hafiz Ahmed Pasha, then governor, examined Dr. Barclay's complaint, he said that no one had been authorized to sell land at Wadi Ferra, and that any such sale would be invalid if it had taken place. Barclay then asked Hafiz Pasha to obtain repayment of his money from the local land owners. The effendis summoned by the pasha averred that Tannoos had given them only 5,480 piasters.

Tannoos, confronted by Barclay, admitted the truth of the claim, but could not account for all of the remaining 11,520 piasters and refused to return any of it. Barclay offered Tannoos 500 piasters for his "services," but the latter said that he had spent much more in bribes, feasts for the landlords and peasants, and his own expenses. Having no alternative, Barclay then went to British Consul Finn to bring suit against the dragoman to recover the 11,000 piasters. Finn, however, supported Tannoos's claim that his expenses had been above 4,000 piasters and awarded Barclay 7,000 piasters to be paid by Tannoos not later than June 25, 1853, The latter signed an obligation, pledging his own land as a surety. When the due date passed without payment of the debt, Barclay had recourse to Finn's court again. This time, the consul ruled that Tannoos had "needlessly and foolishly" written an obligation against himself. He then increased Tannoos's claims against the disputed money by 3,000 piasters and ordered his dragoman to pay only 4,000 piasters to Barclay, reserving the rest for future arbitration."

At no time did Barclay accuse Finn of having profited personally from the peculations of his dragoman. As Finn continued to employ Tannoos, however, he became a party to the dishonesty of his employee.[12]

All of this merely serves to illustrate the difficulties with which foreign non-Moslems, acting as individuals, were faced in purchasing land in Palestine.

It must be remembered that Turkish law further complicated all land purchase by Europeans by requiring a firman for the land purchase itself and a special firman if any structure to be used for non-Moslem religious services was to be built on the land. Nevertheless, during the Crimean War the European consuls at Jerusalem took advantage of the illusory good will they imagined they had earned at Constantinople. The text of a letter from Grand Vizier Ali Pasha to Governor of Jerusalem Kiamal Pasha betrays the nervous reluctance felt by the Turks about any land purchases by Europeans.

> The Imperial [Austrian] Internunciature has addressed us a request to permit the purchase of a property which has been acquired by the Consulate of Austria at Jerusalem in the goal of building a hospice for Austrian pilgrims.
>
> As to the authorization to build the said structure, it will be the object of a special negotiation;…the Sublime Porte does not oppose the purchase alone, of the land in question, so long as there are no local difficulties to prevent it, and it does not trespass upon the rights of any other nations.
>
> Furthermore, in view of the delicate position of the affairs of Jerusalem, it would appear suitable to act in regard to the said property with the same circumspection applied to all questions involving buildings. We recommend, according to your sense of duty and your wisdom, not to neglect these considerations.
>
> But if it is found that there is no…reason for apprehension for the buildings and residences of individuals belonging to other religions, or subjects of other governments, and that the purchase of the said property would offer no motive for dissensions or complaints, then your lordship may permit it.[13]

In the next year, emboldened by his success with the establishment of a pilgrims' hostel, Count Pizzamano sought and obtained a vizirial letter authorizing the purchase of a consulate building. Ultimately, Austria possessed a complex of buildings just within the Jaffa Gate.[14] The interested visitor to Jerusalem today may note the handsome building still bearing the Habsburg coat of arms which was once the Austrian post office, but is today a Catholic information center.

The Prussians, though they had been neutral and indeed friendly to Russia during the Crimean War, took full advantage of the new privilege of land purchase which Constantinople had so reluctantly granted to the British and Austrians. Dr. Rosen arranged the establishment of a Prussian deaconess's house to become a girls' boarding school, in rented premises in 1855. Kiamal Pasha had graciously agreed to visit the first Evangelical Lutheran religious institution at Jerusalem.[15] It may be recalled that the British and Prussian consuls at Jerusalem were bitter enemies, but their respective consuls-general at Beirut drew up an agreement for a joint defense of Protestant interests in Palestine. Thus, Anglican and Lutheran gains continued to be identified at a higher level in all contacts with the Turks at Beirut and Constantinople. That meant that the powerful patronage of Lord Stratford de Redcliffe afforded an umbrella of protection for the Prussians.[16]

After the issuance of the Hatti-Humayun of 1856 and the signing of the Peace of Paris, the Prussians set about buying a consulate building in Jerusalem. For thirteen years they had rented a large house with gardens on Khan Bazar Zeit Street, close to the border of the Moslem and Christian quarters of Jerusalem. In April 1856, the property was purchased in the name of Daood el Koordi, the rayah dragoman of the Prussian consulate. The house had been jointly owned by four cousins, members of the effendi aristocracy and of the Jerusalem medjlis, as well as leading directors of the Wakf. As the sellers continued to own two properties adjacent to the Prussian consulate, they were certainly fully aware that el Koordi was merely a titular owner while genuine possession was in the hands of Christian foreigners. As the whole affair was quite open, the Prussians moved to legalize the transfer from el Koordi to the kingdom of Prussia in the fall of 1856. A vizirial letter authorizing the change was apparently obtained without difficulty.[17]

The most surprising expansion of land ownership in Palestine, however, was Russian. For motives not entirely clear, the sultan gave the entire Meidan, or army parade ground, outside the walls of Jerusalem as a gift to Czar Alexander II, immediately after the signing of the Peace of Paris in 1856. The Turkish grant of 32 acres of prime open land to their recent enemies may have been an attempt to end the ancient enmity of Russians and Turks.[18] More probably, it was intended to confound both the British and the French, whose military aid to the Turks in the Crimea had been accompanied by an arrogance which the Turks resented. It was perhaps no coincidence that the huge new Russian landed property at Jerusalem blocked the path leading from the Damascus Gate and the Christian quarter of Jerusalem to the extensive British missionary-owned farm properties at Kerem Avraham, a mile from the city walls.[19] Surrounded by a high wall, intended to be militarily defensible, the Russian compound enclosed a Russian Orthodox cathedral, bishop's palace, a consulate, an ecclesiastical mission, a hospital, apartments for priests and teachers, and pilgrim hostels. Nor did the Russians stop with the Russian compound. A large-scale land purchasing program was begun in all the Palestinian sanjaks intended to make the Russian Orthodox Church dominant. Since the days of Catherine the Great, Russia had protected Greek Orthodox interests in all of the Ottoman Empire, and the Greek patriarch of Jerusalem had looked to St. Petersburg for political protection. In the new phase of Russian expansion after 1856, the Russians bid fair to engulf their Greek brothers and to submit the Orthodox Christian community, the largest Christian rayah community in Palestine, to the discipline of the Procurator of the Russian Holy Synod rather than that of the rayah patriarch of Jerusalem, Cyril II. Very wisely, the Russians expanded at the expense of their Greek brethren in faith, using native priests trained in Palestinian seminaries.[20]

The Russians also built their political framework in Palestine much more firmly after the Crimean War than it had ever been before 1853.[21] In August 1856, only five months after the Treaty of Paris had been signed, Marabutti, the same man who had been Russian vice consul at Jaffa before the war, was back at his old post.[22] On September 29, 1858, for the first time a Russian consul,

Dr. Kozhevnikov, opened a consulate at Jerusalem.[23] The Russian flag was formally hoisted, and the Turkish guns at the Jaffa Gate citadel saluted Turkey's recent enemy.[24] As a Russian Orthodox bishop had arrived in Jerusalem the previous February and was already resident in an episcopal palace within the Russian compound, the seriousness with which Russia regarded its future role in Palestine was quite clear.[25]

In a short nineteen years, Russia became the greatest foreign property holder in Palestine.[26] When the Russo-Turkish War of 1877–78 began, all Russian property was placed under the care of the German consulate at Jerusalem, and a detailed inventory prepared. The portion of that inventory relating to real estate is interesting enough to be duplicated here.

1. Russian establishments surrounded by a wall [the Russian Compound] and containing: the Consulate House, the Hospital, the Russian Ecclesiastical House with a church, the large church, the male pilgrims' house, the female pilgrims' house, servants' buildings, several shops and 9 cisterns.
2. A small property called "Khomsi" to the east of the Russian Establishments – surrounded by a wall.
3. Land facing the Damascus Gate known under the name of the "Eghnéimi" property – surrounded by a wall and containing a house, a cistern, and several gardens.
4. Land on the Mount of Olives.
5. Land in the city near the Church of the Holy Sepulchre, bought from the Copts and others, containing two shops and a terrace.
6. Land in the city, in the "Bab-Hutta" quarter, containing some trees, cactus, half of an uninhabitable house, and a cistern.
7. Land outside the city below the Mamilla cemetery, surrounded by a wall.
8. Land in the village of Ein Kerem, surrounded by a wall.
9. Land at Haifa.
10. Land at Nazareth.

In addition to the properties above, which were the outright possessions of the Russian Crown, a separate inventory was given of Russian state property administered by the Russian ecclesiastical mission at Jerusalem.

1. On the Mount of Olives, land surrounded by a wall containing a two story house, a servants' building and the foundations of a church.
2. In the village of Siloam a small property with no buildings, containing two sepulchral caverns.
3. In the village of Ein Kerem, a property surrounded by a wall and containing three houses, gardens etc.
4. In the village of Bait Jala – a property surrounded by a wall and containing two houses.
5. In the vicinity of Hebron, at the place called "Sabta," a property surrounded by a wall, and containing two houses, a building for servants, gardens, etc.
6. At Jericho, a property surrounded by a hedge and containing a building under construction.
7. Near Jaffa, a garden with a house, building for servants, wells etc.[27]

The tremendous Russian land acquisition program from 1856 to 1877 was paralleled by Russian efforts to control sea access to the Holy Land. Grand Duke Constantine, brother of Czar Alexander II, took an active interest in promoting the Russian Steam Navigation Company while serving as Minister of Marine. Although Russian steamship routes were opened from the Black Sea to Marseilles, Trieste, and Galatz, the grand duke used his influential position to offer the highest subsidies from governmental funds to the lines running to Alexandria and Jaffa. Ultimately the Jaffa line was tied in with a route which included Smyrna.

The activities of the steamship line were bound intimately to the expansion of the Russian church in Palestine and the increase of pilgrim traffic to the Holy Land. It was Grand Duke

Constantine who had obtained possession of so many properties in Palestine as president of the Palestine Committee. Indeed, the grand duke, his wife, and son visited Jerusalem in the summer of 1859, losing no opportunities to underline the dependence of the Greek and Russian Orthodox Churches upon the Russian State. So active was the grand duke that Prince Alexander Gortchakov, who served as Russian Minister of Foreign Affairs from the Crimean War until after the Russo-Turkish War of 1878, resented him for interfering in Russian foreign policy. Gortchakov feared that the aggressive expansion of the Russian Church in Palestine would offend the Latin Church and its French patron.[28]

The Latins on their side, using the puissant influence of the French consulate, established a vast network of Catholic educational institutions throughout Palestine. Precisely because the Protestants were suspected of hoping to convert Moslems to Christianity, they were under Turkish suspicion. The Latins, because they renounced such goals and because they had a well-rooted native Catholic population to succor, aroused no such Turkish resentment.[29]

Because the French had large orders of teaching nuns, they were prepared to offer education for girls as well as boys, a statement which cannot be made about any other religious communions in the East. In the immediate area of Jerusalem by 1868, the Latins, dominated by French clergy, had four convent schools for boys, four convents for girls, two boys' schools, two girls' schools, and one priests' seminary. The French language became a band of cultural unity binding many disparate communions which recognized the pope as the head of the church, but differed from one another in liturgy and organization.[30]

It is little wonder then that Britain and Prussia early concluded that there was no means whereby they could use religion, or the expansion of the ownership of property in the name of religion, to increase their political influence. Clearly, the Russians and the French were the only contenders in that contest. There was a certain note of wry resignation in the orders sent by the Prussian

embassy in Constantinople to Consul Rosen in Jerusalem at the
end of the crucial year 1858.

> The Cabinet of London has lately addressed the principal
> powers of Europe, in order to expose to them the unsuitable
> results which have ensued from the intrusion of foreign con-
> sulates in the internal affairs of the Ottoman Empire. Accord-
> ing to this exposé, a state of affairs prejudicile to the authority
> of the Sublime Porte and contrary to the principle of its inde-
> pendence, has arisen. The influence of some foreign agents
> has provoked the jealousy of others; all have sought motives
> for disagreement from an abundant source; the pretensions
> of supremacy which the different religious communities es-
> tablished in Turkey have raised against one another. In Syria,
> especially these sorts of litigations have taken a turn which
> tends more and more to efface the authority of the Porte by
> its intervention of foreign consuls in the regular function of
> Ottoman Administration. The Government of Her Britannic
> Majesty have expressed the desire, as much in the interests
> of the Porte's true independence as in that of the peaceful
> relations of the other powers, that we find the most proper
> means to remedy the above mentioned problems. Having
> already enjoined its consuls to abstain from all interven-
> tion in the local affairs of their residences, it hopes to meet
> the same disposition among the other governments.... The
> King's Government have verified with true satisfaction that
> the attitude of its own consulates has always conformed to
> international law and to the sentiments of friendship and be-
> nevolence which Prussia has avowed, for a long time, toward
> the destinies of Turkey. I have been able...myself to receive in
> this regard, the precious testimony of the Ministers of H.M.
> the Sultan. Nevertheless, the King's Government, appreciat-
> ing the justice of the observations presented by that of Her
> Britannic Majesty, and desiring to join its efforts to those of
> England to assure and preserve from all entanglements the

independence…of the Ottoman Empire, thinks that it would be proper…to recall to its organs, the rules of conduct…to follow in their relations with the Ottoman authorities….

…I engage you then, Sir, to limit yourself to guarding the interests of Prussian and German subjects – to confer your protection and to avoid scrupulously mixing in business which is not in that domain….[31]

As will be noted in the chapter dealing with the consuls and the Jewish population of Palestine, the pious sentiments proclaimed above were never realized while Palestine was part of the Ottoman Empire. The temptation to amass property and to claim protégés as a means of increasing a consulate's influence was too great to be easily resisted.

Chapter Twelve
The Old Yishuv and the Consuls

The biblical Book of Genesis refers to Ashkenaz as a great-grandson of Noah.[1] Jewish tradition associates Ashkenaz with Germany. Thus, Jews of German origin, including those in eastern Europe speaking the Germanic dialect called Yiddish, bear the name Ashkenazim.[2] As stated earlier, the history of mid-nineteenth century Palestine corresponds to the dramatic growth of an Ashkenazic majority in the Jewish community, largely occasioned by the arrival of Yiddish-speaking Russian Jews. By the era of the Crimean War, the old native Sephardic Jewry and the newly arrived Ashkenazim constituted clear majorities of the populations of Jerusalem, Safed, and Tiberias. They formed a substantial minority at Hebron. They established viable religious communities in every port city and in many villages of the Galilee.[3] Under Turkish law, and by virtue of commonly accepted practice, only the Sephardic Rishon l'Zion and the other native rabbis enjoyed official status.[4] The Ashkenazim, even as they became majorities in diverse Jewish communities, enjoyed some measure of protection only to the degree that they accepted the authority of the Rishon l'Zion and became "honorary Sephardim."[5]

In the pre-nationalist society of mid-nineteenth century

Palestine, the self-identification of individuals was primarily religious. All matters of personal status from birth to death and including marriage, divorce, inheritance, and even the right of residence rested with the clergy. A secularist individual who stood aloof from the organized religious community became a species of nonperson. No prisons or police were required to ensure obedience to the legal decisions of rabbi or priest. A social deviant would have been shunned and ostracized. Formal excommunication was rarely necessary to ensure conformity to communal norms.[6]

Consequently, as the Ashkenazic community grew it submitted itself to the discipline of the existent Sephardic rabbinate. Nevertheless, the Ashkenazim created their own complex system of kollelim distributing halukah, as previously described. Thus, within the Ashkenazic communities, a Yiddish and German-speaking rabbinate developed, which assumed legal authority over Jews within given kollelim. The Sephardic rabbinate discreetly ignored the emergence of a rival system of religious courts, provided that the Rishon l'Zion was recognized by all Jews as their supreme authority, especially in conflicts between the native Sephardic Jews and their Ashkenazic cousins. So long as the Rishon l'Zion controlled the revenues accruing from self-imposed Jewish communal taxes on the sale of certain kosher foods, for interment in Jewish cemeteries, and for the services of burial societies, it was highly unlikely that an Ashkenazic rebellion against Sephardic control would succeed.[7] There was to be a long and bitter battle within the Jewish community before Rabbi Samuel Salant became the unofficial, though de facto, Ashkenazic Chief Rabbi in 1878.[8]

Precisely because the Ashkenazim survived precariously as tolerated strangers in the Sephardic camp and as foreigners in the eyes of Turkish officialdom, they desperately needed protection. Although there were substantial numbers of Ashkenazic Jews bearing Austrian or Prussian passports and sprinklings of pious pilgrims from Great Britain, Holland, France, and even the

United States, the masses of the new Ashkenazic immigration came from Russia.

Very obviously, mere flight from the brutal anti-Semitism of Czar Nicholas I would not explain the choice of Palestine as a refuge. In the 1840s, there were still many lands which would have accepted Russian Jewish immigration if the primary motive of the immigrant was the attainment of physical security. The Russian Jews who chose a Palestinian refuge were motivated by deep piety. They moved from the hostile Russian environment in which they had, at least, been able to support their families by a variety of trades to a life of grinding poverty in Palestine. Supported by the often meager halukah of their kollel, they abandoned the trade which they had practiced in Russia to devote themselves to full-time prayer and Talmudic study. The Jewish quarter of the walled city of Jerusalem became one vast theological seminary, with individual Jewish families renting homes in the Moslem or Christian quarters of the city as well.[9]

The great dilemma of the impoverished Russian Ashkenazim lay in the fact that they had left their inhospitable homeland with a passport good only for a year-long pilgrimage to the Holy Land. As most such Jews had no intention of returning to Russia, they became stateless persons twelve months after leaving home. They then had a choice of begging for an extension from the Russian vice consul at Jaffa or submitting themselves to Turkish law, without gaining any of the assurance that the indigenous Turkish Jews enjoyed as members of a recognized *dhimmi* community.

Actually, Russia was happy to see the departure of thousands of Jews for Palestine. Therefore, in practice, Russian consuls usually granted renewals of passports, but played a cruel cat-and-mouse game in which expatriate Russian Jews were kept in a constant state of uncertainty about their future. The helplessness and vulnerability of Russian Jews made them pawns easily exploited for the ambitions of the Russian state in the Near East. Like all of the major European powers, the Russians found it politically useful to have a long list of resident protégés in Palestine, whose vicissitudes gave them pretexts for intervention in Turkish affairs.[10] In the case of the Russians, however, the Jews were something of an embarrassment because their domestic policy was blatantly anti-Semitic. Furthermore, the czar already had all the political leverage he needed in Palestine, as the protector of the Greek and Russian Orthodox Churches in all of the Ottoman Empire.[11]

The Russians, therefore, emphasized their Orthodox Christian protectorate and minimized their role as the defenders of Palestine's Russian Jews. To accomplish this feat, the Russian consul general at Beirut named Rabbi Isaiah Bordochan or Bordaki as the consular agent for Russia at Jerusalem. As Rabbi Bordochan, actually an Austrian national, had no consular exequatur and was not recognized by the Turks, he styled himself "Chief Ashkenazic Rabbi." Without having gained the official recognition of anyone as either a consular agent or as a chief rabbi, Bordochan proved to be a useful Russian tool in manipulating the precariously threatened Ashkenazic community.[12] As it suited them from time to time, both the Austrian and Prussian consuls at Jerusalem designated Bordochan a consular agent for their Jewish nationals.[13] Quite unconsciously, the rabbi became an object of amusement, marching pompously through the streets of Jerusalem preceded by a uniformed kawass, pretending to dignities which were more apparent than real.[14]

In March 1847, however, as part of Russia's pre-Crimean War effort to win British support,[15] Russian Foreign Minister Count Carl von Nesselrode made the British an attractive offer. The Russian consul general at Beirut, Constantine Basily, approached British Consul General Hugh Rose. Basily informed Rose that any Jew converted to Anglican Protestantism at Jerusalem would retain all of the privileges and protection given to Russian Christian pilgrims by Russian law. More significantly, the Russians offered to hand over the protection of all Russian Jews in Palestine in a body to the British if the proposal came from Britain.[16]

Rose was perfectly aware of the political uses to which his country could put the sudden accession of thousands of protégés in so sensitive an area as the Holy Land. Both he and Foreign Secretary Lord Palmerston, however, were much too experienced in diplomacy to take the initiative and to approach Nesselrode. Instead, Palmerston ordered Rose to inform Basily that Britain would not intrude into purely Russian affairs. Rose was to add, however, that if the Russians wished to hand over protection of any Jews to the British, they would be accepted. Rose was told to inform all British consular agents in Syria, the Lebanon and Palestine of the new policy,[17] and Palmerston took the additional precaution of writing personally to Consul Finn at Jerusalem on the subject.[18]

Basily's response to Rose was that when he had cleared it with Nesselrode he would be glad to transfer to the British the custody of Russian Jews whose passports had expired. As Rose was about to return to Britain prior to transfer to a new post, he returned no formal answer to the Russians, promising to discuss the matter with Palmerston, face to face.[19]

Actually, there was nothing startlingly new about the policy, in principle. As early as 1839, Palmerston had instructed William Young, then the British vice consul at Jerusalem, to protect the Jews generally, but to submit all disputes involving non-British Jews to the attention of the Ottoman government through the British embassy at Constantinople. Only the claims of bona fide British Jewish subjects were to be submitted directly to the Turkish pasha at Jerusalem under the protecting aegis of the British consul, serving as their advocate.[20] In 1842, at the request of the Netherlands, Dutch Jews in Palestine were placed under British protection exactly as though they were British subjects, inasmuch as there was no Dutch consul nearby.[21] What was new about the Russian proposals of 1847 was that it involved transferring thousands of suddenly stateless persons from the protection of Russia to that of Great Britain, without consulting them or the Turkish government.

It was quite in keeping with Russia's habitual behavior toward its Jewish subjects that Marabutti performed what was purported to be a humanitarian act in a manner designed to be brutal. In March 1849, Vice Consul Marabutti appeared suddenly at Jerusalem and Hebron. All Russian Jews were informed through their rabbis that they would have to surrender their passports for the purpose of a census. Those which were valid were revalidated.

All other Russian Jews, including those whose passports had expired or who had failed to submit to Marabutti's order, were informed that they no longer had any claim to Russian protection unless they returned to Russia within six months and paid all their arrears in taxes. The vice consul's order was given to the Russian rabbis to be read publicly in the synagogues. It ended with the ominous statement that if any Jew lost his Russian status,..."His Majesty's paternal care would provide them with sufficient protection by surrendering them to another power."[22]

Nothing was said about Great Britain as the subject of that reference. Marabutti deliberately allowed the impression to be given that all ex-Russian Jews were to become Turkish rayahs.

The Russian rabbis consulted together and agreed to keep the proclamation secret for a full week to avoid mass panic. Without any knowledge of the discussions which had taken place between the British and Russian governments, the rabbis of Jerusalem and Hebron approached Consul James Finn to ask whether stateless Russian Jews could receive British protection. Finn assured them that any Jew abandoned by Russia would receive British protection.

An attempt was made by the Russians to avoid giving unnecessary offense to the Turks. With British collusion, the pretense was maintained that the mass transfer of Russian Jews to British protection was purely temporary and was rendered desirable by the fact that no Russian consul resided in Jerusalem, Hebron, Safed, or Tiberias. Bahri Pasha, the Turkish governor of Jerusalem, received Basily's note purely as information and raised no protest.[23] Thus, in a flash, Great Britain suddenly found herself with a vast new register of protégés in Palestine, where formerly she had had only a small community of bona fide British subjects.

Ex post facto, Finn's superiors legitimized what had already been completed.[24]

Finn's first response, when informed that Lord Palmerston had approved a blanket extension of British protection to Russian Jews, was to offer certificates of protection to any Russian Jew who called at his consulate requesting such protection. Very shortly, however, he received amended instructions from the Foreign Office, ordering him to issue certificates of protection only to Russian Jews who could produce an *attestat*, or formal notice of dismissal, from Russian protection signed by Marabutti or Basily. Finn then attempted to recover certificates which he had issued without having seen an *attestat*, but the task proved to be impossible. The long-lasting result of Finn's failure to correct records thrown into chaos was a British entanglement with the fate of Russian Jews who clung to the role of British protégés long after the original recipients of Finn's certificates had died. The yellowed documents were passed as a valued heritage by parents to children.[25] By 1870, the official rolls of the British consulate at Jerusalem showed the names of only 285 adult men and women and 441 children who held British protection in Palestine as former Russian Jews. This does not take into account, however, a considerably larger number who claimed such protection based upon the events of 1849.[26]

Whatever the long-term results may have been, the immediate consequences of the transfer of so many Russian Jews to British protection was satisfactory to all concerned. The Russians were freed to pursue their role as Orthodox Christendom's protector. The British suddenly had the means of playing a large role in Palestine, where previously they had had only a minor part as the protector of a small Protestant congregation. For the Ashkenazic Jews, it meant that they could obtain justice in a European consulate when abused by members of other rayah communities. It meant equally that Jews could be assured that a representative of the British consulate would accompany them to the cadi's court and act as their spokesman if they were sued by a Moslem. It should be remembered that non-Moslems could not give sworn testimony in a cadi's religious court. Most subtly, it meant that they had an alternative to trial in a Sephardic rabbinical court where an Ashkenazi did not always feel confident of equal justice if an Ashkenazic plaintiff brought suit against a Sephardic defendant.[27] The enthusiasm of James and Elizabeth Anne Finn for the accession of this great concourse of protégés lay in their goals as missionaries. The Finns, consciously or unconsciously, viewed the vulnerability of the Russian Jews as a means whereby they could be moved to accept Anglican conversion.[28]

Actually, the deeply committed Jewish religious enthusiasm of Russian Jews, which had caused them to settle at Judaism's holiest shrines, made them very poor candidates for conversion to another faith. It became a scandal that the poorest class of Jew was prepared to accept conversion for the rewards offered by missionaries in exchange for baptism. Honest missionaries admitted publicly that conversions motivated only by hope of material reward were not worth much. Such rewards consisted of salaried employment as a dragoman in a consular office or in the London Jews Society Mission, a secular education in mission schools, or medical care in the London Jews Society hospital.[29]

At the height of the depression induced by the cutoff of Russian halukah funds during the Crimean War, the London Jews Society had the greatest illusion of the triumph of their efforts.

Daily Christian services in Hebrew were conducted at Christ Church for the authentic converts, a fluctuating group of about 20 to 30 adult men.[30] A Miss Cook of Cheltenham, England, donated £10,000 for a "House of Industry" where prospective converts, as well as those actually baptized, could work for a salary. A handful of Jews were employed at the Finns' home on the slopes of the Talibiyeh facing Mount Zion as stone cutters and masons. A larger, though indeterminate number of serious candidates for conversion, were sent to labor on the Finns' farm at Artas. In 1855 at the height of the Crimean War Depression, 650 men were employed as farm labor at Kerem Avraham. These latter were observant

Jews who had no intention of accepting conversion, but were willing to work for the missionaries in exchange for a loaf of kosher bread, two hard-boiled eggs, and the equivalent of a few pennies per day. At the same time, Mrs. Finn established the "Sarah Society" inside the city walls, where about 150 Ladino-speaking Sephardic women were taught fine needlework. Like their menfolk at Kerem Avraham, these were regarded as prospective converts. Actual converts were encouraged to work side by side with the unconverted Jews, urging them to accept baptism. In the hospital and in the places where Jews labored for salary, the missionaries meticulously allowed their clients the observance of the Jewish sabbath and holidays, supplied them with kosher food, and used a persuasive rather than a coercive approach to conversion.[31]

Nevertheless, a missionary like Finn was convinced that he was a divinely commissioned instrument for hastening messianic redemption. He wielded a mighty weapon when, as a consul, he served as judge and defender for all stateless protégés otherwise abandoned to the arbitrary justice of the Turks. Using that enormous power, Finn was able to prevent the husbands, wives, parents, or other kinsmen of his converts from threatening physical or economic punishment to his apostate protégés.[32] Every consulate possessed at least one room which could be locked and used as a prison. As the consul was a judge whose interpretation of justice could be arbitrary and unchecked, interference with a consul's control of his protégés was not attempted lightly. A consul could always dangle above the head of obstreperous protégés the threat of being abandoned to the Turks. Allegedly, the pasha of Jerusalem was only too willing to consign prisoners, thus abandoned by their consuls, to a Turkish "inner dungeon," a dreaded place entirely cut off from light and air. Few consular protégés were willing to test the reality of the threat, and preferred the relative amenity of a consulate's prison room to the imagined horrors of a Turkish jail.[33]

The Old *Yishuv*, or pre-Zionist Jewish community of Palestine, was thus caught in a strange love-hate relationship with the consuls. They desperately needed European protection, yet bitterly resented the ease with which wealthy foreigners could intrude upon and manipulate the most sacred institutions of the Jewish community.

If a kollel sent a *meshullach,* or envoy, abroad to collect money for the halukah, the consul was petitioned to provide letters of introduction and other documents ensuring safe passage. The condition on which the consul extended such favors was the recognition of his right to examine the accounts and to approve the financial report of the envoy upon his return. Whereupon, if the kollel was dissatisfied with either the honesty or the productivity of their alms collector, they would have to sue him in a consular court. Ordinarily, such purely Jewish communal quarrels were within the jurisdiction of the rabbinical court, or *beth din.*[34]

In a similar vein, under the heading of consular interference in Jewish communal affairs, consuls frequently imposed their will upon the rabbinate with regard to interment in Jewish cemeteries. The chief rabbinate, as part of its campaign against the missionaries, forbade any observant Jew to accept employment in a missionary establishment. Such a ban was extremely hard to enforce in hard times when the threat of starvation drove hundreds of otherwise faithful Jews to accept income from the missionaries. In more normal times, however, the rabbinate was able to induce most Jews to shun such temptations by simple social pressure, or if need be by threat of excommunication. An excommunicate who died while under the ban was liable to be denied Jewish burial. Such persons, if they had not actually accepted baptism, would be denied Christian burial as well.[35] The Turkish governor, mindful of the fact that the sultan's Hatti-Humayun had specifically given control of burial to the clergy, declined to intervene. In some cases of that sort, the survivors of the deceased were able to obtain Jewish burial for their dead by very generous payments to the communal treasury. In at least one case, a young woman who had died in the London Jews Society hospital remained unembalmed and unburied for so long that the consul finally ordered her to be entombed above ground in a zinc casing until a final resting place could be found for her.[36]

It is not surprising that the Crimean War and the attendant cruel financial hardship which accompanied it proved to be a major turning point in the history of the Old Yishuv.

Because most of the kollel halukah funds came from the Russian Empire, the Ashkenazic community was faced with ruin. It was this calamity which had driven so many hundreds of Jews to seek Christian charity in spite of rabbinic bans against contacts with the missionaries. Horrified by the prospect that the missionaries might succeed in winning souls by their blandishments, Rishon l'Zion Rabbi Jacob Covo set out for a tour of western Europe to raise funds for Palestinian Jewry. Rabbi Covo, who had undertaken this unprecedented journey, never reached his goal, but died at Alexandria in June 1854.[37] Nevertheless, his self-sacrifice was sufficiently dramatic that it brought help from the wealthy Jewish communities of Britain, France, Austria, the German states, and even the United States. The form which that help took, however, was not one which would have pleased Rabbi Covo if he had lived to see it.

The most flamboyant and dramatic of the western Jews who came bringing succor to their Palestinian coreligionists was Sir Moses Montefiore. Reference has already been made in other contexts to Sir Moses' epochal journey of 1855. It may easily be said that of the seven pilgrimages he made to Jerusalem in 1827, 1838, 1849, 1855, 1857, 1866, and 1875, that of 1855 made the greatest impact.[38]

The Chief Rabbi of Great Britain, Dr. Nathan Marcus Adler, had raised a fund of £19,887 for the relief of Palestinian Jewry. In 1855, Sir Moses Montefiore disbursed £11,000 of that total.[39] Although the great philanthropist was an observant Jew, he objected to the prospect of a Palestinian Jewish population devoting a lifetime to study and prayer, supported by foreign charity. It was his intention to establish self-supporting small industries through which Jews might earn a living. He also hoped to establish small farm colonies on which Jews could learn the arts of agriculture. He was not in any sense of the word a political Zionist with aspirations to the creation of a Jewish state.[40] He did entrust part of his money to an evangelical Christian, Colonel Charles Henry Churchill, charging him to train Jews as farmers. Colonel Churchill was an Anglican who hoped to hasten the messianic program by settling Jewish farmers on Palestinian soil without necessarily converting them to Christianity.[41] The most lasting physical monument to Sir Moses' work in 1855 is the great windmill, still standing on the Talibiyeh, and the row of apartments constructed in its shadow. Calling his apartments *Mishkenot Shaananim*, or the "Habitations of Delight," the philanthropist intended to lure twenty-four industrious Jewish families to leave the security of walled Jerusalem and to enjoy pursuing useful craftindustries in the healthy open country near the city. For that purpose, he designated that twelve such families were to be Sephardic and twelve Ashkenazic. Thus was created the nucleus of the first Jewish suburb outside the walls of Jerusalem. The windmill and twenty-four apartments were not completed until 1860, and it was several years after that before Sir Moses' beneficiaries could be induced to spend the night in the open countryside away from the squalid security of the walled city.[42]

Montefiore incurred the wrath of the Ashkenazic rabbis, however, when he laid the foundation for Jewish schools in which secular subjects would be taught. The Ashkenazim, who had witnessed the devastating effect of the secularist *Haskalah*, or "Enlightenment," upon European Jewry, regarded any time spent away from Jewish religious study as subversive to Jewish survival. The native Turkish Jews, who had never been exposed to the destruction of Jewish identity caused by the Enlightenment, tended to be more receptive to Sir Moses' concept of open curricula. In addition, Sir Moses caused widespread discomfort in conservative Jewish circles by a proposal to open schools for the education of girls.[43]

In this latter connection, Montefiore was strongly seconded by Dr. Ludwig August Fränkel of Vienna, who arrived at Jerusalem in 1856 as the agent of a family of wealthy Austrian Jews. He established the Frau Elise von Herz-Lämel School, which was both secularist and coeducational.[44] The British House of Rothschild entered the scene in 1867 when Baroness Lionel de Rothschild founded the Evelina de Rothschild School for Girls, named in memory of her daughter who had died in 1866. It absorbed the Montefiore school for girls, founded in 1863.[45]

At a less controversial level, Montefiore carried a letter from Grand Vizier Ali Pasha authorizing the building of a Jewish hospital. Work on this had already begun, the money for it having been brought to Jerusalem in 1854 by Albert Cohn, an agent of the French branch of the Rothschild family.[46] Thus was established the Misgav Ladach Hospital, which continued its services in the Jewish Quarter from 1854 until it was destroyed by the Jordanians along with the rest of the Jewish Quarter in 1948.[47] It was the evident intention of the French Rothschilds to offer medical care under Jewish auspices in order to provide an alternative to the missionary hospitals, which had become anathema to the rabbinate. Nevertheless, the implantation of so many western-endowed medical and educational institutions was a clear challenge to the conservative order of the Old Yishuv.[48]

The final great accomplishment of Montefiore's mission of 1855 was the presentation of a sultan's firman authorizing the construction of a great new Ashkenazic synagogue at Jerusalem. The firman swept away a rat's nest of confused claims.[49]

In 1701, Rabbi Judah the Pious had arrived in Jerusalem with his Polish followers, intending to build an Ashkenazic community in the Jewish Quarter. They had purchased the right to build on the ruins of a thirteenth-century synagogue, thus honoring the Turkish prohibition against building new non-Moslem houses of worship, though the repair of old structures was permitted. The rabbi's death, only three days after his arrival, demoralized his followers, and by 1720 the debt-encumbered congregation had entirely departed Jerusalem for the more hospitable Galilee. Thus, for more than 150 years, Rabbi Judah's uncompleted synagogue remained known as the *Hurva*, or "ruin." In 1849, the Perushim Ashkenazic community had attempted to continue the long interrupted building of a great synagogue to be called Beit Yaakov, or "House of Jacob." However, 150 years of ruin had left a mass of conflicting claims to the property by Jewish claimants and Moslem creditors.

It was ultimately a partnership between the British embassy at Constantinople, headed by Lord Stratford de Redcliffe and assisted by Francis, Lord Napier of Ettrick, Sir Moses Montefiore, and the French House of Rothschild which elicited an imperial firman authorizing the construction of a synagogue. Credit for the ultimate success of the effort to elicit an imperial firman must also go to James Finn, who maintained pressure on the embassy to continue its efforts throughout the Crimean War. It is part of the dilemma posed by the complex and enigmatic character of the British consul that he worked tirelessly to build a great Jewish monument, at the same period that he was engaged in constant warfare with the Palestinian rabbinate on behalf of his missionary activities. The still uncompleted building was dedicated on May 14, 1856. The completed synagogue, crowned by its magnificent dome, was consecrated in 1864. Congregation Beit Yaakov continued to be known popularly as "the ruin," or the *hurva*, even to the moment when it was truly reduced to ruin by the Jordanian conquest of East Jerusalem in 1948.[50]

In 1865, at the end of that watershed period of Palestinian history marked by the Crimean War and its aftermath, the current British consul submitted an estimated census of the population of the sanjak of Jerusalem. It must be recalled that the sanjak did not comprise central and northern Palestine. Major towns such as Nablus, Haifa, Acre, Nazareth, Safed, and Tiberias were outside its borders. The sanjak of Jerusalem ran from El Arish to the area north of Jerusalem and included Gaza, Jaffa, and Hebron. Consul Noel Temple Moore estimated the total population of the sanjak of Jerusalem to be 200,000, of which 160,000 were Moslem, 30,000 were Christian, and 10,000 Jewish. Nine thousand of the Jews were concentrated in Jerusalem where they constituted a majority of the almost 18,000 people in that city. Jerusalem had 5,000 Moslems and 4,000 Christians.[51]

Between 1855 and 1881, Palestine was in a state of ferment. Precisely because Jews constituted a majority in the largest city of an essentially underpopulated country, they continued to play a role in the considerations of the consuls at Jerusalem out of proportion to their numbers in Palestine. European Jewish philanthropies continued to build schools and hospitals.[52] Because western-endowed schools, regardless of religious denomination, continued to emphasize the use of European languages as the medium of instruction, French, German, or English consuls took an increasing interest in protecting the rights of their protégés.[53] They plainly regarded such schools or hospitals as instruments of European cultural imperialism. Thus, we observe the German consul carrying on a long correspondence with the governor of Jerusalem, demanding that the streets be kept clean and well drained and that sewers be constructed near the German Jewish-endowed hospital Bikur Cholim.[54]

To the very moment when a true Jewish nationalist movement, the precursor of modern Zionism, began to change the face of Palestine in 1881, the consuls did not quite know how to relate to their Jewish protégés. Every one of the European[55] and United States[56] consuls had his list of Jewish protégés who were not citizens of their country, but who had gained the right of protection by one means or another. The consuls and their governments were inconsistent and confused as to whether a list of alien protégés constituted a liability or an asset in their checkered relationship to the Sublime Porte.[57]

Thus on May 12, 1870, we witness North German Consul General Baron von Alten formally notifying the Turkish governor of Jerusalem that nineteen Jewish families were to be surrendered to the Turks as rayahs, no longer protected by the Berlin government.[58] On June 11, 1870, a very embarrassed von Alten wrote to the governor saying that:

A telegram reached me today ordering me to cancel that de-
marche for political motives, and to extend my protection
again, to these persons, who having been protected by this
consulate from a remote date, are not in a condition…to
produce documents strictly conforming to the established
rule…. I thus beg your Excellency to view as non-avenue the
letter which I addressed to you dated May 12….[59]

It undoubtedly gave the Turkish governor great satisfaction
to reply on the same day that the nineteen protégés, abandoned by
von Alten a month before, had become irrevocably rayahs unless
the sultan himself intervened to restore them to the Germans.[60]
On June 18, the unhappy von Alten diminished his request from
the return of nineteen protégé families to the return of only four.[61]
On July 11, the governor, with a great display of magnanimity, returned the four families to the registry of the protégés of the North
German Confederation.[62]

If it is not too cynical, we may note that sovereign nations
rarely inconvenience themselves purely out of humanitarian concern for the weak and defenseless. We may therefore assume that
the nations which clung tenaciously to their lists of Jewish protégés when they could have been so easily abandoned as rayahs, had
strong ulterior motives of national self interest in doing so.

The Old Yishuv has often been dismissed rather contemptu-
ously as a passive victim of misuse by their Moslem rulers and
their foreign Christian protectors. It must be said, however, that
prior to the great social revolution of 1881, both the Sephardic
and Ashkenazic leadership of Palestinian Jewry had learned the
fine art of political manipulation in their own interest. They became adept in the use of petitions to influential Jews, native to
the countries whose help they sought. A Montefiore, a Cremieux,
or a Rothschild could work wonders at a foreign ministry.[63] The
Jews of Palestine learned to invoke the aid of two or more consuls to move the Turks to action. It was the Prussian and British
consuls who eventually enabled the Ashkenazim to obtain control

of the right to slaughter their own kosher animals, thus breaking the former Sephardic monopoly on that essential and profitable activity.[64]

The Old Yishuv which came face to face with the secularist and socialist force of the New Yishuv after 1881 was not nearly so unprepared for the nineteenth century as has been claimed.

Chapter Thirteen
The Golden Age of Consular Supremacy, 1853–66

With the advantage of hindsight, we know that the era of the Crimean War, symbolized by the sultan's concession of Hatti-Humayun, marked the zenith of consular plenipotentiary powers. For approximately a dozen years, three essential conditions coincided, making it possible for foreign consuls to behave like ambassadors. First and foremost, the Turks saw advantages in keeping all foreign powers content and hence less threatening. The second was a general consensus that the status quo ought to be preserved, lest the balance of power be threatened by a disproportionate growth of any nation's strength at the expense of the Turks and to the disadvantage of rivals. Finally, those years were the last in which Palestine was truly isolated by the absence of telegraphic communication with the rest of the world.

Even the one great European military intrusion into the Palestinian area was in the name of the concert of Europe rather than the unilateral decision of one imperial power. France sent an army of modest size to the Lebanon in 1860 to end the endemic civil war, which had degenerated in 1859 to a particularly bloody decimation of the Roman Catholic population primarily at the hands of Druse clansmen.[1] Even Napoleon III, however, had not dared to sing the anthem "Partant Pour La Syrie" without first obtaining a mandate to do so from the other major powers and the consent of the Turks.[2]

Phasael Tower of the Jerusalem Citadel, 1880. The Jaffa Gate and its Turkish guard house can be seen in the rear. From Sir Charles Wilson, Picturesque Palestine, Sinai and Egypt, *London, J.F. Virtue, 1884.*

By the terms of a treaty negotiated at Paris in July and August of 1860, France was to provide six thousand troops for the pacification of the Lebanon and another six thousand were to be provided by some other European power, not designated in the treaty. France, Austria, Prussia, and Russia signed the agreement on August 16, 1860. Turkey and Britain adhered to the treaty on September 5. Ratifications were exchanged on October 18.

As events turned out, the French did not await the formal conclusion of the treaty, but landed their army in the Lebanon at the end of August. The other European powers were either unable or unwilling to touch the Lebanese tar baby. In the end the pacification of the Lebanon was carried out by the tiny French contingent and a greatly enlarged Turkish army. The Turks had been transformed by European pressure from a force in secret collusion with those who were slaughtering Maronite Christians to one imposing order upon the hate-convulsed religious cults of the Lebanon. The rest of Europe confined itself to composing a commission which "supervised" the French expedition without direct involvement.[3] A new Paris Conference in February and March of 1861 decided to extend the French mandate as Europe's policeman to June 5. The last French forces quit Beirut by that deadline, permitting everyone, including the Turks, to save face. The Turks, under the terms of a special pact signed on June 9, created a separate Christian region of the Lebanon under the governorship of an Armenian Christian directly responsible to the sultan. Thus, with skillful diplomacy and a minimum of military force, peace was brought to the Lebanon. Due notice was served to the Moslem and Druse population that Turkey would no longer ignore their slaughter of Christians. At the same time, none of the rival Christian denominations gained an advantage because the sultan's Christian governor did not belong to any of the dominant churches of the country.[4]

Thus, the Eastern Question, by mutual consent, was thrust into the background. No one was prepared to make a war issue of events in the eastern Mediterranean after the close of the Crimean War. Indeed, the rapid development of real threats to world peace elsewhere on the globe permitted Palestine the luxury of isolation until the telegraph tied Jerusalem to Europe in 1865[5] and even to North America in 1866.[6] In rapid succession the statesmen of Europe were tested by an Italian war in 1859, followed by the creation of a united Kingdom of Italy in 1861, Civil War in the United States from 1861 to 1865, French involvement in Mexico from 1861 to 1867, a Polish revolt in 1863, a closely averted Anglo-French war against Russia in that year, a German-Danish War in 1864, the Seven Weeks War of 1866, and a complete reordering of the German balance of power in 1867.

It is little wonder then that those years induced in both the native and foreign residents of Palestine a dreamlike state of unreality, so different from the mood which had preceded the Crimean War and which would follow the extension of the telegraph to Jaffa.

Those years are rich sources of anecdotes demonstrating the imperial arrogance of consular representatives in Palestine, at the precise moment when their home governments were determined not to make Palestinian affairs a pretext for military action.

In March 1857, the United States named John Warren Gorham as its first resident consul in Jerusalem. As far back as 1832, when David Darmon had been named consular agent at Jaffa, the United States had had a consular office in the Holy Land. From 1832 until 1857, a series of rayah agents and vice consuls had spoken for the United States.[7] Warder Cresson's fantastic career had enlivened the exotic history of that post.[8] Nevertheless, Gorham in 1857 was the first authentic United States citizen to reside in Jerusalem officially accredited by the United States and accorded a *berat*, or consular exequatur, by the Turks.[9]

Received into the charmed circle of European consuls at Jerusalem, Gorham quickly learned that the Turks had recognized the right to fly foreign flags only as a consequence of their Crimean War concessions. Therefore, Gorham informed the seraglio that he intended to raise the United States flag at Jerusalem for the first time on July 4, 1857.

Unfortunately, the new governor of Jerusalem, Suraya Pasha, happened to be at Nablus at the moment Gorham's note was received at the seraglio. Consequently, the consul formally notified the commander of the Turkish garrison of his intention to raise his flag and asked that the artillery at the Jaffa Gate citadel fire a twenty-one gun salute. The Turkish colonel, however, had informed Gorham that only kings were entitled to twenty-one gun salutes. The garrison commander averred that he could not take it upon himself to decide the appropriate salute for a mere president and that only the absent governor could settle the delicate question. Unwilling to see President Buchanan or the United States slighted, Gorham informed his fellow consuls that he would raise his flag at 10:00 A.M. on July 4 and hoped that they would raise their flags in friendly salute. Gorham spent the night of July 3–4 in an exchange of written communications with the stubborn commander. Although the United States consulate was within a short walk from the Jaffa Gate, Gorham kept his dragoman busy all night delivering messages and awaiting replies. Neither consul nor garrison commander could have had much sleep that night. Finally, when nothing else availed, the consul threatened that if his flag did not receive a twenty-one gun salute at 10:00 A.M. the case would be reported to the Sublime Porte. At that point the commander capitulated, firing a salute which he evidently believed was far too generous for a mere president. Apparently the colonel concluded that it was less dangerous for himself to be reprimanded by the xenophobic Suraya Pasha for excessive generosity to a president, than it would be to earn reprimand from the grand vizier for having infuriated a foreign legation.[10]

Although the archives are replete with tragicomic examples of consular assertions of national pride at the expense of the Turks, perhaps an example drawn from the records of the other North American state represented at Jerusalem will serve as an example for the entire genus.

Almost as soon as Archduke Ferdinand Maximilian von Habsburg had been enthroned as Emperor Maximilian of Mexico, he had sought diplomatic recognition from every sovereign state in the world, from the kingdom of Hawaii to the Ottoman Empire. Hitting two birds with one stone, he sent his most dangerously reactionary supporters into honorable exile, giving them diplomatic posts in countries whose attitude toward Mexico mattered little.[11] For the embassy to Turkey, Maximilian had chosen

General Leonardo Márquez, whose political views were diametrically opposed to the liberal image which the new emperor hoped to project. Although Mexico had little meaningful contact with Turkey, Márquez set to work with admirable industry to transform his honorable exile from a meaningless sinecure into a monument to his country's aspirations to greatness. He contrived to negotiate and complete the ratification of a Turkish-Mexican treaty of trade and navigation. He also played a role in legitimizing the dispatch of Egyptian conscripts to Mexico.[12] On December 5, 1865, the energetic General Márquez arrived at Jerusalem to install Pedro de Haro as consul general of Mexico.[13] The Mexican empire did not have enough business at Jerusalem to warrant stationing a consular agent there, much less a consul general. Nevertheless, Márquez's dramatic gesture was intended to emphasize Mexico's aspirations as a major Catholic monarchical power.

It is predictable that the new consul general, representing an impoverished government barely able to guard its own capital city against the republican guerrillas in the countryside, would be even more assertively aggressive than the truly great powers of Europe. Of course, the Mexicans knew that the Turks could be bullied only because of the illusion that France, Austria, Britain, and Spain supported Mexican goals. Even so, it was a superb piece of braggadocio when Consul General de Haro, on November 24, 1866, sent the following circular note to all consuls at Jerusalem whose governments recognized Emperor Maximilian:

> This consulate general was insulted last May 27 by Ali Aga, Adjutant Major of the troops of His Majesty the Sultan.... A satisfaction having been asked against the offense committed, it has just been decided between the local government and the consulate general, that the military pasha accompanied by the civil pasha, both in full uniform, will come together tomorrow, Sunday the 25th current, at two o'clock in the afternoon, to present their excuses under the Mexican flag, in the presence of the Consular Corps.

The Ottoman flag will be raised over the fortress at the same hour.

As I desire that the Consular Corps be present at that act, I beg you, Monsieur le Consul, to be pleased to honor me with your presence, assisting in uniform.[14]

This sort of effort to humble the Turks for the smallest slight became regular practice. A British army colonel who was visiting Jerusalem was insulted when a Turkish soldier called him "*ghiaour*," a particularly offensive epithet for Christians. The colonel promptly beat the soldier with his cane, chasing him back to his barracks followed by a large contingent of supportive English tourists. The British consul then summoned the Turkish military commander to his office and demanded that the entire garrison be drawn up and harangued on the necessity of civility to foreigners. The soldier who had committed the offense was then tried and sentenced to fifteen days imprisonment. Two other soldiers who had jostled the colonel's wife were sentenced to a week in jail.[15]

Imperial consular policy went beyond attempts to dominate the Turks. It extended to attempts to enlarge lists of protégés to include rayah populations having no connection whatsoever to their European protector. Precisely because France had hoary claims to the protection of Roman Catholics, the British took an interest in patronizing the Druse clans.[16] Britain also did what it could to throw a protective blanket over the tiny Samaritan community and even assured the prelates of the Armenian and Abyssinian Churches of its willingness to protect them.[17]

It was by no means unusual for one foreigner to be able to invoke the protection of two or more consuls. On January 11, 1858, Frederick Steinbeck, a Prussian subject, was murdered while visiting the home of his father-in-law, Walter Dickson, an American. Four burglars were ultimately found guilty of the murder and of raping Steinbeck's wife and mother-in-law. The three survivors of these crimes had a natural right to United States and Prussian protection. Consuls Gorham and Rosen posted a one thousand piaster reward. The Dicksons had a residual claim upon British protection as well, because prior to the arrival of a United States consul they had been listed as British protégés. The British consulate could afford to take a subordinate role in this case, since the greatest burden of obtaining justice fell upon Dr. Rosen and Mr. Gorham. A United States warship, the u.s.s. *Wabash*, visited Jaffa to show the flag and to coerce Suraya Pasha in a subtle way when he was desultory in making arrests and in pursuing prosecution of the accused.[18]

We have already explored the special relationship of the British to the Jews, but James Finn in 1861 went beyond anything attempted theretofore in an attempt to dominate Jewish protégés.

As noted previously, as early as 1842 the kingdom of the Netherlands had confided the care of Dutch Jews at Jerusalem to the British consul, simply because the Netherlands had no consulate at Jerusalem. By 1861, however, the Dutch had established a consulate general at Beirut with jurisdiction over all of the Lebanon and Palestine, but had not yet established any sort of consular agency at Jerusalem. For actual communication with the Turkish authorities in Palestine, the Dutch availed themselves of the good offices of Prussian Consuls. Effectively then, Prussia spoke for the Netherlands at Jerusalem, but Jewish families who had been registered as British protégés since 1842 continued to regard themselves in that light. Apparently, until 1861 no one had bothered to tidy up this obvious source of future trouble. In that year what should have been a minor lawsuit brought all of the peculiarities of justice under the Turkish capitulatory system into strange juxtaposition.

The crisis had begun when the united kollelim of the Jewish communities of Hebron had sued Joseph Shalom, an authentic British subject rather than a mere protégé in James Finn's British consular court. The defendant was charged with having embezzled funds collected abroad for the kollelim. Finn acquitted Shalom of all charges as there was no evidence that he had pocketed the missing funds.

Joseph Shalom had then brought suit in the same court against two of his own employees, meshullachim or fund-raising emissaries, whom he had sent to Europe to collect money for the kollelim.[19]

One of the defendants, Rabbi Kimchi, was a British subject. The other. Rabbi Israel Elyakim, was a native-born Dutch subject who regarded the British consul as merely a proxy for a Dutch consul. Neither of the defendants raised any objection to being tried in the British consulate. On May 23, 1861, as neither Kimchi nor Elyakim could produce a credible accounting for the funds they had collected in Europe, Finn jailed them in the consulate's prison. Immediately thereafter, protests came from two quarters. The Sephardic Chief Rabbi or Rishon l'Zion, Chaim David Chazan, demanded jurisdiction in the case since the dispute involved Jews exclusively. In a separate action, Rabbi Elyakim appealed to the Prussian consul general at Beirut to invoke the aid of the Netherlands government so that he could be tried by a Dutch consular judge.

Prussian Consul General Theodor Weber at Beirut immediately requested that Finn release Elyakim and surrender him to Prussian custody. Simultaneously, Chief Rabbi Chazan demanded that the prisoners be submitted to his legal authority. Finn refused both requests, stating that neither defendant had denied his authority to try them, and that he could not surrender them to other authorities now that the trial was concluded and a verdict given.[20]

The Prussian response was to raise the matter as a subject for amicable discussion with the British and Netherlands governments. The response of the Rishon l'Zion was to place a ban of excommunication against Joseph Shalom for having sued two rabbis in a consular court when the issue at stake was a Jewish religious and communal matter properly belonging in a rabbinical court, or beth din.

There was nothing very much that Finn could do to effect the resolution of the case of Rabbi Elyakim at London, Berlin, and the Hague, except to send a very full exposition of his position to Foreign Secretary Lord John Russell.

Finn's counterattack against the Chief Rabbi took the form of a public proclamation; henceforth, he would not give justice to any Jew unless the plaintiff signed a specific statement renouncing rabbinical authority as it related to the power of excommunication. Very unwisely, Finn composed a Hebrew language text of his rash proclamation and posted it throughout the Jewish quarter of Jerusalem. He also sent copies to the five principal Jewish communal organizations, ensuring that every rabbi in Palestine had access to a written and signed copy of his ultimatum.[21]

By his action, Finn managed to accomplish what two thousand years of Jewish history had failed to do. He united Jews of all cultural and religious backgrounds against him in a common cause. The Palestinian rabbinate, Sephardic and Ashkenazic alike, inundated Sir Moses Montefiore with complaints about Finn. Sir Moses, as President of the London Committee of Deputies of the British Jews, visited the Foreign Office to explain the situation.[22] Lord John Russell took the time to intervene in the matter, though he was certainly far more preoccupied with the Trent Affair, danger of war with the United States, Mexican finances, and Italian unification. Russell sent an unusually cold rebuke to Finn. It said:

> I entirely disapprove of that notice which you had no authority whatever to issue, for no Consul ever closes his Consular Court against a British suitor or dependant or makes his disposition of justice in any case conditional upon the act of others not parties to the cause, or upon the subscription on the part of the parties themselves to a declaration bearing on a matter of religious law or observance.
>
> I have therefore to desire that you will immediately and publicly withdraw that notice as by direction of the Secretary of State.

As regards Jews not British Subjects, although you may allow them to stand in your Consular Court on the same footing as British Subjects, you have no right to compel them to resort to it: as regards those who are British Subjects, if they are hindered illegally from pursuing their plaints in your Consular Court, you will refer to the Judge of the Supreme Court at Constantinople for instruction and be guided by his directions: but you will not take upon yourself without authority to publish…notices of so offensive a character as that to which I am alluding….[23]

In the end, Finn lost both his battles. He was forced to surrender custody of his prisoner, Rabbi Israel Elyakim, to the British, Prussian, and Dutch consuls general at Beirut. His unabashed, continued interference in Jewish communal affairs[24] gave the Foreign Office the excuse they needed to end in 1862 his seventeen-year career in Palestine.[25]

It must be emphasized, however, that throughout the long brouhaha of the Finn Affair, as the British, Prussians, Dutch, as well as the several Jewish communities fought for their respective jurisdictional power, no one proposed that the Turkish authorities should be consulted or granted jurisdiction.

Indeed, the Sephardic Jewish community of Hebron, which had precipitated the crisis in the first place, saw no difficulty at the end of 1861 in binding themselves to other foreign consuls for protection. The Prussian consul, for example, was formally requested by all the Hebron kollelim, as well as institutional spokesmen from Jerusalem, to agree to receive money coming from Europe and to channel it to them through that same Mr. Joseph Shalom whom they had sued in the British consulate earlier that year.[26] On its side, the Netherlands foreign ministry in July 1862 tidied up its Palestinian affairs by obtaining a list of all authentic Jewish subjects of the Netherlands known to be living in Palestine, including their minor children. The lists, divided by their communities of origin in the Netherlands, were handed over to the Prussian government which was thenceforth charged with the protection of both Christian and Jewish Netherlanders in Palestine.[27]

If, for the greater glory of their country, the consuls sought to increase the numbers of their protégés, the honor must have seemed less than splendid at times. Consuls became the guarantors for land claims, the witnesses for debts,[28] and the executors of wills.[29] They found themselves setting fair value on such items of disputed wealth as "three silver spoons" or "one gold watch."[30]

Nevertheless, the years 1853–66 remained years of happy nostalgia for Europeans who experienced much less freedom in the next generation under Ottoman rule in Palestine.

Chapter Fourteen
The Telegraph and the End of the Plenipotentiary Consulate

In all the long history of diplomacy, the greatest single change in the way in which nations relate to one another was wrought by the invention of the telegraph. In the classic "old diplomacy," each government gave its envoys broad general instructions describing the limits of their powers. Within those limits, the diplomat was permitted truly plenipotentiary discretion. It was a calamity much feared, but seldom experienced, when an ambassador so far exceeded his discretionary powers that he had to be repudiated. Because instructions could be sent and received only as quickly as a courier could carry them, no sudden shifts of policy were possible.[1] Because the majority of the population was illiterate, newspapers played almost no role in disseminating accurate information about such policy changes that took place. In the "old diplomacy" the men who made policy were aristocrats sharing a common view of world order, even with enemies across international borders. It was thus possible to move slowly, unpressed by events transpiring days, weeks, or months away.[2]

The old order ended with dramatic speed in 1844 when

Samuel F.B. Morse launched the first commercially useful telegraph line connecting Washington to Baltimore. Within the next six years most of western Europe was united by wires. The Crimean War had necessitated the linking of the western European complex and Constantinople. By the spring of 1855, Constantinople was linked to the Russian Crimea by a suboceanic cable. Immediately after the war, St. Petersburg, Russia, joined the European telegraphic system. A line from Constantinople reached Jaffa in 1864. This was extended to Jerusalem in 1865. In August 1866, the North American and European telegraphic systems were joined by transatlantic cable.[3]

Italian language petition to the Consular Corps bearing the seals and signatures of the leaders of Jerusalem's Ashkenazic Jews, asking intercession with the Turks to obtain permission to slaughter and sell kosher meat. Copy of document presented to the author by Dr. P.A. Alsberg, State Archivist of Israel.

As the telegraphic octopus spread its tentacles, plenipotentiary diplomacy as practiced for centuries came to a sudden end. Diplomats, thenceforth, were given very specific instructions and allowed almost no discretion. On all major questions, an envoy was only a matter of minutes away from his government if he needed advice. The likes of Lord Stratford de Redcliffe were gone forever. In the "new diplomacy," the greatness or mediocrity of a diplomat rested upon bringing the force of his personality and his mastery of language to the task of transmitting his government's views. The diplomat became a teamworker, rarely allowed a virtuoso performance. What rescued the diplomat from becoming a mere messenger boy was his individualized genius for making the views of his government seem reasonable without diluting hard and unpleasant truths which had to be clearly understood.

For men of the old school of diplomatic practice, the crisis atmosphere induced by the union of the continents by wire and cable was a genuine shock. Napoleon III, who certainly lent the full prestige of his government to the spread of the new technology, confessed that it befuddled him. In an intimate note he remarked, "I cannot say more to you for policy changes color three times a day."[4]

The foreign consuls in Palestine continued to be treated by their governments as though they had diplomatic functions. Capitulatory control of judicial proceedings by consuls continued to be a major part of their function until 1917.[5] Precisely because the use of the telegraph was so expensive, however, even wealthy governments reserved its use only for the most vital matters. Between 1865 and 1880, consuls found the conduct of the most ordinary business drawn out over protracted periods of time by the necessity of obtaining clearance not only from the local authorities, but from the home government as well.

One example of that sort will suffice. When in 1870 the Jerusalem authorities decided to demolish all purely decorative vaults and archways blocking the narrow streets of walled Jerusalem, consular property was affected as well. Baron von Alten, the consul of the North German Confederation which was shortly to become the German Empire, was asked to give his consent to the removal of vaults attached to the walls of his building. The ornamental stonework apparently had no function in terms of supporting the consular walls, and the expense of their removal would be borne by the Jerusalem authorities.[6] Von Alten was obliged to consult his superiors at Berlin and gave no reply until June 1871. The fact that Germany and France were at war may explain the delay. Nevertheless, von Alten was merely authorized to discuss the demolition, not to agree to it. Berlin had a complete blueprint for the Jerusalem consular property and pointed out that the sculptured gazelles which crowned the vaults actually did support a roof which funneled rainwater into a cistern. Baron von Alten was ordered by his government to obtain assurances that if the consular cistern ran dry during the rainless summer because the removal of part of the roof reduced the amount of rainwater captured during the winter, the local government would supply water free of charge to the consulate.[7] By the end of 1871, the Jerusalem authorities, perhaps exhausted by the slowness of protracted negotiations over what had originally seemed a routine matter, abandoned plans to clear the market area near the consulate of archways. It was now the turn of the Germans to court the Jerusalemites, admitting that the roof was dilapidated and could not endure the stress of winter storms for many more years.[8] Once the Jerusalem authorities had determined to abandon their plans for urban renewal, they allowed the Germans to stew in their own juice until 1877. What should have been a very simple matter within the discretion of the local consul, but which had become the subject of seven years of negotiation, thanks to Berlin's overwhelming supervision of minute details, was finally settled. A document in French and Turkish in two identical copies including a preamble and four articles, set forth the details of the work to be done and the responsibilities of both parties. Its tone resembled a treaty between two sovereigns more than it resembled a simple agreement between a municipal authority and a property holder. It was obvious that neither side was taking any chance on either being cheated or allowing the "gazelle terrace" to become a pretext for armed intervention.[9]

As another aspect of the hazards to which telegraphic communication exposed the consuls, more use of cipher codes became routine. Diplomats have always used codes to prevent hostile agents from learning confidential information. Prior to the age of telegraph, chancellories had distributed the keys to cipher codes very sparingly to minimize the chance of foreign agents laying hands on the key. It is a mark of the importance attached to the Palestinian consulates that cipher keys were given to some of them routinely for use when telegraphic messages were sent.[10]

In a positive context, the telegraph accelerated the cooperation of two or more foreign consulates in Palestine on matters of common interest. One such issue would appear at first glance to be entirely outside the province of consular jurisdiction. Nevertheless, it became a consular question by a circuitous route. Reference is made to the slaughter and sale of kosher animals.

As noted previously, the Rishon l'Zion, or Sephardic Chief Rabbi, had always exercised tight control over the licensing of *shochetim*, or ritual slaughterers. For each animal slaughtered, a tax was paid to the Turkish authorities and a separate tax was paid to the Sephardic communal treasury for the support of the poor and for the other expenses of the Rishon l'Zion. These taxes applied only to meat slaughtered for sale. Individuals who slaughtered poultry or other small animals exclusively for the use of their own family were not affected. Obviously, however, in a hot climate prior to the invention of refrigeration, no individual family was likely to slaughter and consume the meat of a large animal exclusively for its own use. This raised no problem for the Sephardim because their butchers were accustomed to removing the specific categories of fat, veins, and sinews which may not be eaten by observant Jews. Thus, the entire animal could be sold by a Sephardic butcher to Sephardic purchasers. Even with the government and Jewish communal taxes, it remained economically feasible for a person of moderate income to afford meat.

The Ashkenazim, however, presented special problems. Their rabbis held to a stringent interpretation of religious law which said the hindquarters of quadruped animals were to be sold to Gentiles. The butcher would thus avoid risking the inadvertent failure to remove the fat, sinews, and veins concentrated in those portions of the carcasses. Appropriate dissection of the hindquarters required a greater skill at anatomical dissection than the strict Ashkenazic rabbis attributed to an average butcher.

Consequently, as soon as Ashkenazim had become a majority of the Jewish population in Jerusalem, and perhaps in Safed, Tiberias, and Hebron as well, they had attempted to slaughter their own meat, independent of the Sephardic chief rabbinate. Inasmuch as the hindquarters were sold to Arab butchers, the quantity of meat available to the Gentile population increased even as the price of such meat fell. Thus, the Arab butchers absorbed the cost of the government tax. The Ashkenazic shochetim, not having been licensed by the Rishon l'Zion, did not pay the communal tax. It was argued that as the Ashkenazim were the poorest class of Palestinian Jews, most of them subsisting on support from the kollelim, only the elimination of the two taxes would put red meat within reach of their modest budgets.

The Sephardic chief rabbinate, however, regarded the Ashkenazim as merely attempting to evade paying their fair share of Jewish communal taxes. Therefore, the Rishon l'Zion invoked the aid of the governors of Jerusalem, alleging that the Ashkenazim were evading the government tax, as well. In 1853 and in 1862, the united Ashkenazic communities had attempted to obtain the consent of the pashas of Jerusalem for their program of selling only the forequarters of animals without paying the two taxes. Each time they had been beaten by the united front presented by the Rishon l'Zion and the pashas, who recognized him as the leader of the Jewish community.[11]

By 1866, however, because the Ashkenazic Jews were so clearly the majority of the Jewish community of Jerusalem, and the Jews were so clearly a majority of the population of the city, it was no longer possible to maintain the status quo. The leadership of the five Ashkenazic communities, Volhynia, Warsaw, the Perushim, Germany and Holland, and Austria and Galicia, met to plan strategy. Before they could take action, the Sephardic Chief Rabbi, Chaim David Chazan, sent a formal notice to the consul of Prussia as dean of the consular corps that he would oppose any interference by the consuls in a purely Jewish communal quarrel.[12] Evidently the Rishon l'Zion had heard rumors that the Ashkenazim planned to obtain their independence through consular aid. As a majority of the Ashkenazim claimed Russian, Austrian, Prussian, or British protection, the consuls would be their logical champions if they had no chance of winning a law suit in the Rishon l'Zion's beth din. As the Russian consul had no interest in fighting battles for the Jews, the Prussian, Austrian, and British consuls were their only possible advocates.

On February 3, 1867, a formal petition composed in Italian and signed by twenty of the most outstanding lay and rabbinic leaders of the Ashkenazic community, was presented to the Prussian consul. It bore the seals of the five Ashkenazic communities. The burden of the request was that the Ashkenazim wished to open legal proceedings to end the Sephardic monopoly on the right to collect a Jewish communal meat tax.[13] Dr. Georg Rosen, in the last year of his fifteen years of service at Jerusalem, undertook to arbitrate the quarrel, hoping to avoid formal legal proceedings. Associating himself with British Consul Moore and Austrian Acting Consul Pascal, he invited Rabbi Chazan to designate three Sephardic representatives to meet with three Ashkenazic representatives at the Prussian consulate.[14] The proposed meeting took place on March 5, but broke up with the quarrel more exacerbated than ever.[15] The three consuls, therefore, visited the governor of Jerusalem, Izzet Pasha, the next day to obtain his intervention on the side of the Ashkenazim. The governor seemed sympathetic, but first had to be convinced that the Ashkenazim were authentic Jews. The rumor had spread, undoubtedly inspired by Sephardim angered by the quarrel, that the Ashkenazim were members of an exotic cult which did not observe Jewish law. The Moslems took an interest in that question because Moslem religious law recognized the Jewish method of animal slaughter as acceptable to the standards of Islam. They were not prepared to give full faith and credit, however, to members of a foreign cult calling themselves Jewish but not resembling the familiar native Sephardic Jews in language, dress, or physical appearance.

The three Christian consuls then found themselves in the peculiar position of having to give a Turkish governor basic lessons in Jewish history and religion. Fortunately, Prussian Consul Rosen was the sort of linguist and scholar who was equal to the task. British Consul Noel Temple Moore seems to have seconded him ably. Austrian Acting Consul Pascal, who was merely carrying on his country's business prior to the expected arrival of a new consul, Count Caboga, assumed a minor role. It is sufficient to say that the consuls must have been persuasive, because Izzet Pasha gave the Ashkenazim what amounts to independence of the Rishon l'Zion in the preparation and sale of kosher meat, in mid-March, 1867.[16]

Unfortunately for the Ashkenazim, the matter was far from settled, however. A new governor of Jerusalem, Mohammed Nazif Pasha, replaced Izzet Pasha in the fall of 1867. On October 26, he sent an order to the consuls in Turkish, Italian, and French, specifically restoring the old supremacy of Chief Rabbi Chazan. He took refuge in the argument that the imperial firman of Hatti-Humayun, as well as the Treaty of Paris, guaranteed the supremacy of the Sephardic chief rabbi in the Jewish community. The new governor stated that he had specific orders from the Turkish Ministry of Foreign Affairs, dated September 19, 1867, to restore the old system.[17]

Under the circumstances, the whole business was referred to the consul general of the North German Confederation at Beirut to negotiate with his administrative counterpart in the Turkish administration, Reshid Pasha, the wali, or governor general, at Damascus.[18]

There the matter lay for the next five years. The Turks obviously felt safer from foreign intervention if they rested their case solidly on the existent system, even if it contained inequities. They apparently feared that any challenge to the Rishon l'Zion could be interpreted as persecution of the Jews, even though the evident intention of allowing the Ashkenazim freedom from Sephardic domination was actually a gesture of tolerance.

In January 1873, a way was found to circumvent all the thorny questions so as to satisfy everyone but the Rishon l'Zion. The first mayor of Jerusalem, as distinct from the pasha of the sanjak of Jerusalem, was an Arab merchant. Joseph al-Khalidi. The municipal council imposed its own tax on carcasses sold by butchers. Al-Khalidi was perfectly prepared to allow the Ashkenazim to open their own abattoirs and to sell the hindquarters of the animals to Arab butchers, provided that both parties paid the municipal tax. The entire matter of the guarantee given to the Rishon l'Zion under Hatti-Humayun was finessed. Apparently the new Sephardic Chief Rabbi, who was named, ironically, Abraham Eskenasi, either could not or chose not to pursue the matter further. The imperial German consul general at Jerusalem, Baron von Alten, undertook to serve as guarantor that those Ashkenazic butchers who were German subjects would be supervised closely by him and obliged to pay the tax. Thus ended one of the stranger and more complex tangles of Turkish, consular, and native Palestinian controversies.[19]

More than any other single factor, it is probable that the Ashkenazic victory in the battle to free their meat supply from Sephardic supervision led to the creation of an unofficial Ashkenazic chief rabbinate in 1878. Rabbi Samuel Salant, until his death in 1909, enjoyed de facto leadership of Ashkenazic Palestinian Jews.[30] To the very end of Turkish rule in Palestine, however, only the Rishon l'Zion enjoyed an official position recognized by the government.

With the benefit of hindsight, we recognize that the fifteen years between the coming of the telegraph to Jerusalem and the advent of true Jewish nationalist immigration in 1881 were quiet ones for Palestine. However, no one who had lived through the years from 1865 to 1881 could have predicted that. The great powers with a stake in the Eastern Question justly regarded Palestine as one of the many powder magazines in which the explosion leading to the next war might be sparked. Great Britain, Austria, Russia, and Germany watched one another nervously.[31]

In October 1870, Russia had announced her intention to remilitarize the Black Sea, unilaterally renouncing the single most important clause of the 1856 Treaty of Paris. In the next year the other great powers, having no intention of fighting the Russians to keep the Black Sea neutralized, recognized as legal that which they could not prevent. Once again Russia was in a position to expand in the Balkans and to threaten the Turkish Empire as she had before the Crimean War. Britain and Austria stood watchfully on guard to keep the Russians out of the Mediterranean. Discounting the role of the French and the Italians, neither of them capable of playing a major role in the Near East, Germany was determined to prevent a Russo-Turkish war which could only be to Berlin's disadvantage.[22] The Germans, the greatest military power in the world after 1871, fully realized that any war bringing major powers into collision would give France an opportunity for revenge. Only peace could keep the French isolated and harmless. To accomplish that, imperial Germany had to convince the world that she was not only a satiated power, but that she had no aggressive ambitions anywhere. Prince Otto von Bismarck, Chancellor of the new German Empire, had to bind the hands of the Austrian and Russian rivals by assuring both of Germany's friendship. The Dreikaiserbund of 1873, the pact between the three conservative emperors, was designed primarily to assure nervous Austria and Russia that Germany, seeking no additional power for herself, would see to it that each of the rivals might expect to profit equally in any changes affecting the Ottoman Empire.[23] To ensure that the German consulate general in Palestine did not become a factor in the power struggle there, the German envoy to Turkey sent the following stern warning:

> The political and religious dissensions which have erupted in different places, and which sometimes have taken an acute character, impose on the representatives of Germany a greater prudence and a greater reserve than in the past.
>
> It is evident that the parties attach a great price to spreading the opinion that they are supported by one of the great powers of Europe and they have always tried to distort even the smallest act of personal interest which the representatives of a foreign power may have expressed to them, and to consider his line of conduct as having been prescribed to him by his government.
>
> Acts of this nature have given occasion in recent times to misunderstandings which must be absolutely avoided in the future.
>
> By special order of the Ministry of Foreign Affairs, I therefore must give you instruction to abstain completely from all political and religious questions which may arise, unless you have been specially authorized to do so by me.
>
> I am authorized to impose immediate provisional suspension of service for any official who does not conform strictly to the present instructions.
>
> You will bring what precedes to the attention of all officials subordinated to you in order that they may conform to it.[24]

However much Prince Bismarck wished to keep the eastern Mediterranean quiet and his Russian and Austrian neighbors peaceful, events got out of his control. In 1874, Great Britain bought the khedive of Egypt's shares of the Suez Canal and became the dominant force in an institution which France had created.[25] Ironically, what Britain had tried to prevent coming to life had now become her domain.[26] In the next year, Prime Minister Benjamin Disraeli, flamboyant and theatrical, had named Queen Victoria Empress of India. In a gesture, Britain had underlined the importance of the Near East as the highway to the Far East.[27] In that same gesture, Britain had reaffirmed her role as Turkey's defender against Russian ambitions.[28]

In 1875–77, the Bulgars had rebelled against the Turks, and, while the rest of Europe debated the extent of the Turkish massacres of Balkan Christians, Russia took up arms once more as the champion of Orthodox Christendom.[29]

In 1877–78, Russia and Turkey had fought still another war, the Turks astonishing everyone by the good account they gave of themselves on the battlefield.[30] Triumphant at last in January 1878, within striking distance of Constantinople itself, Russia imposed a Carthaginian peace upon Turkey. By the Peace of San Stefano of March 3, 1878, a large Bulgarian client state was created which would have given Russia bases on the Mediterranean. By including much of Macedonia inside the new Bulgaria, the new order bid fair to block the southward expansion of Austria and the nationalist goals of Greece. Britain and Austria found common cause in ripping San Stefano to shreds and in pushing Russia and her Bulgar clients away from the Mediterranean shore and the Macedonian *Lebensraum*.[31]

Bismarck offered his services as the honest broker, the friend of Britain, Austria, and Russia alike. He presided over the Congress of Berlin, rewriting the Peace of San Stefano. Too late, Bismarck realized that he could no longer remain everyone's friend. At Berlin, faced with the unavoidable choice, Germany became the prop of weak Austria against threatening Russia. The genius of Bismarck managed to keep the telegraph lines open to St. Petersburg and to renew the Dreikaiserbund twice again. Nevertheless, Germany had lost her innocence. She was now bound irrevocably to her Austrian neighbor. In the Dual Alliance of 1879, whether he willed it or not, Bismarck made Germany a party to the revived Eastern Question. The best that he might hope to do for the rest of his career was to assure Austria and Russia equal success in expanding at the expense of Turkey.[32]

England, which had come to Berlin dominant at the Suez Canal, left Berlin with a 99-year protectorate over the Island of Cyprus. London gave the Turks no assurances of their future in Europe but guaranteed what was left of their empire in Asia.[33]

The Turks, relieved that they had recovered much that they had lost at San Stefano, sobered up on the morrow of Berlin to realize that they were merely keeping real estate open for ultimate occupancy by Austria and Russia. In only twenty years, the Turks were ready to regard Germany rather than England as their best guarantor against Russia.[34]

A diplomatic revolution had been achieved. Palestine was not left untouched by the forces which it released.

Chapter Fifteen

Palestinian Self-Concept; the Concrete Hardens, 1870–80

It may be said that your true self-concept is the essential loyalty which you express at three o'clock in the morning. If you are asked at 3:00 A.M. whether or not you would be willing to die for a cause, your answer might be in terms of love for your nation, family, religion, ethnic ties, or political creed. There would also be some happy, but singularly uninvolved creatures, who would answer, "None of the above." In searching for true self-concept, we are not interested in the sort of answer given smoothly at noon. The sophisticated smoke screen, which most educated folk can emit when fully alert, does not correspond to the truth uttered from visceral reaction, when half-conscious.

If it is difficult to psychoanalyze the living, the task is almost impossible for the dead. To try to discover the self-concept of a mass of people who lived more than a century ago defies the limits of possibility. Examining the population of Palestine in the years before the great Jewish and Arab immigrations began, the honest historian will confess frustration.

One statement may be made with confidence. Nationalist

loyalty was virtually nonexistent. A minuscule minority among the Moslem and Christian population were influenced either to a pan-Turkish or a pan-Arabic loyalty. Interestingly, Christian Arab intellectuals at Beirut were at the center of such Arab national feelings as existed.[1] It is doubtful that more than a handful of urban Palestinian intellectuals even knew the names of Nasif Yazeji or Butrus el-Bustani, who defined Arabism long before those usually described as Arab nationalists had a following.[2]

It is equally difficult to find either Ashkenazic or Sephardic Jewish Palestinians who were nationalists in a modern sense. Jews who crossed the narrowly defined boundaries of their own cultural and religious circle were likely to find themselves ostracized. Joshua and David Yellin, father and son, dared to give their children a secular education. They were consequently deprived of their share of the halukah and virtually banned by their own Ashkenazic community. As a teacher in secular schools, David Yellin composed the first textbooks in Arabic for the use of Arabic-speaking Jewish children. He interested himself not only in Sephardic culture, but was one of the first Ashkenazic Jews to study Moslem ideas in a systematic way. Because the Yellins favored Jewish agricultural settlement, they were among the few Jews of the Old Yishuv to form a link with the Zionists who began large-scale immigration after 1881.[3]

Almost the entire population defined themselves religiously. Moslems, Christians, or Jews who accepted "the nation" as the most important force in their lives were mostly individuals who had studied in Europe, or at a European or American-sponsored school located in Palestine or the Lebanon.[4]

Rabbi Zvi Hirsch Kalischer and his son Ludwig, usually described as among the earliest Zionists to wed traditional Jewish religious devotion to the Land of Israel with a nationalist desire to see Jews laboring as farmers in that land, worked within the framework of older, conservative, non-nationalist institutions. When Rabbi Kalischer of Thorn, Prussia, bought three dunams of land near Rachel's Tomb at Bethlehem in October 1875, he carried out the entire transaction without leaving Europe. The Perushim congregation, which had built Jerusalem's Hurva Synagogue, acted as purchaser and owner with money supplied by the Kalischers. The purchase was registered at the German consulate-general. In other words, German Consul General Baron Thankmar von Münchhausen thought of the transaction as a service to a German national who chose to donate land to a Jewish religious organization.[5] To contemporaries, Kalischer's work seemed to be philanthropy with a German label, just as the establishment of an agricultural school called Mikve Israel in 1871 bore a French label.[6] Charles Netter, who was commissioned by the Alliance Israélite Universelle to begin the training of Jewish youth for life as Palestinian farmers, had no Zionist impulse. The school's curriculum was secularist. The language of instruction was French. It proposed merely to rescue urban Jews from the city's squalor in the name of humanitarianism.[7] The intellectual impact of men like the Kalischers, Moses Hess, and Peretz Smolenskin was upon European Jews in Europe before Jewish nationalism became a force to be reckoned with in Palestine.[8]

Similarly, the earliest settlements of Jerusalem's Old Yishuv outside the walled city had nothing to do with nationalism either, though they provided part of the infrastructure upon which Zionist immigration would build. Sir Moses Montefiore's first Jewish suburb outside the walls of Jerusalem, Mishkenot Shaananim, was a simple attempt to induce Jews to pursue self-supporting crafts in a healthy environment.[9] The second Jewish suburb outside the walled city, Mea Shearim, was a walled enclosure built by extreme pietists, who wanted to pursue their own way of life, free of the corrupting influences of a city grown by 1875 to almost 30,000 inhabitants, in which the Jewish majority, constrained to its own quarter, had outgrown its living space.[10] A third Jewish population explosion from the walled city resulted in the establishment of a religious farming community called Petach Tikvah in 1878.

It nearly foundered in the marshy land near Jaffa, but somehow survived to provide the foundation for the city bearing that name today.[11]

Certainly, however, the decade of the seventies was not marked by any liberalization of the Turkish attitude toward foreigners and their ideas.

The brief thaw in Turkish xenophobia ended immediately after the Crimean War. The death of Sultan Abdul Medjid in 1861 concluded a reign which had begun the Age of the Tanzimat and had been crowned by Hatti-Humayun as a statement of good intentions. He was succeeded by his brother Abdul Aziz, who contrived to build a harem of wives and former wives, destined to include nine hundred women and three thousand eunuchs. By an unprecedented extravagance, he veered close to repudiating the interest on Ottoman debts until the enraged financial community insisted upon the control of Turkish finances by an International Commission. Abdul Aziz was deposed in 1876, dying allegedly by suicide a few days after his imprisonment. His four nephews, Murad v, Abdul Hamid II, Mahomet v, and Mahomet vi, turn by turn, were the last Turkish sultans. The one moment when it seemed that the Turkish dynasty might yet save itself was during that brief period when Grand Vizier Midhat Pasha, in the service of Abdul Hamid II, moved vigorously to implement constitutional reform. The grand vizier's reward was deposition, followed by murder at the sultan's command.[12]

It must not be supposed, however, that the sultan was indifferent to nationalism as a dangerous force. Certainly in the century between the Congress of Vienna and the outbreak of World War I, Europe had witnessed the successful secession of Greeks, Serbs, Rumanians, and Bulgars from the Ottoman Empire, In Asia, however, contemporary observers saw no evidence of a viable Arab nationalism.[13] Indeed, Ibrahim, the son of Nasif Yazeji, might compose and recite fiery Arab nationalist poetry to eight select members of the Syrian Scientific Society, but it scarcely reached the consciousness of the Arab masses. Students conspiratorially reciting poetry at Beirut or Damascus in 1868 failed to set off alarm bells at Constantinople.[14] Arab notables, who seemed too ambitious to build a political following for the advancement of their own power, locally could be easily silenced. The sultan's government would invite them to be "guests" at the capital. There, they were treated as honored men of distinction but kept under discreet police surveillance. Arabs of note were appointed to posts at the Sublime Porte. An honor guard composed of Arab recruits was on duty at the imperial palaces. Indeed, at the moment when Turkey was losing its European provinces, the Ottoman ensign was advancing into previously unsubdued portions of the Arabian Peninsula.[15]

Precisely because Christians were at the vanguard of such modest Arab nationalism as existed, the Ottoman government consciously promoted pan-Islamic revivalism.[16]

An independent thinker such as Sayyed Jamaluddin al-Afghani, residing in Egypt from 1871 to 1879, formed a devoted band of disciples who preached the revival of the Moslem Golden Age which in the seventh century had seen the Islamic world united under one caliph. Even the much-maligned Sultan Abdul Hamid II had the shrewd common sense to win the support of Moslem religious notables at Mecca and to get them to throw their support to him as the true Commander of the Faithful, the caliph who would unite the Moslem world.[17]

If nationalism in Asia was perceived as unthreatening at Constantinople, it was treated as totally irrelevant by the pashas of Jerusalem. They had no incentives to adopt liberal practice. By 1879. access to the Temple Mount had been closed again to non-Moslems, just as in the pre-Crimean period. Except for very prominent foreign visitors, exclusion had been in effect for twenty years. The British consul was reduced to complaining to London that water supplies from the large cisterns at Al Haram on the Mount were available only to Moslems and to those Jews and Christians able to hire a Moslem to carry water to them.[18]

More predictably, the Turks began to press the consulates

to surrender protégés to Turkish protection.[19] The authorities at Constantinople were particularly anxious to end protégé status for persons born on Turkish soil of Turkish parents, who had gained foreign protection in order to evade taxes. The Turks did not repudiate the capitulations under which foreign consulates had judicial rights over their own subjects, however painful such concessions may have been to their pride. They were determined, however, to cut the number of Palestinian residents who used any subterfuge available to evade rayah status. The consulates, on their side, were of two minds on the subject. On one hand, they wished as much as ever to have an impressive list of protégés, as an extension of their own power.[20] On the other, they were perfectly willing to surrender protégés on a selective basis if their maintenance on consular registers was likely to cause more trouble than they were worth as political pawns.[21] Until 1917, however, the numbers of foreigners listed at all the consulates as protégés continued to grow. Russian-born Jews and their descendants formed the largest bloc of that class.[22]

The decade of the seventies saw other evidences which were harbingers of a maturing sense of local self-determination, though scarcely a proof of a separatist tendency in Palestine. The governors of the sanjak of Jerusalem began to style themselves governors of Palestine. On January 1, 1872, the German consul general received a note from the governor of Jerusalem, with a newly printed letterhead for the *Gouvernment de Palestine*. Baron von Alten underlined the letterhead as though to dramatize his surprise at the low-keyed way in which the governor had enlarged his jurisdiction from that of a mere sanjak to all of Palestine. Thenceforth, the Turks referred to the Government General of Palestine in all their official notes.[23] Previously the pashas of Jerusalem had been simply the equals of pashas at Nablus and Acre. Thenceforth, the city of Jerusalem was the seat of the government of all Palestine. The governor of Palestine behaved as though he were the equal of the musheer of Beirut, their common superior being the wali of Damascus.[24]

Simultaneously, Jerusalem which had been governed for so long by the pasha assisted by a medjlis, or council, began to develop true municipal institutions on the western model. As mentioned previously, a wealthy Arab merchant, Joseph al-Khalidi, assumed the post of president of the Municipal Council, equivalent to the office of mayor. He was assisted by an elaborate appointive official staff, including a director of Municipal Finances. All of these persons held office at the pleasure of the Turkish governor, but seem to have enjoyed full autonomy in everything relating to such city services as traffic, property condemnation, sewer maintenance, water supply, and cleanliness.[25] The growth of a small but powerful Arab middle class in a society which only forty years before had seen commerce almost entirely in Armenian, Greek, and Jewish hands is worthy of comment. It is also worthy of note that the aristocratic Arab effendi class which had previously been the only influential Moslem element under the Turks found themselves sharing power with Arab merchants.[26]

As both Arab and Turkish Moslem particularism grew in intensity, the consulates heightened their sense of national particularism. Every effort was exerted to fill all responsible consular positions with authentic nationals of the country represented.

Since the establishment of the first consulate at Jerusalem in 1838, the consuls had been heavily dependent on Ottoman subjects of all ethnic stocks, especially in the crucial office of dragoman. Suddenly, the foreigners in European service had become an embarrassment. On March 13, 1868, Professor Heinrich Julius Petermann, the scholarly and gentle consul of the North German Confederation, formulated a note in Italian to Daood el Koordi, the Arab dragoman who had been in Prussian and German service for twenty-five years. In a tone of evident embarrassment, Dr. Petermann informed his faithful employee that he had just received a telegram from Count von Bismarck ordering him to dismiss any foreign dragoman on his staff. That the consul signed his note, "Bene affezionato," cannot have made it easier for the man so summarily dismissed.[27] El Koordi seems to have been in a state of shock, because it was not until three months later that he sent a begging note requesting that he receive his salary as a pension for the rest of his life, since he was the sole support of a family of ten. The present writer has no clue as to the denouement of that pathetic drama.[28]

Notwithstanding the wishes of Count von Bismarck, the practical realities of life at Jerusalem made it necessary to continue the employment of persons who knew the languages spoken in Palestine. Out of necessity, such employees were in collusion with their European employers to befog their legal nationality. One such case is that of Serapian Murad, the third generation of his family in consular service. In the era when Mehmet Ali had opened Palestine to foreign consuls, the United States had employed a prosperous Armenian merchant, a Turkish rayah as vice-consul at Jaffa.[39] Murad Aroutin had adopted his nephew by marriage, one Jacob Serapian, who thenceforth signed himself Jacob Serafin Murad. At the death of Murad Aroutin, his adopted son had become vice consul at Jaffa for both the United States and Prussia.[30] As noted previously, such double service was common in the early period of the European penetration of Palestine. In 1868, the young son of Jacob Serafin Murad had become dragoman at the consulate of the North German Confederation, signing himself as Serapian J. Murad. Unlike his father and grandfather, Serapian Murad had learned to speak and write a correct German and, like them, knew French and several of the more useful native languages as well. Intending to pursue a career in the service of the German Empire, he had gone to Berlin in 1875 to familiarize himself with the personnel and structure of the imperial foreign office. In 1876, he had petitioned the government for naturalization. The petition was refused in May of that year. He was also told confidentially by the counsellor of the German legation at Constantinople that any hope that he might have for advancement in the service was illusory. Nevertheless, as late as February 1876, the German consul general at Jerusalem formally requested the Turkish governor to regard Serapian Murad as a

German rather than as a Turkish subject. There is no reason to believe that Baron von Münchhausen was trying to mislead Faïk Pasha.[31] All that can be concluded is that there was sincere confusion on all sides as to the dragoman's nationality. In May 1877, convinced of the fatuity of attempting to become a German or to hope for advancement in German service, Serapian Murad ended forty-odd years of his family's service to foreign interests in Palestine by voluntary resignation.[32]

The Turkish-Russian War of 1877–78 is another case in point. It offers a remarkable contrast to the previous conflict between those two empires in 1853–56. During the Crimean War, the Turks in Palestine had shown restraint with regard to the treatment of Russian nationals and interests. As noted previously, the Turks had not harassed Russians who found themselves in Palestine when war began in 1853. There had been some rumors that the Turks wished to expel Russian Jews who did not enjoy consular protection, but nothing was done to carry out such a threat. Indeed, the British consul had concluded that the Turkish officials who had sparked such rumors were more interested in extorting bribes than in actually victimizing stateless persons by expulsion.[33]

In 1877, however, the situation was markedly different. In part this was due to the fact, as previously noted, that Russia had vast property holdings in Palestine in 1877 which she had not held in 1853. Primarily, however, the situation had changed because the Turks were much less tolerant of anyone associated with the Russian foe. German Consul General von Münchhausen was named custodian of all Russian imperial and church property in Palestine, as well as the protector of all Russian subjects unable to leave Palestine before the formal declaration of war.[34] As the Russian consul at Jerusalem, Nicholas Ilarianov closed his consulate, he gave von Münchhausen detailed inventories of all property and a list of all Russian subjects stranded in Palestine. There were forty-six Russian Christian pilgrims who were to be gotten out of Palestine, if it were possible. There were also 131 Jewish passport holders, representing an unknown number of dependents, who were certified as Russian subjects in good standing, but who had no intention of leaving Palestine.[35] The Russian Christian pilgrims were all gotten safely out aboard an Austrian vessel going to Trieste.[36] The Turkish governor, however, not only insisted on the expulsion of such Russian transients, but demanded that the German consul cooperate in arranging the departure of all Russian clergy and the employees of Russian church institutions.[37] Von Münchhausen had no means of protecting Russian priests who were authentic Russian subjects. He did, however, firmly resist the application of the decree of expulsion to the numerous Greek subjects who had been employed by Russia and to Arab Christians who were authentic Ottoman subjects.[38] Münchhausen's protests did little good, however. Even Turkish rayahs, who had served Russian institutions in Palestine before the war, were obliged to leave the country during the war. It required the intervention of the German envoy at Constantinople to obtain exemptions for a handful of such persons. A note from the Naib Assad, the acting Turkish governor at Jerusalem in June 1877, to the German consul conveys the emotional tone of Turkish xenophobia even toward rayahs who collaborated with Russia in peacetime.

> Although the Sublime Porte has ordered the expulsion of the honorary Dragomans of the Russian Consulate, they have agreed to make an exception at the request of the German Embassy at Constantinople, in favor of Hanna El Khouri who is in charge of Russian church property at Haifa and who is in charge of the construction of Russian church property. The exception has been made because he is an inoffensive person and he alone knows the languages, and the facts concerning the buildings.[39]

It must be said to their credit that the Turkish authorities protected Russian property from vandalism during the period when it was in German custody. It must also be said that in that gentler age, the Russian consul was back in Jerusalem on June 16, 1878, a mere five months after the end of hostilities.[40]

At the close of the 1870s, no one observing Palestine would have had any reason to predict the enormous changes about to take place in the country as political Zionism emerged. In 1880, Jerusalem boasted a population of 30,000. Acre's population had fallen to 8,500 from a previous high of 10,000. Nearby Haifa, with its superior harbor, had risen to 6,000. Jaffa had 10,000 inhabitants, Gaza 19,000, Hebron 10,000, Nablus 12,500, Nazareth 6,000, Tiberias 3,000, and Safed 7,500.[41]

Essentially, however, between 1838 and 1880, Palestine had remained an empty land, dominated by marginal agriculture, small villages, and endemic disease. The marauding Bedouin remained the bane of every Turkish governor's existence. Two great changes had occurred in the economic structure of the country. The first was that small farms had been consolidated into the hands of great landlords. The second was the growth of an Arab commercial bourgeoisie.[42] By way of historic irony, the former was to make it easier for Zionist pioneers to buy land and to establish a Jewish agricultural base in the land.[43] The latter provided a base for the later development of Arab nationalist feeling.[44]

On March 13, 1881, two bombs exploded in St. Petersburg, Russia. Hideously mangled, Czar Alexander II died at the hands of assassins.[45] His son, Alexander III, a completely sincere reactionary, was convinced that only an alliance between himself and the uncontaminated Russian peasantry could save the purity of Russia's soul.[46] For the czar, the urban and cosmopolitan Jew became the embodiment of the devilish forces which had killed his father. His government returned zealously to the policies of his grandfather, Nicholas I, to force the Jews to accept conversion or to leave Russia. From 1881 and onward until the outbreak of World War I, the Russian army and police actively abetted bloody massacres of the Jews.[47] In May 1882, the "May Laws" pushed Jews back to that pale of settlement which had been vigorously maintained until the succession of the late czar. Jews were confined to cities with more than 10,000 inhabitants. Many thousands of Jews were driven to penury and, perhaps worse than that, deprived of the revival of spirit which the sight of open fields, green trees, and unpolluted nature affords humanity. It was not necessary for Alexander III's lay procurator of the Orthodox Church, Constantine Pobedonovstyev, to utter his notorious threat. A large minority of Russian Jewry did not wait to see if he would truly convert one-third, expel one-third and starve one-third. In 1881, the great flight began which ultimately created the great American Jewish community.[48] In that year, however, seven thousand Jews entered Palestine. In raw numbers, the figure was small. Most of them were pious folk who belonged to the Old Yishuv. Nevertheless, seven thousand were a greater number than had entered Palestine in any one year since the Romans had destroyed the Second Temple. Among the seven thousand were a score of young people determined to become Jewish peasants farming Jewish earth. Among them also was a young Lithuanian Jew, a dropout from a French medical school, who had vowed to make Hebrew a living tongue. Eliezer Ben Yehudah's Hebrew and the philosophy of labor of his fellows gave life to Zionism fifteen years before Theodor Herzl penned *Der Judenstaat*.[49] Palestine was to be quiet no longer.

Turkish Governors, Non-Moslem Religious Leaders, and Foreign Consuls

Listed below are the consuls, religious leaders, and Turkish governors of Jerusalem 1838–1880. Where the dates of an official's tenure of office are known, they appear after his name. When the date of an official's death or resignation is uncertain, only the date of his appointment is given. When only the surname of an official is ascertainable, it appears without first name or initials. When a consulate is known to have been open, but the names of its tenants are uncertain, the dates during which the consulate functioned are given without the names of the consuls.

ANGLICAN BISHOPS

Michael Solomon Alexander (1842–45)
Samuel Gobat (1846–78)
Joseph Barclay (1879–81)

ARMENIAN PATRIARCHS

Gabriel of Nicomedia (1818–40)

Zakaria of Koph (1840–45)
Kyriakus (1846–50)
Hovhannes of Smyrna (1851–60)
Bishop Vertanes, *Locum Tenens* (1860–64)
Yessai of Talass (1864–85)

AUSTRIAN CONSULS

Count Josef de Pizzamano (1847–61)
August Lenk von Wolfsberg (1861–64)
Leopold Walcher von Moltheim (1864–67)
Bernhard, Count Caboga-Cerva (1867–82)

FRENCH CONSULS

Gabriel, Count de Lantivy (1843–45)
Joseph-Marie-François Helouis-Jorelle (1845–48)
Paul-Emile Botta (1848–55)
Edmond de Barrère (1855–68)
Joseph-Adam Sienkiewicz (1868–70; Acting Consul until February
    1872)
Ernest Crampon (1871–74)
Salvator Patrimonio (1874–81; Acting Consul from October 30,
    1873)

CONSULS OF GREECE

Sporadic attempts were made to establish a Greek consulate at
Jerusalem 1851–58. The Greek government maintained a vice-
consulate at Jaffa during those years, except during the Crimean
War. A royal decree of July 8, 1858, established a Greek consulate
at Jerusalem, but no consul was in residence until 1862.

Stamatis Lekatis (1862)
Ioannis Metaxas (–1866)
Constantinos Afthonidis (1867)
Ioannis Pervelis (1868–69)
Theodore Xenos (1869)

[Diplomatic Rupture] (1869–70)
Mich. Aivazidis (1872–78)
George Pakmor (1878)
Ioannis Pervelis (1878)
N. Mihos (1878–80)
Ag. Vougioukas (1880)

GREEK ORTHODOX PATRIARCHS

Athanasios IV (1827–44)
Cyril II (1845–72)
Procopios II (1872–75)
Ierotheos (1875–82)

CONSULS OF PRUSSIA, THE NORTH GERMAN CONFEDERATION, AND THE GERMAN EMPIRE

Dr. Ernst Gustav Schultz (1842–51)
Dr. Georg Rosen (1852–67)
Professor Heinrich Julius Petermann (1868–69)
Baron Karl von Alten (1869–73)
Baron Thankmar von Münchhausen (1874–81)

CONSUL OF MEXICO

Pedro de Haro (1865–67)

CONSULS OF PERSIA

Consular Agent, name unknown (1857–)
[Consul] Mohammed Hadi (1873–)

KINGDOMS OF SARDINIA-PIEDMONT AND ITALY

Name of Consul unknown (1843–49)
Names of Consuls unknown (1873–)

LATIN PATRIARCHS

Augustus Foscolo, titular, non-resident (1830–47)
Joseph Valerga (1847–72)

Vincent Bracco (1872–89)

TURKISH GOVERNORS
Tayar Pasha (1841–44)
Mehemed Bahri Pasha (1845–49)
Adhem Pasha (1849–51)
Hafiz Ahmed Pasha (1851–54)
Kara Osman Oglu Yakoob Pasha (1854)
Kiamal Pasha (1855–57)
Suraya Pasha (1857–64)
Izzet Pasha (1864–67)
Mohammed Nazif Pasha (1867–69)
Kiamal Pasha (1869–72)
Mohammed Nazif Pasha (1872–73)
Kiamal Pasha (1873–74)
Ali Pasha (1874–75)
Faïk Favlallah Pasha (1875–77)
Reouf Pasha (1877–)

CONSULS OF RUSSIA
Dr. B. Kozhevnikov (1857–)
Dorgobouginov (1859–60)
Sokolov (1860–61)
Names Unknown (1862–64)
Dr. B. Kozhevnikov (1865–75)
Nicholas Ilarionov (–1877)
Diplomatic Rupture (1877–78)
Nicholas Ilarionov (1878–)

RISHON L'ZION, CHIEF RABBI, OR CHACHAM BASHI
Abraham Chaim Mercado Gaguine (1843–47)
Jacob Covo (1848–54)
Chaim Nissim Abulafia (1854–60)
Chaim David Chazan (1860–69)
Abraham Eskenasi (1870–80)

CONSULS OF SPAIN

Pío de Andrés García (1854–55)
Fernando Vara (1856)
Miguel de Tenorio (1857–59)
Mariano Prellezo e Isla (1860–62)
Ramón de Valladares y Saavedra (Served *ad interim* during portions of 1860–62)
Luis Dodice (1864–68)
Tomás Magdalena de Tejada, Count of Casa Sarria (1869–77)
José Alcalá-Galiano (1878)
Salvador Ramés y Villanueva (1879)
Antonio Vázquez (1880)

CONSULS OF THE UNITED KINGDOM OF GREAT BRITAIN

William Tanner Young (1838–45)
James Finn (1846–62)
Noel Temple Moore (1863–90)

CONSULS OF THE UNITED STATES

John Warren Gorham (1856–60)
William R. Page (1860)
Franklin Olcott (1861–62)
Albert Rhodes (1863–65)
Victor Beauboucher (1865–70)
Richard Beardsley (1870–73)
Frank S. de Hass (1873–77)
Joseph G. Willson (1877–82)

Notes

CHAPTER 1 – THE LAND; PALESTINE IN 1841

1. Detailed documentation for this chapter can be found in Arnold Blumberg. *A View From Jerusalem, 1849–1858: The Consular Diary of James and Elizabeth Anne Finn* (East Brunswick, N.J.: Fairleigh Dickinson University Press, 1980).

2. Benjamin Mazar, *The Mountain of the Lord: Excavating in Jerusalem* (Garden City, N.Y.: Doubleday, 1975), p. 291.

3. For a particularly valuable study of early trade routes see Alexander Schölch, "European Penetration and the Economic Development of Palestine, 1856–1882," in *Studies in the Economic and Social History of Palestine in the Nineteenth and Twentieth Centuries,* edited by Roger Owen (Carbondale and Edwardsville: Southern Illinois University Press, 1982), pp. 10–87.

4. Consul J. Warren Gorham to Secretary of State Lewis Cass, January 19, 1859, Jerusalem, United States National Archives, State Department Correspondence (hereafter abbreviated as U.S.N.A., S.D.C.), Microcopy M453. Roll 1.

5. A wealth of travel literature contains descriptions of journeys in Palestine 1840–80. A few representative primary source accounts would include Peter Amann, "Prophet in Zion: the Saga of George J. Adams," *The New England Quarterly* 37 (1964): 477–500; James Turner Barclay, *The City of the Great King: or Jerusalem As It Was, As It Is, and As It Is To Be* (Philadelphia: J. Challen, 1858); John Ross Browne, *Yusef, or the Journey of the Frangi: A Crusade in the East* (New York: Harper, 1853); Samuel Sullivan Cox, *Orient Sunbeams, or From the Porte to the Pyramids by Way of Palestine* (New York: 1882); William Francis Lynch, *Narrative of the United States Expedition to the River Jordan and the Dead Sea* (Philadelphia: Lea & Blanchard, 1849); Herman Melville, *Journal of a Visit to Europe and the Levant, October 11 1856–May 5, 1857* (Princeton: Princeton University Press, 1955); Mark Twain, *The Innocents Abroad* (New York: Harper & Brothers, 1911). The works by Barclay, Browne, and Cox were all reprinted by Arno Press, New York, in 1977.

6. An excellent primary source for the nationalities of seamen engaged in the coastal trade is the large collection known as "Files of British Consulate in Jerusalem," preserved at the Israeli State Archives. The collection has been assigned the Record Group Number 123–1. *The Consulate's Instructions to Consular Agents,* containing extensive documentation concerning seamen, is known as file number 14. Hereafter, materials from this collection will be cited simply as "British Consulate, R.G.N. 123–1," followed by the appropriate file number by which the document is identified at the Israeli State Archives, at present.

7. With surprising frequency, residents of Palestine corresponded with foreign consuls in Italian. Elsewhere in the world in the nineteenth century, French would have been the normal language of correspondence between educated persons of different nationalities. The author's examination of British, Austrian, and German consular correspondence, as part of the research for this work, reveals Italian to be more widely used than French.

8. For a detailed treatment of this phenomenon, see Albert Hourani, *The Emergence of the Modern Middle East* (Berkeley and Los Angeles: University of California Press, 1981), pp. 104–17; Frank Edgar Bailey, *British Policy and the Turkish Reform Movement; A Study in Anglo-Turkish Relations 1826–1853* (New York: Howard Fertig, 1970), p. 9.

9. Howard Robinson, *Carrying British Mails Overseas* (New York: New York University Press, 1964), p. 165.

10. See Note 5 for references to travel journals as primary sources.

11. For frequent and detailed references to the specific techniques for building a complex system of protective alliances see Blumberg, *A View From Jerusalem.* The system used for the purchase of protection for travelers prior to the growth of consular power is described in Amnon Cohen, *Palestine in the 18th Century: Patterns of Government & Administration* (Jerusalem: Magnes Press, 1973), pp. 256–57.

12. For topographical statistics see Zev Vilnay, *The Guide to Israel* (Jerusalem: Hamakor Press, 1972), pp. 12–13.

13. Joan Dash, *Summoned to Jerusalem; the Life of Henrietta Szold* (New York: Harper & Row, 1979). pp. 88–89, 108–11, 143.

14. These figures are drawn from a contemporary source. See J. Thomas and T. Baldwin, *Lippincott's Pronouncing Gazetteer* (Philadelphia: Lippincott, 1866). More modern sources are in basic agreement, varying by only as much as 1,000 persons. See Schölch, "European Penetration," p. 57.

15. Vilnay, *Guide to Israel*, p. 192.

Notes

CHAPTER 2 – THE SUBLIME PORTE AND ITS PASHAS

1. George, Lord Eversley, and Sir Valentine Chirol, *The Turkish Empire from 1288 to 1924* (New York: Howard Ferlig, 1969), pp. 281–86, 288–89; Frank Edgar Bailey, pp. 38–62, 145–50; Vernon John Puryear, *France and the Levant, From the Bourbon Restoration to the Peace of Kutiah* (Berkeley: University of California Press, 1941), pp. 208–18.
2. P.M. Holt, *Egypt and the Fertile Crescent 1516–1922* (Ithaca, N.Y.: Cornell University Press, 1969), pp. 176–92; Sir Charles Webster, *The Foreign Policy of Palmerston 1830–1841* (New York: Humanities Press, 1969), 2:753–76.
3. Moshe Maoz, *Ottoman Reform in Syria and Palestine 1840–1861; the Impact of the Tanzimat on Politics and Society* (Oxford: Clarendon Press, 1968).
4. These developments are traced in Blumberg, *A View From Jerusalem.*
5. David Finnie, *Pioneers East, The Early American Experience in the Middle East* (Cambridge, Mass.: Harvard University Press. 1967).

CHAPTER 3 – THE CONSULS OF THE THREE HORSE TAILS

1. Garrett Mattingly, *Renaissance Diplomacy* (Baltimore: Penguin Books, 1955), pp. 58–60.
2. Abdul Latif Tibawi, *British Interests in Palestine 1800–1901; A Study of Religious and Educational Enterprise* (London: Oxford University Press, 1961), pp. 30–31.
3. A revealing exchange of correspondence on this subject is contained in the Israeli State Archives. It is evident from the documents cited that the French pretensions were resented and resisted, by the foreign consuls, but generally accepted by Roman Catholic clergy of all nationalities. See Spanish Consul Pío de Andrés García to Prussian Consul Georg Rosen, February 26, 1855. Jerusalem No. 5, Mss., Collection of Files from the German Consulate at Jerusalem, Israeli State Archives, Jerusalem, Record Group Notation 67, Israeli File Number 120. This large and valuable collection will be cited hereafter simply as "German Consulate, R.G.N. 67," followed by the appropriate file number by which the given materials are identified in the Israeli State Archives at present.
4. Mattingly, *Renaissance Diplomacy*, pp. 152–55.
5. Tibawi, *British Interests in Palestine*, p. 30.
6. Sir Bernard Pares, *A History of Russia* (New York: Knopf, 1946), pp. 265–66, 338–39.
7. James Finn, *Stirring Times, or Records from Jerusalem Consular Chronicles of 1853 to 1856* (London: Kegan Paul, 1878), 1:55–100.

8. Albert M. Hyamson, ed., *The British Consulate in Jerusalem in Relation to the Jews of Palestine 1838–1914* (London: Edward Goldston, 1939), p. ix.

9. Albert Hourani, *The Emergence of the Modern Middle East* (Berkeley: University of California Press, 1981), pp. 12–18.

CHAPTER 4 – PALESTINIAN ISLAM, 1841

1. The *Encyclopedia Britannica* of 1885 bases its estimates of population on Turkish government statistics for the sanjaks of Jerusalem, Belka, and Acre. The sanjak of Jerusalem ran down to El Arish on the Mediterranean and included Jaffa and Hebron. The sanjak of Belka straddled both sides of the Jordan River and included Nablus, Jenin, Ajlun and Es Salt. The sanjak of Acre included the districts of Haifa and Safed. The three sanjaks had a total of 54,007 households. The *Encyclopedia,* estimating an average household at five persons, places the population in 1885 at slightly more than 270,000, not counting Bedouin tribesmen who had been missed in the Turkish statistics. The *Encyclopedia* admits the inadequacy of these figures and implies that the new Jewish, Algerian, and Circassian as well as nearby Arab immigration which was in progress by 1885 may have carried the total Palestinian population as high as 650,000 on both sides of the Jordan. It seems safe to say, however, that the total population in 1841 did not exceed 300,000 persons. Better figures exist for the principal towns, based on Western sources. The total population of Jerusalem, Acre, Haifa, Jaffa, Ramle, Gaza, Hebron, Bethlehem, Nablus, Nazareth, Tiberias, and Safed in 1840 is estimated at 70,000. See Schölch, "European Penetration." pp. 48–57.

2. Vilnay, *Israel Guide*, pp. 34–37; Finn, *Stirring Times*, 1:18–22.

3. For a survey of the personality and characteristics of the Turkish officials stationed in Palestine at this period, see Blumberg, *A View From Jerusalem.*

4. Mia Brandel-Syrier, *The Religious Duties of Islam as Taught and Explained by Abu Baker Effendi* (Leiden: E.J. Brill, 1971), pp. 83, 124, 127, 131.

5. Finn, *Stirring Times*, 1:25–100,

6. David S. Landes, "Palestine Before the Zionists," *Commentary* 61 (February 1976): 52–53.

7. Edwin, Lord Samuel, *A Lifetime in Jerusalem; the Memoirs of the Second Viscount Samuel* (Jerusalem: Israel Universities Press, 1970), pp. 104–10.

8. Sir Moses Montefiore, the celebrated Jewish philanthropist, ultimately received permission to increase the height of the wall to make such malicious mischief more difficult. It was esteemed a great concession when in 1866

Sir Moses was permitted to erect an awning before the *Kotel Ha-Maaravi* or Western Wall to provide shade and protection from falling objects for Jews visiting this holiest shrine. See Paul Goodman, *Moses Moniefiore* (Philadelphia: Jewish Publication Society of America, 1943), p. 180. An international committee of the League of Nations in 1933 reaffirmed the Ottoman *status quo ante bellum*, and declared that the Kotel remained the property of the Moslem Waqf. See Y. and M. Alexander and M.S. Chertoff. eds., *A Bibliography of Israel* (New York: Herzl Press. 1981), p. 155.

9. William H. Bartlett, *Walks About the City and Environs of Jerusalem; Summer, 1842* (Jerusalem: Canaan Publishing House, 1974), pp. 148–68.

10. The first verse of Sura 17 of the Koran describes a mystic Night Journey by Mohammed. Moslems believe that while he slept near the Kaaba in Mecca the Angel Gabriel appeared to him and that they rose together to heaven to meet Abraham, Moses and Jesus. Some Moslems hold that Mohammed made the journey while awake and actually traversed the ground of the Temple Mount.

11. Shimon Ben-Eliezer, *Destruction and Renewal; the Synagogues of the Jewish Quarter* (Jerusalem, Alpha Press, 1975),

12. Moshe Aumann, *Land Ownership in Palestine 1880–1948* (Jerusalem: Israel Academic Committee on the Middle East, undated), pp, 1–2.

13. Blumberg, A View *From Jerusalem*, pp. 103, 109, 111, 121, 124, 199, 260, 293, 297.

14. For an excellent survey of Syrio-Palestinian land tenure see Doreen Warriner, "Land Tenure in the Fertile Crescent," in *The Economic History of the Middle East 1800–1914*, edited by Charles Issawi (Chicago: University of Chicago Press, 1975), pp. 71–78.

15. For special reference to the relationship of the landlords to their peasants, see Gabriel Baer, "The Evolution of Private Landownership in Egypt and the Fertile Crescent," *ibid.*, pp. 79–90.

16. Aumann, *Land Ownership in Palestine*, pp. 1–3.

17. Finn, *Stirring Times*, 1:226–27.

18. Elizabeth Anne Finn, *Reminiscences of Mrs. Finn, Member of the Royal Asiatic Society* (London: Marshall, Morgan and Scott, 1929), p. 112.

19. The complexities of land tax collection led to extensive tax farming in which wealthy entrepreneurs bought the right to collect the taxes of a specific district. The government supplied soldiers to assist the tax farmers with the actual collection. They had the right to quarter the soldiers and their beasts on the villagers, without compensation. Villagers were usually willing to pay more than their obligation to get rid of their unwelcome guests. See Baer, "Private Landownership," p. 82.

20. Blumberg, A *View From Jerusalem*, pp. 72,. 77, 82, 105, 106, 133, 137, 142, 157, 187, 197, 202, 259, 310.

CHAPTER 5 – PALESTINIAN JUDAISM, 1841

1. In the vast mass of scholarly literature on the subject, the following multi-volume works provide an examination of the unbroken history of Jewry in Palestine, in depth. See Salo W. Baron *et al., A Social and Religious History of the Jews,* 12 vols. (New York: Columbia University Press, 1952–67); Heinrich Graetz, *History of the Jews,* 6 vols., (Philadelphia: Jewish Publication Society, 1891–98).

2. *Encyclopedia Judaica* (Jerusalem: Keter Publishing House, 1971), 13:1452.

3. As noted elsewhere, only a Moslem could strike a Moslem with impunity. The right of a non-Moslem to employ a kawass was a privilege specifically conferred on non-Moslem dignitaries, such as foreign consuls and church prelates. When an individual not enjoying Turkish authorization to employ a kawass did so, it became the object of jealous attention. See James Finn to British Foreign Secretary Lord Palmerston, March 12, 1847, Jerusalem, No. 11, Public Record Office, Foreign Office (hereafter cited as P.R.O. F.O.), 78/2068; same to same, March 23, 1849, Jerusalem, No. 12, *ibid.* Pre-World War I P.R.O. F.O. documents cited in this work are part of the microfilm collection of The Central Archives for the History of the Jewish People at the Hebrew University in Jerusalem. All reference to P.R.O. F.O. documents after 1918 are drawn from the microfilm collection at the Israel State Archives.

4. Ben-Eliezer, *Destruction and Renewal*, p. 15. For the impact of the Turkish reforms of 1839 and 1856 upon the Jews, see Hayyim J. Cohen, *The Jews of the Middle East, 1860–1972* (New York: John Wiley, 1973), pp. 14, 16, 177.

5. See Blumberg, *A View From Jerusalem*, pp. 20, 30–47, 51–56, 60–63, 66–68, 97, 110, 152, 175.

6. Chief Rabbi Chaim David Chazan to Prussian Consul Dr. Georg Rosen, May 17, 1866, Jerusalem, German Consulate, R.G.N. 67, file no. 348; Rosen to Chazan, February 28, 1867, *ibid.*

7. German Consul General, Baron von Alten to Joseph Al Khalidi, President of the Municipal Council, January 10, 1873, *ibid.*, file no. 351; British Consul Noel Temple Moore to British Ambassador to Turkey Lord Lyons, March 19, 1867, Jerusalem, Hyamson, 2:342–44.

8. Finn Diary, November 10, 1849; February 25, 1850; in Blumberg, *A View From Jerusalem*, pp. 55, 66, 67.

9. Emile Marmorstein, "European Jews in Muslim Palestine," *Middle Eastern Studies II* (1975): 74–87; Ben-Eliezer, *Destruction and Renewal*, p. 21.

10. *Ibid.*, pp. 21–22.
11. *Lippincott's Pronouncing Gazetteer*, pp. 1640, 1877.
12. Marmorstein, "European Jews in Moslem Palestine," p. 77.
13. Finn, *Reminiscences*, pp. 53–58.
14. A. Lobanov-Rostovsky, *Russia and Europe, 1825–1879* (Ann Arbor, Mich.: George Wahr, 1954), p. 138.
15. Finn, *Stirring Times*, 1:100–102; *Encyclopedia Britannica*, 1881, 13:654.
16. Finn to Palmerston, November 7, 1851, Jerusalem, Hyamson, I, 179. See also Salo W. Baron, "The Jewish Question in the Nineteenth Century," *Journal of Modern History* 10 (1938): 51–65.
17. Max L. Margolis and Alexander Marx, *A History of the Jewish People* (Philadelphia: Jewish Publication Society of America, 1927), pp. 668–74.
18. W.E. Mosse, "Russia and the Levant, 1856–1862: Grand Duke Constantine Nicolaevich and the Russian Steam Navigation Company," *The Journal of Modern History* 26 (1954): 39–48: Derek Hopwood, *The Russian Presence in Syria and Palestine 1843–1914; Church and Politics in the Near East* (Oxford: Clarendon House, 1969); Howard Robinson, *Carrying British Mails Overseas* (New York: New York University Press, 1964).
19. Finn, *Reminiscences,* pp. 53–58.
20. Marmorstein, "European Jews," p. 77.
21. Bartlett, *Walks About the City*, pp. 80–81, 188–94.
22. *Halukah* means "a share" or "a portion."
23. See Blumberg, *A View From Jerusalem*, pp. 37, 46, 55, 63, 69, 199, 202, 214–15, 220, 275, 308.
24. During the economic depression induced by the Crimean War, Sephardic Chief Rabbi Jacob Covo actually set out on an unprecedented journey to western Europe to beg funds for all the poverty stricken Jews of Palestine. As will be noted later in this work, he died en route (*ibid.*, p. 179). As late as 1866, before plunging into a battle to keep control of both the native and European Jewish communities, Sephardic Chief Rabbi Chaim David Chazan consented to negotiations, even while threatening excommunication of anyone who openly defied his religious authority (Rabbi Chazan to Consul Georg Rosen, May 17, 1866, Jerusalem, German Consulate, R.G.N. 67, file no. 348).
25. Christian evangelical religious enthusiasts, and literary romantics, were optimistic about the immediate practicability of the establishment of a Jewish state in Palestine. These included such prominent British thinkers as Lord Shaftesbury, George Eliot, Holman Hunt, Colonel George Gawlor, Laurence Oliphant, Edward Cazalet, and Colonel Charles Henry Churchill.

See Samuel Katz. *Battleground – Fact and Fantasy in Palestine* (New York: Bantam Books, 1973), Chapter 4.

CHAPTER 6 – PALESTINIAN CHRISTIANITY, 1841

1. For valuable surveys of the origins of Christianity, see Maurice Goguel. *The Primitive Church* (London: George Allen & Unwin, 1963): Michael Gough. *The Early Christians* (New York: Frederick A. Praeger, 1966); B.J. Kidd. *A History of the Church to A.D. 461* [in 3 vols.] (Oxford: Clarendon Press, 1922); Gerd Theissen, *Sociology of Early Palestinian Christianity* (Philadelphia: Fortress Press, 1978).

2. For the impact of Islam upon Byzantium, see Aziz S. Atiya, *History of Eastern Christianity* (Notre Dame, Ind.: University of Notre Dame Press, 1968); Speros Vryonis, *The Decline of Medieval Hellenism and the Process of Islamization from the Eleventh Through the Fifteenth Century* (Berkeley: University of California Press, 1971).

3. See Romilly Jenkins, *Byzantium, the Imperial Centuries A.D. 610–1071* (New York: Random House, 1966); B.J. Kidd. *The Churches of Eastern Christendom from A.D. 451 to the Present Time* (New York: Burt Franklin, 1973); George Ostrogorsky, *History of the Byzantine State* (New Brunswick: Rutgers University Press, 1969).

4. Tibawi, *British Interests in Palestine*, p. 65.

5. Sultan Abdul Medjid to Governor of Jerusalem Hafiz Ahmed Pasha; copies given to all consuls at Jerusalem, April 1853, German Consulate, R.G.N. 67. file no. 18.

6. Finn Diary, April 6, 1852, March 20, 1853; April 26, 1856, April 18, 1857, April 3, 1858, in Blumberg. *A View From Jerusalem*, pp. 103, 104, 117, 149, 225, 243, 256, 286.

7. Lobanov-Rostovsky, *Russia and Europe*, p. 138; Hyamson, *The British Consulate in Jerusalem*, 2:331.

8. Schölch, "European Penetration," pp. 39–42.

9. Finnie, *Pioneers East*, pp. 168–81; Tibawi, *British Interests in Palestine*, pp. 3–4, 37–40.

10. *Ibid.*, pp. 162–63.

11. British Consul General Patrick Campbell to Vice Consul William T. Young. November 21, 1838, Cairo, Hyamson, *British Consulate in Jerusalem*, 1:2–3; Young to Foreign Secretary Lord Palmerston, March 14, 1839, Jerusalem, *ibid.*, 1:3–4.

12. Bailey, *British Policy and the Turkish Reform Movement*, pp. 129–78; Tibawi, *British Interests in Palestine*, pp. 32–33.

13. *Ibid.*, pp. 41–42.
14. *Ibid.*, p. 34.
15. *Ibid.*, p. 33.
16. *Ibid.*, p. 37.
17. Palmerston to British Ambassador to Turkey Lord Ponsonby, April 21, 1841, London. Hyamson, *British Consulate in Jerusalem*, 1:39–40; Young to Viscount Canning. January 13, 1842, London, *ibid.*, 1:41–46.
18. Tibawi, *British Interests in Palestine*, pp. 33–36.
19. Campbell to Palmerston, July 20, 1833, *ibid.*, p. 37.
20. *Ibid.*, p. 38.
21. Register of British Subjects at Jerusalem. 1855–73. R.G.N. 123–1, Israeli file no. 3.
22. Tibawi, *British Interests in Palestine*, pp. 40–41.
23. *Ibid.*, p. 99.
24. *Ibid.*, pp. 45–86.

CHAPTER 7 – THE TANZIMAT AND THE PALESTINIAN CONSULS, 1839–50

1. Eversley and Chirol, *The Turkish Empire*, pp. 287–311.
2. Bailey. *British Policy and the Turkish Reform Movement*, pp. 129–205.
3. United States Minister to Turkey Carroll Spence to United States Secretary of State William Marcy, June 19, July 18, November 25, 1854. February 12, April 6, 1855, United States National Archives, State Department Correspondence (hereafter abbreviated as U.S.N.A., S.D.C.), Microcopy M46, Roll 16; Spence to Secretary of State Lewis Cass, April 8, 1857, Constantinople, No. 41, *ibid.*
4. Tibawi, *British Interests in Palestine*, p. 144.
5. W.E. Mosse, "Russia and the Levant, 1856–1862: Grand Duke Constantine Nicolaevich and the Russian Steam Navigation Company," *The Journal of Modern History* 26 (1954): 39–48; Derek Hopwood, *The Russian Presence in Syria and Palestine 1843–1914; Church and Politics in the Near East* (Oxford: Clarendon House, 1969); Howard Robinson, *Carrying British Mails Overseas* (New York: New York University Press, 1964).
6. For numerous examples of consular techniques for remaining in touch with superiors while taking risky initiatives, see James Finn's Diary in Blumberg, *A View From Jerusalem.*
7. Tibawi, *British Interests in Palestine*, pp. 16, 22, 27.
8. *Ibid.*, pp. 32–33; Hyamson, *The British Consulate in Jerusalem*, 1:xviii.
9. Sultan Abdul Medjid to Cadi of Jerusalem, Moslem Date Second Decade

of Tiel Hege 1259 (1843 in Gregorian Calendar), German Consulate, R.G.N. 67, file no. 2.

10. Hyamson, *The British Consulate in Jerusalem*, 1:66.

11. The microfilm services of the Austrian State Archives have graciously prepared selected copies of the correspondence of Count Pizzamano during his long career at Jerusalem, 1847–61. These documents were selected from volumes at the Haus-Hof und Staatsarchiv, but are not identified by number. Material from that microfilm, in the personal possession of the author, will be here after cited as H.H.U.S.A.

12. Finn Diary, March 23, November 30, 1854, in Blumberg, *A View From Jerusalem*, pp. 161, 176, 178.

13. *Ibid.*, pp. 38–44, 59, 85, 95, 108, 109.

14. *Ibid.*, pp. 22, 51, 52. The unified Kingdom of Italy opened a consulate in 1872 (Notification to German Consul General, Baron von Alten, March 7, 1872, German Consulate, R.G.N. 67, file no. 163).

15. *Ibid.*, pp. 22, 49, 85, 97, 234, 256. The Kingdom of Greece reopened its consulate in 1862 (Notification to Prussian Consul Dr. Georg Rosen, November 2. 1862, *ibid.*).

16. Prior to the establishment of a United States Consulate at Jerusalem, the most revealing source for the consular involvement of the secondary maritime powers in the eastern Mediterranean can be found in the reports of United States Consuls at Beirut. See U.S.N.A., S.D.C., Microcopy T367, Rolls 1 and 2.

17. On May 17, 1844, Warder Cresson had been appointed U.S. Consul at Jerusalem, without pay, by John C. Calhoun, Secretary of State. On May 25, Calhoun rescinded the appointment upon receiving information that Cresson was psychotic. The latter, however, was already en route to Jerusalem and continued to claim the rights and title of a United States Consul even after he had received word that plans for a Jerusalem consulate had been abandoned. He voluntarily "resigned" his office in 1848, following his conversion to Judaism. He died in 1860, at Jerusalem. See Frank Fox, "Quaker, Shaker, Rabbi: Warder Cresson, The Story of a Philadelphia Mystic." *The Pennsylvania Magazine of History and Biography* (April 1971): 146–94.

18. There had been a United States Consular Agency for Jaffa, serving Jerusalem, as far back as 1832, when David Darmon held the post. For the earliest reports by a permanent U.S. Consul at Jerusalem, see those of John Warren Gorham, beginning on March 24, 1857 in U.S.N.A., S.D.C., Microcopy 453, Roll 1.

19. Finn's Diary, December 24, 1857, March 15, 1858, in Blumberg, *A View From Jerusalem*, pp. 271, 285.

20. *Ibid.*, pp. 99–100.

21. Prussian Consul General Theodor Weber to James Finn, August 7, 1861. Beirut, enclosed with Finn to British Consul General Niven Moore, August 21, 1861, Jerusalem. P.R.O. F.O., 78/2068; Finn to Weber, August 12, 1861. Jerusalem, enclosed with *ibid.*

22. Blumberg, *A View From Jerusalem,* pp. 54, 62, 109, 115, 137, 142, 157, 171–76, 182–84.

23. For the annual fluctuations in attitude toward royal birthdays and national holidays, see Finn's Diary, *ibid.*

24. The Prussian and German Consuls at Jerusalem kept a separate dossier of notes received from other consuls defining the niceties of protocol (R.G.N. 67, file no. 163).

25. A. Portales to Dr. Schultz, March 7, 21, 1843, Constantinople, R.G.N. 67, file no. 228.

26. Murad to Schultz, April 28, 1843, Ramla, *ibid.*

27. Murad to Schultz, June 16, 1844, R.G.N. 67, file no. 2.

28. The complex network of consular agents, consular correspondents, and other British employees in Palestine can be discovered in a bound register at the Israeli State Archives titled *The Consulate's Instructions to Consular Agents,* British Consulate, R.G.N. 123–1, file no. 14. Frequent references, by name, to the consular agents of the other major powers, confirm the fact that they had an equally complex support structure in Palestine.

29. Finn Diary, May 26, June 13, 1853, in Blumberg, A *View From Jerusalem,* pp. 128, 130, 151.

30. Ibid., p. 179.

31. German Consulate, R.G.N. 67, file no. 491.

32. Finn to Foreign Secretary Lord John Russell, January 20, 1864, Private, Gloucester, England, P.R.O. F.O., 78/2068; Finn Diary, July 24, 1854, in Blumberg, *A View From Jerusalem,* p. 168.

33. Spanish Consul Pío de Andrés García to Prussian Consul Rosen. Jerusalem, German Consulate, R.G.N. 67, file no. 120.

34. German Consular Dragoman Serapian J. Murad to Consul General Baron von Münchhausen, March 6, 1877, Jerusalem, Note 514, German Consulate, R.G.N. 67, file no. 47.

35. Finn Diary, March 13, 17, 1850, in Blumberg, *A View From Jerusalem,* pp. 68–69; Finn, *Reminiscences,* pp. 102, 125.

36. Blumberg, *A View From Jerusalem,* pp. 230, 246, 250, 254, 256, 273, 276, 283, 287, 305.

37. US Consul Gorham to John P. Brown, U.S. Consul-General at Constantinople, January 17, 1858, Jaffa, U.S.N.A., S.D.C., microcopy 453, roll 1; Gorham to U.S. Secretary of State Cass, November 12, 1858, Jaffa, no. 70, *ibid.*

38. Blumberg, *A View From Jerusalem*, pp. 90, 97, 98, 138, 174, 183, 202, 206, 264–66, 271, 282, 290, 295, 300.
39. Issawi. *The Economic History of the Middle East 1800–1914*, pp. 71–90. 203–47, 258–73.
40. Finn Diary, February 23, 26,1850. in Blumberg, *A View From Jerusalem*, pp. 66–67.
41. Finn Diary, October 7, 1850, November 3. 1851, November 23, 1852, November 17, 1853, *ibid.*, pp. 76, 92, 113, 144.
42. Finn Diary, March 4, 1851, March 15, 1853, *ibid.*, pp. 85, 124. 148.
43. G.S. Murad to Dr. Schultz, June 2, 1848, Jaffa, Prussian Consulate. R.G.N. 67, file no. 2.
44. Register of British Subjects at Jerusalem, British Consulate, R.G.N. 123–1, file nos. 2, 3.
45. Chasseaud to U.S. Secretary of State Daniel Webster, September 6, 1843. Beirut, U.S.N.A., S.D.C., Microcopy T367. Roll 1.
46. Chasseaud to U.S. Minister to Turkey D.S. Carr, August 10. 1849. Beirut, *ibid.*
47. Murad to Schultz, April 18, 1843, German Consulate, R.G.N. 67, file no. 228; T. Weber to Chasseaud, July 7, 1847, *ibid.*, file no. 2.
48. J. Chasseaud to Dr. Schultz, September 13, 1847, Beirut, *ibid.*, file no. 16; Y.B. Catafago to Dr. Schultz, undated September 1847, Beirut, *ibid.*
49. Chasseaud to U.S. Secretary of State John Forsyth, January 2, 1849, Beirut, No. 1. U.S.N.A., S.D.C., Microcopy T367, Roll 1; same to same, August 3, 1839, Beirut, No. 4, *ibid.*
50. Same to same, March 24, 1840, Beirut, No, 12. *ibid.*
51. For accounts of the Damascus Blood Ritual Murder Accusation of 1840, see Cyrus Adler and Aaron M. Margalith, *With Firmness in the Right; American Diplomatic Action Affecting Jews 1840–1945* (New York: The American Jewish Committee, 1946), pp. 3–5; Jacob Ezekiel, "Persecutions of the Jews in 1840," *Publications of the American Jewish Historical Society* 10 (1902): 119–28; Heinrich Graetz, *History of the Jews* (Philadelphia: Jewish Publication Society of America, 1895), 5:632–63.
52. This refers to his rival Catafago whom he regarded as having usurped his Prussian office.
53. Chasseaud to Clayton, April 27, 1850, Beirut, U.S.N.A., S.D.C., Microcopy T3 67, Roll 1.
54. J. Hosford Smith to U.S. Secretary of State Daniel Webster, January 22, 1851. New York, *ibid.*

CHAPTER 8 – PALESTINE AND THE CRIMEAN WAR

1. Philip Warner, *The Crimean War; A Reappraisal* (New York: Taplinger, 1973). pp. 5–12.

2. Joseph Redlich. *Emperor Francis Joseph of Austria: A Biography* (New York: Macmillan, 1929), pp. 118–82.

3. Paul W. Schroeder, *Austria, Great Britain, and the Crimean War: the Destruction of the European Concert* (Ithaca and London: Cornell University Press. 1972), pp. 47–51.

4. Czar Nicholas I to Emperor Franz Josef, October 23, 1851, Redlich, pp. 124–25.

5. Barbara Jelavich, *The Habsburg Empire in European Affairs, 1814–1918*, (Chicago: Rand McNally, 1969), pp. 69–79.

6. Tibawi, *British Interests*, p. 65.

7. Pares, *History of Russia*, pp. 338–39.

8. Tibawi, *British Interests*, pp. 50–75, 101–104.

9. Ibid., p. 89.

10. *Ibid.*, pp. 101–104.

11. Finn Diary, September 3, 6, 1852, in Blumberg, *A View From Jerusalem*, p. 109.

12. The writer is grateful to Reverend Arten Ashjian, Canon Sacrist of St. Vartan Cathedral and to His Eminence Archbishop Torkom Manoogian, Primate of the Armenian Church of America, for information about the Armenian Patriarchs of Jerusalem, 1838–1880. The former has indicated the preferred spelling of the patriarchs' names in Latin letters, and the writer has accepted his guidance.

13. Blumberg, *A View From Jerusalem*, pp. 118, 149, 151, 157, 217, 242, 247, 274, 304, 306, 307.

14. The last of the non-resident titular Latin patriarchs of Jerusalem immediately preceding Joseph Valerga was Augustus Foseolo, who was appointed in 1830 and who served until asked to resign by Pope Pius IX in 1847.

15. Prussian Consular Agent Murad to Consul Schultz, January 14, 1848, Jaffa, German Consulate, R.G.N. 67, file no. 16.

16. Spanish Consul Pío de Andrés García to Prussian Consul Dr. Georg Rosen, February 26, 1855, no. 5, Jerusalem, *ibid.*, file no. 120; Rosen to Andrés García, March 3, 1855, Jerusalem, *ibid.*

17. Monsignor Valerga, in spite of a brave show of optimistic confidence, was privately deeply worried about the condition of his Roman Catholic flock, as he found them in 1847. He confessed, privately, that the masses were ignorant and that the native clergy were poor in number and quality. He regarded the Greek Orthodox clergy and the Protestant missionaries as very

effective and dangerous rivals. Therefore, the building of schools and the training of native clergy became his first priorities (Valerga to Monsignor Lueget, Bishop of Nezebon and Papal Envoy to Switzerland, October 12, 1848, Jerusalem, Vatican Archives, Vatican City, Propaganda Fide Collection, Mss, *Relazione intorno al patriarcato*). In the course of his own research in the Vatican Archives, the writer's colleague Bruce Kupelnick of the Harvard University Law School Fund arranged the microfilming of almost five hundred pages of Valerga's correspondence consulted for this work. Hereafter, all references to that material will be cited as "Vatican, Propaganda Fide."

18. A. Lobanov-Rostovsky, *Russia and Europe, 1825–1879* (Ann Arbor, Michigan: George Wahr, 1954), p. 138.

19. Tibawi, *British Interests*, pp. 64–66.

20. A. Loftus, *The Diplomatic Reminiscences of Lord Augustus Loftus, 1837–1862* [in 2 vols.] (London: Cassell, 1892), I, 170–73.

21. Finn, *Reminiscences*, pp. 83, 99, 101; Finn, *Stirring Times*, 1:450–51.

22. Finn Diary, September 14, 1852, in Blumberg, *A View From Jerusalem*, p. 109.

23. Finn, *Stirring Times*, 1:18–22.

24. Sullan to Governor of Jerusalem Hafiz Ahmed Pasha, 1852, contained as an enclosure with circular letter from Hafiz Ahmed Pasha to the consuls at Jerusalem, April or May 1853, German Consulate, R.G.N. 67, file no. 18.

25. *Ibid.*

26. British Foreign Secretary Lord Malmesbury to British Ambassador to France Lord Cowley, December 20, 1852, London, Earl of Malmesbury, *Memoirs of an Ex-Minister; an Autobiography* (London: Longmans, Green, 1885). pp. 287–88.

27. The Prussian Envoy at Constantinople, General von Wildenbruck, knew the essential details of Menshikov's instructions. It must be assumed then, that a substantial circle shared the secret (Wildenbruck to Georg Rosen, February 18, 1853, Pera, German Consulate, R.G.N. 67, file no. 18). The writer is grateful to his colleague Professor Armin Mruck who prepared an English translation of this document from the German Gothic script manuscript.

28. Schroeder, *Austria, Great Britain and the Crimean War*, pp. 30. 409–11; Jelavich, *The Habsburg Empire*, pp. 72–73.

29. Eversley and Chirol, *The Turkish Empire*, II, 292–98.

30. Wildenbruck to Rosen, May 22, 1853, Constantinople, German Consulate, R.G.N. 67, file no. 18. Translation from German Gothic script by Professor Armin Mruck.

31. Case, *Edouard Thouvenel et la Diplomatie du Second Empire*, p. 66.

32. Eversley and Chirol, *The Turkish Empire*, pp. 301–307; Warner, *The Crimean War,* pp. 9–12.
33. Enclosures in Finn to Rosen, January 30, 1856, Jerusalem, German Consulate, R.G.N. 67, file no. 491.
34. Schroeder, *Austria, Great Britain, and the Crimean War,* pp. 187–90.
35. Rondo Cameron, *France and the Economic Development of Europe 1800–1914* (Chicago: Rand McNally, 1965), p. 253.
36. At crucial moments in the war crisis, the European consuls at Jerusalem went to Beirut or Constantinople to be closer to dependable sources of information (Finn, *Stirring Times,* 1:26–27).
37. Finn Diary, June 3, 6, 1853, in Blumberg, *A View From Jerusalem,* p. 129.
38. E.T. Rogers, British Vice Consul at Haifa, to Finn, October 28, 1853, Haifa, no. 3, Hyamson, *The British Consulate in Jerusalem,* 1:217.
39. Finn Diary, September 16, 19, 1853, in Blumberg, *A View From Jerusalem,* pp. 137–38.
40. *Ibid.,* pp. 115–16.
41. Finn Diary, July 1, 9, 18, 19, 25, 28, 29, 30, 1853, *ibid.,* pp. 131–34.
42. Walter P. Zenner and David Gutmann, "Aquili Agha: The Strongman in the Ethnic Relations of the Ottoman Galilee." *Cooperative Studies of Social History* 14 (1972): 169–92.
43. Blumberg, *A View From Jerusalem,* pp. 83, 105, 107, 109, 111, 115, 128, 129, 133, 139, 140, 147, 152, 159, 172, 174. 185, 188, 190, 192, 194, 196, 208: Prussian Envoy to Spain von Galen to King Frederick William IV, November 7, 1854, German Consulate, R.G.N. 67, file no. 17: Spanish Consul Andrés García to Prussian Consul Rosen, February 26, 1855, *ibid.,* file no. 120; Rosen to Andrés García, March 3, 1855, *ibid.*
44. Procès Verbal of the Consular Meeting at the Jerusalem Seraglio. June 12, 1855, *ibid.,* file no. 491.
45. Finn, *Reminiscences,* p. 82.
46. Pizzamano to Count Karl von Buol-Schauenstein, Austrian Chancellor and Foreign Minister, November 20, 1853, unnumbered rough draft, H.H.U.S.A.
47. Finn, *Reminiscences,* p. 102.
48. *Ibid.,* p. 121; Finn, *Stirring Times,* 1:87–88.
49. See chapter 9.
50. Finn. *Reminiscences,* pp. 11–25.
51. See Blumberg, *A View From Jerusalem,* which explores Finn's career in detail.
52. Finn Diary, July 2, 1854, in Blumberg. *A View from Jerusalem,* p. 167.
53. Finn, *Reminiscences,* pp. 102, 125.

54. Finn Diary, December 17, 1853, January 14, 1854, in Blumberg, *A View From Jerusalem*, pp. 145, 158; Finn, *Stirring Times*, 1:395.

55. Finn Diary, January 27, 1854, in Blumberg, *A View From Jerusalem*, p. 158.

56. Finn Diary, March 16, 1854, *ibid.*, p. 161.

57. Finn Diary, October 20, 1854, *ibid.*, p. 174; Finn. *Reminiscences*, p. 125; Finn, *Stirring Times*, 1:450–51.

58. Finn Diary, February 15, 1855, in Blumberg, *A View From Jerusalem*, p. 187.

59. Finn, *Reminiscences*, p. 128; Feroz Ahmad, "The Relations of Great Britain with the Young Turks Between the Years 1908–1914." *Middle Eastern Studies* 1 (1906): 302–29.

60. Finn, *Reminiscences*, pp. 239, 248.

61. It was profoundly disturbing to Turkish sensibilities to offer cannon salutes to foreign sovereigns and to allow foreigners to raise their flags on their national holidays. See Blumberg, *A View From Jerusalem*, pp. 171–72, 182–84, 202–206, 221, 223, 260–63, 277, 295, 297. On at least one occasion, a bold consul kept his flag flying daily, without authorization, to coerce the Pasha of Jerusalem into arresting and trying a notorious gang of rapists and murderers (U.S. Consul J. Warren Gorham, February 3, 1958, Jaffa, No. 4, U.S.N.A., S.D.C., Microcopy M453, Roll 1). The Turkish governor protested the daily raising of the flag, alleging that the only motive for such a provocative act was "for the annoyance of the Sublime Porte...." (Suraya Pasha to Gorham, enclosed in *ibid.*).

62. Finn Diary, August 22, October 26, 1849, October 16, 1850. October 6, 1851, September 24, 1852, September 13–14, 1853, September 3–4, 1854, June 5, 1856, August 11–12, 1856, July 31, 1857, in Blumberg, *A View From Jerusalem*, pp. 51, 54, 76, 91, 109, 137, 171, 227, 231, 263.

63. Finn Diary, March 13, April 5, 1855, *ibid.*, pp. 189,191–92; Finn, *Reminiscences*, pp. 128–32.

64. Pizzamano to Count Buol, May 10, 1855, Jerusalem, No. XLVIII, H.H.U.S.A. Pizzamano to Austrian Internunzio to the Sublime Porte Anlon. Baron Prokesch von Osten, August 6, 1856, Jerusalem, *ibid.*

65. Finn Diary, June 28, 30, July 1, 2, 1855, in Blumberg, *A View From Jerusalem*, pp. 195–96; Finn, *Reminiscences*, p. 137; Egon Caesar, Count Corti, *Maximilian and Charlotte of Mexico*, 2 vols. (New York: Alfred A. Knopf, 1928).

66. Finn Diary, July 18, 20, 23, 25, 26, 27, August 7, 14, 1855, in Blumberg, *A View From Jerusalem*, pp. 197–99, 211–12; Paul Goodman, *Moses Montefiore* (Philadelphia: Jewish Publication Society of America, 1943), pp. 48, 52, 100, 117, 159, 185; Finn, *Reminiscences*, p. 137; *Diaries of Sir Moses and Lady Montefiore*, edited by L. Loewe (Chicago: Belford-Clarke, 1890).

67. Finn Diary, January 18, 22, 1856, in Blumberg, *A View From Jerusalem*, p. 219: Finn, *Reminiscences*, p. 151–52.

68. Sultan Abdul Medjid's Hatti Humayun, February 18, 1856, J.C. Hurewitz, *Diplomacy in the Near and Middle East, A Documentary Record: 1535–1914*, 2 vols. (New York: Octagon Books, 1972), 1:149–53.

69. Tibawi, *British Interests*, p. 116.

70. Finn Diary, March 31, April 1, 1856, in Blumberg, *A View From Jerusalem*, pp. 221–22.

71. Finn Diary, April 5, 10, 13, 19, 21, 23, 28, 29, *ibid.*, pp. 222–25; Tibawi, *British Interests,* p. 116; Finn, *Stirring Times*, 2:424 – 26.

CHAPTER 9 – THE HEBRON AFFAIR

1. Finn Diary, January 18, 29, May 24, 26, 27, 28, 29, June 7, August 4, 5, 6, 19, 25, October 6, 1852, Jerusalem, in Blumberg, *A View From Jerusalem*, pp. 101–10.

2. In July 1855, Botta received his orders to assume the consular post at Tripoli. His replacement, Edmond de Barrère, did not reach Jerusalem until September. Consequently, the greater part of the French role in the Hebron Affair was borne by Monsieur Legueux, the consular chancellor.

3. Procès Verbal of the Consular meeting at the Jerusalem Seraglio, June 12, 1855, German Consulate. R.G.N. 67. file no. 491.

4. Kiamal Pasha to Rosen, November 15, 1855, Jerusalem, *ibid.*

5. Blumberg, *A View From Jerusalem*, p. 198.

6. *Ibid.*: David el Kurd to Rosen, August 3, 1855, Hebron, German Consulate. R.G.N. 67. file no. 491; Legueux to Rosen, November 15, 1855, *ibid.*

7. Blumberg, *A View From Jerusalem*, pp. 198–99.

8. *Ibid.*, pp. 197–200.

9. Pío de Andrés García to Rosen, November 10, 1855, Jerusalem, German Consulate. R.G.N. 67, file no. 491; E. de Barrère to Rosen, November 11, 1855, Bethlehem, *ibid.*; Kiamal Pasha to Rosen, November 15, 1855, Jerusalem. *ibid.*

10. Enclosures in Finn to Rosen, January 30, 1856, Jerusalem, *ibid.* Finn might claim that his own contacts with the rebels had been to serve as mediator. There is no doubt, however, that he had had at least one secret meeting at his country house, with Abderrahman's brother Mahmoud and with Hhamdan et Taamri, one of the more important Bedouin sheiks in the rebel camp. See Finn Diary, May 30, 1853, in Blumberg, *A View From Jerusalem*, p. 128.

11. Enclosures in Finn to Rosen, January 30, 1856, Jerusalem, R.G.N. 67, file no. 491.

12. Jelavich, *The Habsburg Empire,* p. 73; Heinrich Friedjung, *The Struggle for Supremacy in Germany, 1859–1866* (London: MacMillan, 1935). pp. 8–11; Redlich, *Emperor Francis Joseph,* pp. 156–57; Queen Victoria to the King of Prussia, March 17, 1854, Osborne, in Dr. Kurt Jagow, ed., *Letters of the Prince Consort 1831–1861* (New York: E.P. Dutton, 1938), pp. 209–12; Albert, Prince Consort of Great Britain to Prince William of Prussia, May 31, 1854. London, *ibid.,* pp. 213–14.

13. Baron Otto von Manteuffel to Rosen, September 29, 1855, Berlin. German Consulate, R.G.N. 67. file no. 491.

14. The Prussian Consul had been away from Jerusalem when the dispatch arrived, which further delayed his receipt of it. See Finn Diary, November 6, 1855, in Blumberg, *A View From Jerusalem,* p. 203.

15. Rosen to Finn, November 6, 1855, Jerusalem, No. 58 rough draft, German Consulate, R.G.N. 67, file no. 491.

16. Finn to Rosen, November 7, 1855, Jerusalem, No. 327, *ibid.*

17. Rosen to Finn, November 7, 1855, Jerusalem, unnumbered rough draft, *ibid.*

18. Finn to Rosen, November 8, 1855, Jerusalem, private note, *ibid.*

19. Rosen to Finn, November 8, 1855, Jerusalem, private note, *ibid.*

20. Rosen to Kiamal Pasha, Pío de Andrés García, de Pizzamano, and de Barrère, November 9, 1855, Jerusalem, *ibid.*

21. Blumberg, *A View From Jerusalem,* p. 204.

22. Kiamal Pasha to Rosen, November 15, 1855, Jerusalem, German Consulate, R.G.N. 67, file no. 491.

23. Pío de Andrés García to Rosen, November 10, 1855, Jerusalem, *ibid.*; Edmond de Barrère to Rosen, November 11, 1855, Bethlehem, *ibid.*; Legueux to Rosen, November 15, 1855, Jerusalem, *ibid.*

24. Pizzamano to Rosen, November 17, 1855, Jerusalem, *ibid.*

25. Rosen to Manteuffel, November 17, 1855, No. 70 rough draft, Jerusalem, *ibid.*

26. Same to same November 18, 1855, private, *ibid.*

27. Finn's Register of British protégés in Palestine, British Consulate, R.G.N. 123-1, file no. 3. Finn and Gobat had conceived a strong personal dislike for each other because of widely differing views of missionary goals. It is not surprising that Gobat would have been happy to support Rosen and to undercut Finn. See Tibawi, *British Interests in Palestine,* pp. 133–38.

28. Rosen to Finn, November 21, 1855, Jerusalem, No. 72 rough draft, German Consulate, R.G.N. 67, file no. 491.

29. Finn to Rosen, November 22, 1855, Jerusalem, No. 330, *ibid.*

30. Rosen to Wildenbruck, November 22, 1855, Jerusalem, No. 73, *ibid.*

31. It is typical of Finn that he casually noted in his Consular Journal: "Numerous Despatches to Constantinople chiefly to the prejudice of Kiamal Pasha." Blumberg, *A View From Jerusalem*, p. 204.

32. The Malakoff Fortress fell on September 8, 1855. Sebastopol, the city whose capture had been the chief object of the campaign, fell immediately thereafter. Thenceforth, fighting was desultory and came to an end in December. A telegraph cable had connected the Crimea to western Europe since the spring of 1855. Consequently, by the time the consuls at Jerusalem were really well launched in their recriminations, peace negotiations were under way in Europe.

33. Finn to Rosen, January 30, 1856, Jerusalem, No. 337, German Consulate, R.G.N. 67, file no. 491. Bernstorff had written to inform Manteuffel that Lord Clarendon intended to force Finn to admit his error. Manteuffel wrote promptly to Rosen to share the good news (Bernstorff to Manteuffel, December 22, 1855, enclosed in Manteuffel to Rosen, December 28, 1855, Berlin, No. 2, *ibid.*). It is improbable, however, that Manteuffel's dispatch arrived prior to the date when Finn made his surly and reluctant submission, with such bad grace.

34. Blumberg, *A View From Jerusalem*, p. 219.

35. This referred to the affidavits collected by Rosen from Kiamal Pasha, the other consuls, and Bishop Gobat.

36. Lord Clarendon, by declining to accept the affidavits, took refuge in the diplomatic fiction that they had not been shown to him and consequently could be ignored. Bernstorff had assured himself that Clarendon knew the contents of the affidavits "unofficially."

37. Rosen to the Consuls of Austria, France and Spain, February 6, 1856, Jerusalem, German Consulate, R.G.N. 67, file no. 491.

38. Rosen to Finn, February 8, 1856, Jerusalem, No. 19, *ibid.*

39. Finn to Rosen, February 9, 1856, Jerusalem, No. 340, *ibid.*

40. Rosen to Wildenbruck, February 10, 1856, Jerusalem, No. 20, rough draft, *ibid.*

41. Clarendon to Finn, September 9, 1856, Foreign Office, London, copy contained in Manteuffel to Rosen, date unclear, *ibid.*

42. Wildenbruck to Rosen, October 2, 1856, Constantinople, No. 60, *ibid.*

43. The posthumously published memoirs of both James and Elizabeth Anne Finn are silent on the quarrel with Prussia. Mrs. Finn refers to Georg Rosen only in a complimentary social context. See Finn, *Reminiscences*. Consul Finn's work makes references to foreign attempts to stir rebellion in Palestine, but the only specific charge made refers to the native Greek Christians. He alleges that many of them were actively engaged in smuggling weaponry

into the country, in support of Russia against Turkey, during the Crimean War. See Finn, *Stirring Times*, 1:25.

CHAPTER 10 – PALESTINE AND THE FIRMAN OF HATTI-HUMAYUN

1. Case, *Edouard Thouvenel et la Diplomatie du Second Empire*, pp. 95–101.
2. Bailey, *British Policy and the Turkish Reform Movement*, pp. 288–89.
3. *Ibid.*, p. 290.
4. *Ibid.*, p. 288; Case, *Edouard Thouvenel*, p. 97.
5. *Ibid.*, p. 98.
6. *Ibid.*, pp. 100–101.
7. Eversley and Chirol, *The Turkish Empire*, pp. 307–308, 310.
8. Finn Diary, March 3, 1856, in Blumberg, *A View From Jerusalem*.
9. Finn Diary, April 6, 1856, *ibid.*, p. 222.
10. Finn, *Reminiscences*, p. 153.
11. Finn Diary, July 28, 1856, in Blumberg, *A View From Jerusalem*, p. 230.
12. Finn, *Reminiscences*, pp. 166, 183.
13. Finn Diary, March 14, 19, April 1, 1857. in Blumberg, *A View From Jerusalem*, pp. 253–55.
14. Finn Diary, March 23, 1857, *ibid.*, p. 255.
15. Finn Diary, April 13, May 2, 1857, *ibid.*, pp. 256–57.
16. Finn, *Reminiscences*, p. 183.
17. F. Ollendorf, "Jerusalem's Russian Compound." *The Jerusalem Post*, December 24, 1975; Vilnay, *Israel Guide*, pp. 88–89.

CHAPTER 11 – LAND PURCHASE AND THE EXPANSION OF EUROPEAN INFLUENCE IN PALESTINE

1. Schölch, "European Penetration," pp. 21–26.
2. Baily, *British Policy*, p. 290.
3. Finn Diary, March 19, September 8, November 9, 1852; March 17, 1853: August 14, 1855; June 24, 1857; August 10, 1858, Blumberg, *A View From Jerusalem*, pp. 103, 109, 111, 124, 199, 260, 293.
4. Finn, *Reminiscences*, p. 88; Finn Diary, August 14, 1855, in Blumberg, *A View From Jerusalem*, p. 199.
5. Aumann, *Land Ownership in Palestine*, p. 1.
6. Finn, *Reminiscences*, p. 174.
7. *Ibid.*, pp. 105–108.

8. Finn, *Reminiscences*, pp. 61, 71, 76, 89, 101, 103; Finn, *Stirring Times*, 1:120–21.

9. Records of the Supreme Consular Court of the Levant at Jerusalem, July 6, 1863, British Consular Records, R.G.N. 123–1, file no. 27.

10. Benjamin Mazar, *The Mountain of the Lord: Excavating in Jerusalem* (Garden City, N.Y.: Doubleday, 1975), p. 134.

11. Certified legal documents and witnesses' affidavits enclosed in U.S. Consul J. Hosford Smith to the Department of State, May 27, 1854, Beirut, no. 60, U.S.N.A., S.D.C., microcopy T367, roll 2.

12. Blumberg, *A View From Jerusalem*, p. 149.

13. Grand Vizier to Kiamal Pasha, July 30, 1855, Constantinople, German Consulate, R.G.N. 67, file no. 228.

14. Rosen to Wildenbruck, October 23, 1856, Jerusalem, German Consulate, R.G.N. 67, file no. 228.

15. Rosen to Kiamal Pasha, March 29, 1856, Jerusalem, German Consulate, R.G.N. 67, file no. 323.

16. Observations on the Protestant representation in Palestine, probably written 1856, document unsigned, German Consulate, R.G.N. 67, file no. 323.

17. Rosen to Wildenbruck, October 23, 1856, Jerusalem, German Consulate, R.G.N. 67, file no. 228.

18. F. Ollendorf, "Jerusalem's Russian Compound," *The Jerusalem Post*, December 24, 1975.

19. Finn, *Reminiscences*, p. 177.

20. For a detailed treatment of this subject see Hopwood, *The Russian Presence in Syria and Palestine 1843–1914; Church and Politics in the Near East.*

21. Tibawi, *British Interests in Palestine*, pp. 174–75.

22. Murad to Rosen, August 19, 1856, Jaffa, German Consulate, R.G.N. 67, file no. 16.

23. Finn Diary, September 29, September 30, October 1, 2, 4, 15, 1858, in Blumberg, *A View From Jerusalem*, pp. 299, 300, 310.

24. Russian Consul to Rosen, October 1, 1858, Jerusalem, German Consulate, R.G.N. 67, file no. 163.

25. The young bishop, Cyril Naumov, had previously been inspector at the St. Petersburg Ecclesiastical Academy. See Hopwood, *The Russian Presence in Syria and Palestine*, pp. 50–55, 62–65. Bishop Naumov was accompanied by Dr. V.A. Levinsohn, a Jewish convert to Russian Orthodoxy, who was to serve as a missionary among Palestine's Jews. See Finn, *Reminiscences*, p. 177.

26. The ambitious Russian program was reported in detail by the United States

Consul. See Gorham to Cass, January 19, 1859, Jerusalem, No. 5, U.S.N.A., S.D.C., Microcopy M453, Roll 1.

27. Formal agreement accompanied by property inventories signed by German Consul Baron von Münchhausen and Russian Consul Nicolas Ilarionov, April 27, 1877, Jerusalem, German Consulate, R.G.N. 67, file no. 161.

28. W.E. Mosse, "Russia and the Levant, 1856–1862: Grand Duke Constantine Nicolaevich and the Russian Steam Navigation Company," *Journal of Modern History* 26 (1954): 39–48.

29. William Henry Bartlett, *Jerusalem Revisited* (Jerusalem: Ariel Publishing, 1976), pp. 25, 41, 46, 47.

30. Tibawi, *British Interests in Palestine*, pp. 170–73.

31. Eichmann to Rosen, December 5, 1858, Constantinople, German Consulate, R.G.N. 67, file no. 95.

CHAPTER 12 – THE OLD YISHUV AND THE CONSULS

1. *Genesis.* 10:3.

2. Rabbi J.H. Hertz, *The Pentateuch and Haftorahs: Hebrew Text, English Translation and Commentary, Genesis* (London: Oxford University Press, 1929), pp. 88–89.

3. In addition to previous discussions of this subject in this work, see Schölch, "European Penetration," pp. 47–87.

4. *Encyclopedia Judaica* (Jerusalem: Keter Publishing House, 1971), 13:1452.

5. Rabbi Chaim David Chazan to Prussian Consul, May 17, 1866, Jerusalem, German Consulate, R.G.N. 67, file no. 348.

6. Arnold Blumberg, "The British and Prussian Consuls in Jerusalem and the Strange Last Will of Rabbi Hershell," *Zionism: An International Journal of Social, Political, and Intellectual History* 1 (1980): 1–8.

7. Chief Rabbi Chazan to Consul Rosen, March 5, 1867, Jerusalem, German Consulate, R.G.N. 67, file no, 351.

8. *Encyclopedia Judaica*, 14:674.

9. Blumberg, *A View From Jerusalem*, pp. 36–39.

10. British Consul General Hugh Rose to Palmerston, March 27, 1847, Beirut, no. 18, P.R.O., F.O., 78/2068.

11. Rose to Palmerston, March 27, 1847, Beirut, *ibid.*

12. Finn to Palmerston, March 12, 1847, March 23, 1849, Jerusalem, P.R.O., F.O., 78/2068.

13. Austrian Consul General Adelburg to Rabbi Bordachi, February 12, 1845, Beirut, German Consulate, R.G.N. 67, file no. 2; Young to Adelburg, March 10, 1845, Jerusalem, *ibid.*

14. Finn to Palmerston, March 12, 1847, Jerusalem, no. 11, P.R.O., F.O., 78/2068.

15. See Harold N. Ingle, *Nesselrode and the Russian Rapprochement with Britain, 1836–1844,* (Berkeley: University of California Press, 1976).

16. Rose to Palmerston, March 27, 1847, Beirut, no. 18, P.R.O., F.O., 78/2068.

17. Palmerston to Rose, May 14, 1847, London, no. 5, *ibid.*

18. Palmerston to Finn, May 19, 1847, London, no. 1, *ibid.*

19. Rose to Palmerston, July 9, 1847, November 20, 1848, Beirut, *ibid.,* Rose to Addington, October 28, 1848, Broumans, Private, *ibid.*

20. Previous instructions of January 31, 1839, April 1, 1841, enclosed as copies in Finn to Palmerston, March 12, 1847, Jerusalem, *ibid.*

21. Stratford Canning to Lord Aberdeen, December 10, 1842, Buyukdery, no. 250, *ibid.*

22. Finn to Palmerston, March 23, 1849, Jerusalem, no. 12, *ibid.*

23. Basily to Bahri Pasha, Beirut, 28 Djemez 2nd, 1265, Moslem calendar; Basily to Moore, May 9/21, 1849, Beirut, both enclosed in Moore to Palmerston, May 22, 1849, Beirut, no. 19, *ibid.*

24. Palmerston to Moore, August 6, 1849, London, no. 5, *ibid.*

25. Finn to Henry L. Keeling, January 6, 1864, London, Private, *ibid.;* Keeling to Finn, January 6, 1864, London, Private, *ibid.;* Finn to Russell, January 20, 1864, Gloucester, Private, *ibid.*

26. N.T. Moore, to Foreign Office, April 22, 1870, Jerusalem, no. 256, Hyamson, *The British Consulate in Jerusalem,* 2:347.

27. See Blumberg, "The British and Prussian Consuls in Jerusalem and the Strange Last Will of Rabbi Hershell," *Zionism* 1 (1980): 1–8.

28. In all correspondence with his superiors, Finn denied being engaged in active proselytization. The British government, however, was made fully aware of Finn's aggressive work as a missionary by complaints from the Jerusalem rabbis and by the testimony of Russian Consul General Basily and the Austrian Consul at Jerusalem, Count Pizzamano, given to the British Consul General at Beirut. See Moore to Palmerston, July 2, 1849, Beirut, P.R.O., F.O., 78/2068.

29. Tibawi, British Interests in Palestine, pp. 78, 161–63.

30. Finn, *Stirring Times,* 1:127–28.

31. *Ibid.*, 1:120–21; *ibid.*, 2:73–74; Finn, *Reminiscences*, pp. 61, 71, 76, 89, 101, 133.

32. Finn Diary, October 21, 25, 1852; June 10, November 25, 1853; January 30, March 14, 1854, in Blumberg, *A View From Jerusalem*, pp. 110, 111, 129, 144, 159, 160.

33. *Ibid.*, pp. 67, 73, 74, 78, 80, 84, 92, 107, 116, 124, 132, 135, 136, 153, 155, 167, 178, 197–201, 221, 236, 256, 257.

34. J.H. Marcus and Selig Hausdorff to the Austrian Consul General at Jerusalem, February 3, 1864, German Consulate, R.G.N. 67, file no. 348; Rabbi Nissim Back to Baron von Alten, May 14, 1872, Jerusalem, *ibid.*, file no. 489; Charles Netter to von Alten, May 15, 1872, Mikveh Israel, *ibid.;* Abraham Beer Cohen, May 20, 1872, Jaffa, *ibid.*

35. Finn Diary. October 2, 14, 1849; February 25, 1850, in Blumberg, *A View From Jerusalem*, pp. 53, 66, 67.

36. A. Hastings Kelk, Secretary of the London Jews Society Hospital to British Consul John Dickson, October 19, 1897. Jerusalem, Hyamson, *The British Consulate in Jerusalem*, 2:508–509.

37. Finn Diary, June 8, 1854, in Blumberg, *A View From Jerusalem*, pp. 165, 179; Finn, *Reminiscences*, pp. 117–18. 123.

38. Goodman, Moses Montefiore, pp. 48, 52, 100, 117, 159, 185.

39. Blumberg, *A View From Jerusalem*, p. 213.

40. Goodman, *Moses Montefiore*, pp. 119–20.

41. *Ibid.*, pp. 113–14; Simon Dubnov, *History of the Jews* (New York: Thomas Yoseloff, 1973), 5:251.

42. Blumberg, *A View From Jerusalem*, pp. 45, 83, 278.

43. Goodman, *Moses Montefiore*, pp. 119–20.

44. Finn Diary, June 27, 1856, in Blumberg, *A View From Jerusalem*, pp. 228, 245.

45. Consul John Dickson to Sir Philip Currie, January 20, 1896, Jerusalem, Hyamson, *The British Consulate in Jerusalem*, 2:502.

46. Finn Diary, July 11, July 26, 1854; July 23, 1855, in Blumberg, *A View From Jerusalem*, pp. 167, 168, 180, 181, 197.

47. "Misgav Ladach at 120 Takes A Look Ahead," *The Jerusalem Post*, November 3, 1975. Since 1948, Misgav Ladach has continued its service on Kovshei Katamon Street. (Letter from Dr. Maccabi Salzberger, medical director of Misgav Ladach Hospital, November 9, 1975, Jerusalem, in possession of the writer.)

48. Emile Marmorstein, "European Jews in Muslim Palestine." *Middle Eastern Studies* 11 (1975): 78, 79. Although Finn knew that Cohn's work was designed to render the missionaries impotent, he preferred to maintain the fiction that their efforts and those of the Western Jewish charities were united against the "backwardness" of the rabbis (Finn, *Reminiscences*, pp. 125, 141).

49. See Blumberg, *A View From Jerusalem*, pp. 62, 63, 84, 95, 121, 149, 179, 180, 212, 213, 244.

50. Ben-Eliezer, *Destruction and Renewal; the Synagogues of the Jewish Quarter,* pp. 20–27.
51. British Consular Reports on the Trade and Commerce of Jerusalem in 1864 and 1865, March 3, 1864, March 1865, Hyamson, *The British Consulate in Jerusalem,* 2:331, 336.
52. Misgav Ladach Hospital, founded in 1855, is clearly the oldest hospital in Jerusalem in continuous existence. Nevertheless, Bikur Cholim Hospital contests that claim because it ultimately absorbed a small clinic founded in 1843 by Sir Moses Montefiore. A Prussian Jewish physician, Dr. Simon Fränkel, presided over that modest medical institution for thirteen years (French Consul. Count de Lantivy to Baron de Rothschild, October 6, 1844. Jaffa, *ibid.,* 1:66–67).
53. One of the principal motives for reestablishing the Latin Patriarchate of Jerusalem in 1847 was an acute consciousness of the inadequate religious instruction given to Roman Catholic children of the oriental rites who used Arabic or Greek rather than Latin in the celebration of the mass. The patriarch regarded it as his first duty to train a native clergy, fluent in Arabic or Greek, while teaching the native children a European language, usually French or Italian. (The titular Archbishop of Thessalonica, Secretary of the Congregation of Propaganda Fide to the prelates attached to Propaganda Fide, January 31, 1847, Rome, Vatican, Propaganda Fide.) Even before the restoration of the Latin Patriarchate of Jerusalem, the Franciscan Custodian of the Terra Santa presented an impressive inventory of Roman Catholic educational and charitable institutions located in every Palestinian town with a viable Catholic population. (Minister General Giuseppe M. di Alessandria's Memorial to Propaganda Fide, February 20, 1842, Araceli, *ibid.*)
54. Baron von Alten to Governor of Jerusalem, November 25, 1884, Jerusalem, German Consulate, R.G.N. 67, file no. 348.
55. Mohammed Raouf, Governor of Jerusalem, to British Consul Noel Temple Moore, September 10, 1887, Jerusalem, Hyamson, *The British Consulate in Jerusalem,* 2:439–40.
56. Prior to 1881, the Jewish citizenry of the United States was mostly of western European origin. Few Russian Jews could claim United States protection. Victor Beauboucher, consul at Jerusalem, even resisted the appointment of an American Jew to his consular staff. See Beauboucher to Secretary of State Hamilton Fish, July 8, 1869. Jerusalem, U.S.N.A., S.D.C., microcopy 453, Roll 1. Beauboucher was succeeded in 1870 by Consul Richard Beardsley who supported sympathetically the petition of stateless Russian Jews to become United States protégés. The State Department informed him that he was to

afford protection only to authentic American citizens. See Petition of the Jews of Jerusalem to President Grant, July 31, 1870, *ibid.* Roll 2; Beardsley to Fish, August 5, 1870, Jerusalem, *ibid.* In 1873, however, Consul Frank de Hass, an enthusiastic evangelical Christian, warmly sympathetic to the Jews, became consul at Jerusalem. When the Russo-Turkish War broke out in 1877, de Hass extended United States protection to approximately one hundred Russian Jews. When ordered by telegraph to withdraw that protection, de Hass evaded obeying his order by an ingenious variety of expedients. See de Hass to Secretary of State W.M. Evarts, May 3, 1877, Jerusalem, no. 64, *ibid.*, de Hass to Third Assistant Secretary of State J.A. Campbell, July 12, 1877, Jerusalem, no. 67, *ibid.* Thus at the close of the period covered by this study, the United States joined the great Western European powers in maintaining a roll of Russian Jewish protégés in Palestine, some of whom had no legal claim to such protection.

57. British Military Attaché at Constantinople G. Jackson Eldridge to the Earl of Dufferin, Ambassador to Turkey, June 20, 1884, Aleih, Hyamson, *The British Consulate in Jerusalem*, 2:418–21.

58. Von Alten to Kiamal Pasha. May 12. 1870, Jerusalem, no. 41. German Consulate, R.G.N. 67, file no. 122.

59. Same to same, June 11, 1870, Jerusalem, no. 52, *ibid.*

60. Kiamal Pasha to von Alten, June 11, 1870, Jerusalem, personal and unnumbered, *ibid.*

61. Von Alten to Kiamal Pasha, June 18, 1870, Jerusalem, rough draft, *ibid.*

62. The writer has no information as to the strength of the claims of the four families to German citizenship. Two or three of the names of the heads of the families in question are typical Sephardic or oriental Jewish names. Derivation of a claim to German protection may have been by marriage to or maternal descent from a German subject, service to a German state, or citizenship in a country represented in Palestine by the German consul. The four heads of family were Abraham Bechor Cohen, Isaac Elshech, Nissim Ezra Mandil, and Meyer Mattlon (Kiamal Pasha to von Alten, July 11, 1870, Jerusalem, no. 50. *ibid.*).

63. Sir Moses Montefiore to Lord John Russell, November 26, 1861, Ramsgate, P.R.O. F.O. 78/2068; Charles Netter to von Alten, May 18, 1872, Jaffa, telegram, German Consulate, R.G.N. 67, file no. 489; Rabbi Zvi Hirsch Kalischer's purchase of the three dunams of land at Bethlehem transferred to the Perushim Congregation, October 26, 1875, German Consular Certificate no. 1782. *ibid.*, file no. 349.

64. Von Alten to Mayor of Jerusalem Joseph al Khalidi, January 10, 1873. Jerusalem, *ibid.*, file no. 351.

·CHAPTER 13 – THE GOLDEN AGE OF CONSULAR SUPREMACY, 1853–66

1. General Georges Spillman, "150 Ans de Relations Franco-Libanaises." *Revue Historique des Armees* 3 (1976) :32–54.

2. A token of the interest taken by all European powers in Lebanon can be found in the detailed analysis of events there by an unidentified pair of Prussian agents who sent their comments to the consul in Jerusalem. (Unsigned journal of the Lebanese massacres, August 14, 1859, Mt. Lebanon, German Consulate, R.G.N. 67, file no. 19.)

3. Case, *Edouard Thouvenel el la Diplomatic du Second Empire*, pp. 341–44.

4. *Ibid.*, p. 348.

5. Tibawi, *British Interests in Palestine*, p. 144,

6. An earlier attempt made in 1857 was abandoned when the cable broke, four hundred miles from Ireland.

7. See the introduction to the microfilmed State Department Correspondence of United States Consuls at Jerusalem, U.S.N.A., S.D.C. Microcopy 453. roll 1.

8. Frank Fox, "Quaker, Shaker, Rabbi: Warder Cresson, the Story of a Philadelphia Mystic." *The Pennsylvania Magazine of History and Biography* (April 1971): 146–94. See chapter 7, note 17.

9. Gortiam to Secretary of State William L. Marcy, March 25, 1857, Jerusalem, no. 2, U.S.N.A., S.D.C., microcopy 453, roll 1.

10. Gorham to Secretary of State Lewis Cass, July 12, 1857, Jerusalem, no. 6, *ibid.*

11. Arnold Blumberg, *The Diplomacy of the Mexican Empire, 1863–1867* (Philadelphia; American Philosophical Society, 1971), pp. 15–39.

12. *Ibid.*, pp. 26, 37–38, 52, 65, 96, 108.

13. Márquez to Rosen, December 6, 1865, Jerusalem, no. 102, German Consulate, R.G.N. 67, file no. 163.

14. Pedro de Haro to the Jerusalem Consular Corps, November 24, 1866, Jerusalem no. 117, *ibid.*

15. Finn Diary, April 9, 1854, in Blumberg, *A View From Jerusalem*, p. 162.

16. Charles Henry Churchill, *The Druzes and the Maronites under the Turkish Rule from 1840–1860* (London: Arno Reprint, 1862).

17. Finn Diary, October 11, 1850; April 25, 1851; August 14, 1854; January 12, 1858; in Blumberg, *A View From Jerusalem*, pp. 76, 83, 86, 170, 181, 281, 304.

18. Gorham to John P. Brown, U.S. Consul General at Constantinople, January 17, 1858, Jaffa, U.S.N.A., S.D.C., microcopy 453, roll 1.

19. Prussian Consul General Weber to Finn, August 7, 1861, Beirut, enclosed

with Finn to British Consul General Moore, August 21, 1861, Jerusalem, P.R.O. F.O., 78/2068.

20. Finn to Weber, August 12, 1861, Jerusalem, enclosed with *ibid.*
21. Finn's Proclamation to the Jerusalem Rabbis, June 11, 1861, enclosure no. 1 in Finn to Russell, June 21, 1861, Jerusalem, no. 33, *ibid.*
22. Montefiore to Russell, November 26, 1861, Ramsgate, England, *ibid.*
23. Russell to Finn, December 12, 1861, London, no. 17, *ibid.*
24. Joseph Mayer Montefiore to the Foreign Office, June 20, September 18, October 1, 3, 1862, London, *ibid.*
25. James Murray, Chief of the Consular Service to Russell, June 21, 1862, London, *ibid.*
26. Letters bearing the seals and signatures of more than 30 institutions or individuals in Hebron and Jerusalem, sent to Consul Rosen, December 24, 1861, Hebron, German Consulate, R.G.N. 67, file no. 348.
27. A. Lehren, President, and J.A. Roos, Secretary of the Pekidim and Amarcalim of Amsterdam to the Netherlands Foreign Minister, November 17, 1862. Amsterdam, *ibid.,* file no. 115; Netherlands Foreign Minister to Chargé d'affaires in Constantinople, November 18, 1862, The Hague, *ibid.;* Netherlands Chargé d'affaires to Prussian Consul Rosen, December 24, 1862, Constantinople, *ibid.* A valuable doctoral dissertation explores the origins of the Dutch Jewish community in Palestine. Although the text is Hebrew, an English title page and summary are included. See Arie Morgenstern, *The Pekidim and Amarcalim of Amsterdam and the Jewish Community in Palestine, 1810–1840*, approved by the Senate of the Hebrew University in January 1981.
28. Judgment given in Sir Edmund Hornby's Supreme Consular Court of the Levant, July 8, 1863, Jerusalem, British Consulate, R.G.N. 123–1, file no. 27.
29. A copy of the Will of Rabbi David B. Hershell, November 10, 1851, German Consulate, R.G.N. 67, file no. 494.
30. J.H. Marcus and Selig Hausdorff to Austrian Consul General Walchen, February 3, 1864, *ibid.,* file no. 348.

CHAPTER 14 – THE TELEGRAPH AND THE END OF THE PLENIPOTENTIARY CONSULATE

1. Mattingly, *Renaissance Diplomacy*, pp. 15–22, 181–91, 201–19.
2. Sir Harold Nicolson, *The Evolution of Diplomacy* (New York: Collier Books, 1966), pp. 99–125.
3. Tibawi, *British Interests in Palestine*, p. 144.

4. Arnold Blumberg, *The Diplomacy of the Austro-Sardinian War of 1859* (Ann Arbor, Mich.: University Microfilms, 1962), p. 236.
5. Consul P.J.C. McGregor to Sir L. Mallet, British Ambassador to Turkey, March 15, 1914, Jerusalem, Hyamson, *The British Consulate in Jerusalem*, 2:583–84.
6. Joseph Al-Khalidi to von Alten, December 7, 1870, Jerusalem. German Consulate, R.G.N. 67, file no. 229.
7. Von Alten to Al-Khalidi, June 8, 1871, Jerusalem, *ibid.*
8. Acting German Consul Kersten to Al-Khalidi, October 16, 1871, Jerusalem, *ibid.*
9. German Consul Baron von Münchhausen's Compact with the Jerusalem municipal government, January 29, 1877, *ibid.*
10. Hadolinski to German Consulate at Jaffa, April 27, 1877, telegram, Pera, Turkey, *ibid.*, file no. 161.
11. Petition of the Ashkenazic Rabbis and Kollelim to the British Consul at Jerusalem, 4 Iyar, 5622, enclosed in Finn to British Ambassador to Turkey Sir Henry Bulwer, May 22, 1862, Jerusalem, Hyamson, *The British Consulate in Jerusalem*, 2:296–301.
12. Rabbi Chazan to Consul Rosen, May 17, 1866, Jerusalem, German Consulate, R.G.N. 67, file no. 348.
13. Ashkenazic Petition to Rosen, February 3, 1867, Jerusalem, *ibid.*, file no. 351.
14. Consul Rosen to Rabbi Chazan, February 28, 1867, Jerusalem, *ibid.*, file no. 348; Chazan to Consuls Moore, Pascal, and Rosen, March 1, 1867, Jerusalem, *ibid.*
15. Chazan to Rosen, March 5, 1867, Jerusalem, *ibid.*, file no. 351.
16. Resolution of Gratitude from the Ashkenazic Communities of Palestine to British Consul N.T. Moore, undated, enclosed in Moore to Richard, Earl Lyons, British Ambassador to Turkey, March 19, 1867, Jerusalem, Hyam son, *The British Consulate in Jerusalem*, 2:342–44.
17. Nazif Pasha to the acting consul of the North German Confederation Frangois de Geran, October 26, 1867, Jerusalem. German Consulate, R.G.N. 67, file no. 351.
18. Géran to Consul General T. Weber, October 28, 1867, Jerusalem, telegram. *ibid.*; Weber to Géran, October 28, 1867, Beirut, telegram, *ibid.*, file no. 348; Weber to Reshid Pasha, Wali at Damascus, November 6, 1867, Beirut, *ibid.*, *file no. 351.*
19. Baron von Allen to Joseph Al-Khalidi, January 10, 1873, Jerusalem, *ibid.*
20. *Encyclopedia Judaica* (Jerusalem: Keter Publishing House, 1971), 14:673.

21. Jelavich, *The Ottoman Empire, the Great Powers, and the Straits Question,* pp. 5–24.
22. *Ibid.,* pp. 25–84.
23. Raymond James Sontag, *European Diplomatic History, 1871–1932* (New York: Appleton-Century-Crofts, 1961), pp. 3–26.
24. German Ambassador to Turkey R. von Keudell to Acting Consul at Jerusalem Kersten, March 25, 1873, Pera, Turkey, no. 397, German Consulate, R.G.N. 67, file no. 95.
25. Charles Beatty, *De Lesseps of Suez; The Man and His Times* (New York: Harper & Brothers, 1956), pp. 272–74.
26. Arnold Blumberg, "An Early Project for a Suez Canal: the Aborted Plan of 1847." *The Mariner's Mirror* 68 (1982):317–23.
27. Queen Victoria to Prime Minister Benjamin Disraeli, March 11, 15, 16, 17, 18, 1876, Windsor, George E. Buckle and W.F. Monypenny. *The Life of Benjamin Disraeli, Earl of Beaconsfield* (New York: MacMillan, 1920), 5:467–69.
28. Jelavich, *The Ottoman Empire, the Greal Powers, and the Straits Question,* pp. 5–24.
29. Disraeli to Queen Victoria. June 29, 1876, London, Buckle and Monypenny, *The Life of Benjamin Disraeli,* 6:35–36: Queen Victoria to Disraeli, February 14, 1877, *ibid.,* 6:122–23.
30. Disraeli to Lord Derby, September 1, 1877, *ibid.,* 6:177–78.
31. *Ibid.,* 6:284; Lord Beaconsfield to Queen Victoria, July 20, 1878, Osborne. *ibid.,* 6:334–35.
32. Jelavich, *The Habsburg Empire,* pp. 122–24; Oscar Jaszi, *The Dissolution of the Habsburg Monarchy* (Chicago: University of Chicago Press, 1964), p. 115; Redlich, *Emperor Franz Joseph,* pp. 398–401.
33. Foreign Secretary Lord Salisbury to Sir Henry Layard, Ambassador to Turkey, August 13, 1878, Private, Kenneth Bourne, *The Foreign Policy of Victorian England, 1830–1902* (London: Oxford University Press, 1970), pp. 416–17.
34. Count G. zu Münster, German Ambassador to France to German Chancellor Count Leo von Caprivi, February 26, 1891, Paris, in *German Diplomatic Documents, 1871–1914,* E.T.S. Dugdale, editor (New York: Barnes & Noble, 1969), 2:70–72; Count Paul Hatzfeldt-Wildenburg, German Ambassador to Great Britain, to Baron F. von Holstein at the German Foreign Ministry, July 31, 1895, London, Private, *ibid.,* 2:329–31.

CHAPTER 15 – PALESTINIAN SELF-CONCEPT; THE CONCRETE HARDENS, 1870–80

1. Hassan Saab, *The Arab Federalists of The Ottoman Empire* (Amsterdam: Djambattan Press, 1958), p. 201.

2. George Antonius, *The Arab Awakening* (New York: Capricorn Press, 1946), pp. 45–55. Antonius' seminal work on Arab nationalism fully documents the role of Protestant missionaries from the United States and Great Britain and Roman Catholic missionaries, mostly French, who created the two elements essential to modern nationalist movements. These are Arabic printing presses and Arabic language schools teaching secular subjects. This accounts for the leadership given to early Arab nationalism by Christians centered in Lebanon and northern Syria. See *ibid.*, pp. 35–45.

3. Emile Marmorstein, "European Jews in Muslim Palestine." *Middle Eastern Studies* 11 (1975): 80–82.

4. A careful reading of George Antonius' *The Arab Awakening* will make it clear that he regarded the primarily Christian nationalist circle at Beirut as merely a modest beginning of the movement. He emphasizes the fact that the mass appeal of Arab nationalism dates only from World War I. Nevertheless he has been attacked for having allegedly assigned a greater importance to the Beirut movement than it deserved. See William W. Haddad, "Nationalism in the Ottoman Empire," *Nationalism in a Non-national State; the Dissolution of the Ottoman Empire,* edited by W.H. Haddad and W. Ochsenwald (Columbus: Ohio State University Press, 1977), pp. 9–10.

5. German Consular Registration Certificate no. 1782, with memoranda, October 26, 1875, German Consulate, R.G.N. 67, file no. 489.

6. Charles Netter was one of the six young French Jews who had founded the *Alliance* in 1860. See Graetz, *History of the Jews*, 6:701–702.

7. Maurice Samuel, *Harvest in the Desert* (Philadelphia: Jewish Publication Society, 1945), p. 45. The school, which exists to this day, ultimately became Zionist in philosophy and adopted Hebrew as the language of instruction. Charles Netter, regardless of his limited view of the school, apparently regarded it as more than simply another *Alliance* school, and resided in Palestine to direct it. He became actively involved in the power structure of the Old Yishuv in matters totally unrelated to the school. (Charles Netter to German Consul General von Alten, May 8, 12, 1872, German Consulate, R.G.N. 67, file no. 489; Netter to Murad, May 15, 1872, Mikveh Israel, *ibid.*; Baron von Alten to Netter, May 18, 1872, Jerusalem, *ibid.*)

8. Max L. Margolis and Alexander Marx, *A History of the Jewish People*, pp. 679–80, 687, 703.

9. A part of the support for Montefiore's project was provided by a bequest

from the American Jewish philanthropist Judah Touro (Goodman, *Moses Montefiore*, p. 122).

10. Vilnay, *Israel Guide*, pp. 124–25.

11. *Ibid.*, pp. 243–44.

12. Eversely and Chiral, *The Turkish Empire*, p. 312.

13. Haddad, "Nationalism in the Ottoman Empire," pp. 8–10.

14. Antonius, *The Arab Awakening*, pp. 54–55.

15. *Ibid.*, pp. 71–72, 88.

16. Until the late eighteenth century, the term *rayah* was sometimes used to describe all of the sultan's subjects. By the early nineteenth century, the term referred only to non-Moslem subjects. This distinction reinforced the sense of superiority felt by all Moslems. It should be noted that in 1876 the best estimates show that Turks constituted only 35 percent of the population of the Ottoman Empire. Arabs made up 13.8 percent. Islamic populations enjoyed a bare majority thanks to Moslem Albanians, Kurds, and Circassians. See Davison, "Nationalism in a Non-national State." pp. 30, 35, 36. For more on the conscious promotion of Islamic enthusiasm as a counter both to reform and to nationalism, see Uriel Heyd, *Foundations of Turkish Nationalism: The Life and Teachings of Ziya Gökalp* (London: Harvill Press, 1950), pp. 19–20. 24–27.

17. Antonius, *The Arab Awakening*, pp. 768–71.

18. British Consul N.T. Moore to British Ambassador to Turkey Sir Austen Henry Layard, November 12, 1879, Jerusalem, Hyamson, *The British Consulate in Jerusalem*, 2:410–11.

19. Circular of the Sublime Porte to all embassies at Constantinople, October 29, 1874, *Ibid.*, 2:396–98.

20. It is relevant to reiterate that certain consuls extended protection, even against orders from their superiors, for humanitarian reasons. Individual consuls extended protection to stateless Jews because their own religious convictions regarded Jewish settlement in the Holy Land as part of the Messianic scheme for universal redemption. (U.S. Consul R. Beardsley to Secretary of State Hamilton Fish, August 5, 1870, Jerusalem, U.S.N.A. S.D.C., microcopy 453, roll 2; Consul F.S. de Hass to Undersecretary of State W. Hunter, February 5, 1876, Jerusalem, *ibid.*; de Hass to Secretary of State W. Evarts, May 3, 1877. Jerusalem, no. 64, *ibid.*; de Hass to Third Assistant Secretary of State J.A. Campbell, July 12, 1877, Jerusalem, no. 67, *ibid.*)

21. Von Alten to Kiamal Pasha, May 12, 1870, Jerusalem, no. 41, German Consulate, R.G.N. 67, file no. 122; R.G. Kerin, Netherlands chargé d'affaires to Prussian Consul Georg Rosen, December 24, 1862, Constantinople, no. 2, German Consulate, R.G.N. 67, file no. 115. For estimates of the numbers of

rayahs who improperly claimed foreign protégé status see Davison, "Nationalism in a Non-National State." pp. 42–43.

22. E.A. Finn to Secretary of State for Foreign Affairs Balfour. June 26, 1918, London, P.R.O. F.O., 371/3380.

23. Kiamal Pasha to von Alten, January 2, 1872, Jerusalem, German Consulate, R.G.N. 67, file no. 168.

24. The new status of the Sanjak of Jerusalem was not regularized until it was defined in a *Regiement Organique* of 1887. At that time, although still designated merely as the Sanjak of Jerusalem, historic Palestine was declared to be administratively distinct from the Vilayet of Aleppo, the Vilayet of Beirut, the Vilayet of Syria and the Sanjak of Lebanon. See Antonius, *The Arab Awakening*, pp. 65–66.

25. Al Khalidi to von Alten, December 7, 1870, Jerusalem, German Consulate, R.G.N. 67, file no. 229; von Alten to Al Khalidi, June 8, 1871, Jerusalem, *ibid.*; Acting German Consul Kersten to Al Khalidi, October 16, 1871, Jerusalem, *ibid.*; Pact defining the property rights of the German Consulate and the Municipality of Jerusalem, January 29, 1877, *ibid.* See also Schölch, "European Penetration," p. 36.

26. *Ibid.*, pp. 30, 36, 68–70.

27. Petermann to El Koordi, March 13, 1868, Jerusalem, no. 33A, German Consulate, R.G.N. 67, file no. 47.

28. El Koordi to Bismarck, June 11, 1868, Jerusalem, no. 53A, *ibid.*

29. United States Vice Consul Murad Aroutin was described by a dissatisfied American traveler as speaking no English. See Finnie, *Pioneers East*, p. 253.

30. Six United States Citizens to Consul J. Hosford Smith, June 1, 1853, enclosed in Smith to U.S. Secretary of State W.L. Marcy, June 23, 1853, Beirut. U.S.N.A. S.D.C. microcopy T367, roll 2.

31. Münchhausen to Faïk Pasha, February 26, 1876, Jerusalem, German Consulate. R.G.N. 67, file no. 47.

32. Murad to Münchhausen, March 6, 1877, Jerusalem, no. 514, *ibid.*

33. Finn, *Stirring Times,* 2:57.

34. Hadolinski to Münchhausen, April 23, 1877, Pera, Turkey, Telegram. German Consulate, R.G.N. 67, file no. 161; Formal Pact signed by Russian Consul Nicholas Ilarionov and German Consul General von Münchhausen defining Germany's role in protecting Russian persons and property, April 27. 1877, no. 733, *ibid.*

35. *Ibid.*

36. Russian Vice Consul A. Marabutti to Münchhausen, May 5, 1877, Jaffa, Telegram, *ibid.*

37. Faïk Favlallah Pasha, Governor General of Palestine, to Ilarionov, May 10, 1877, Jerusalem, *ibid.* The Russian Consul had left Palestine before the orders for expulsion were received. (Hadolinski to German Consul at Jaffa, April 27, 1877, ciphered telegram, *ibid.*) It therefore became Münchhausen's unpleasant duty to negotiate the rights of Russians stranded in Palestine.

38. During the period of his guardianship of Russian interests, Münchhausen corresponded directly with Senator N.K. Giers at the Russian Foreign Ministry at St. Petersburg. (Münchhausen to Giers, May 10, 1877, Jerusalem, no. 865, *ibid.*; Giers to Münchhausen, June 1, 1877, St. Petersburg, no. 1418, *ibid.*)

39. Naib Assad to Münchhausen, June 21, 1877. Jerusalem, *ibid.*

40. Ilarionov to Münchhausen, June 15, 1878, Jaffa, telegram, *ibid.*; Ilarionov to Turkish Governor, June 26, 1878, Jerusalem, no. 1288, *ibid.*

41. Schölch, "European Penetration," p. 57.

42. *Ibid.*, p. 56.

43. Samuel, *Harvest in the Desert*, pp. 68–71, 79–80, 96–101, 104–109.

44. Raphael Patai, *The Arab Mind* (New York: Charles Scribner's Sons, 1976). pp. 196, 224, 260, 261. An extremely interesting case can be made of the thesis that the formerly colonial territories which comprise the Arab States today attained independence as a consequence of conflict with Europeans, but did not discover true nationalism until after they had become nations. See Haddad, "Nationalism in the Ottoman Empire." pp. 19–21.

45. Pares, *History of Russia*, p. 387.

46. *Ibid.*, pp. 391–92.

47. *Ibid.*, pp. 412–13.

48. Margolis and Marx, *A History of the Jewish People*, pp. 695–97.

49. Samuel, *Harvest in the Desert*, pp. 47–59, 148–58.

Glossary

Ahl Ud-Dimma: The "Protected Peoples"; usually Christians or Jews conceded to have received authentic divine revelation, but regarded as possessing an incomplete faith in having rejected Mohammed and the Koran. The Dhimmi were denied the prestigious role of warriors and had to pay a head tax in lieu of military service.

Aqsa, Mosque El: The third holiest Moslem religious shrine in the world. Located on the Temple Mount, Judaism's holiest shrine, it marks the point from which Mohammed is said to have made a night journey to Paradise.

Ashkenaz: Biblical Hebrew term for Germany. By derivation, it refers to all Jews of German ancestry or whose forebears spoke Yiddish, a Germanic language written in Hebrew letters. By extension, the Ashkenazim are Jews who share similar religious practices and who accept a common pronunciation of Hebrew, albeit differing widely in dialect.

Attestats: Legal documents affirming that stateless persons have lost the protection of their government. In the context of this book, they were required of persons seeking the protection of another country.

Bashi-Bazouk: A term most commonly used to refer to locally conscripted draftees, as contrasted with regular Turkish soldiery.

Beg [Bek]: Turkish title usually equated with the rank of colonel.

Berat: Equivalent to a Consular Exequatur, signifying Turkish government recognition of a consul's status and rights.

Beth Din: Literally a "House of Law" but usually referring to a Jewish rabbinic court, sometimes involving three or more judges sitting *en banc*.

Blood ritual murder accusation: A fabricated claim that Jews use the blood of Gentiles to make unleavened bread for Passover. The same false accusation was levelled against early Christians by the Romans concerning the baking of wafers used in the celebration of the Mass.

Cadi: A Moslem judge in a court operated under Koranic law.

Caliph ul-Islam: Commander of the Faithful, a title claimed by Turkish sultans, implying that they were the supreme religious authority of Islam throughout the world, beyond the borders of the Turkish Empire of which they were the temporal sovereign. The use of the word "Caliph" implies that its user is the "successor" to the world leadership of Islam.

Capitulations: From the Latin "Capitula" referring to clauses in treaties recognizing that foreign consuls enjoyed diplomatic immunity, extraterritorial privileges on consular property, and the right to dispense justice to their own nationals.

Cicerone: A tourist guide.

Corban Beiram: Moslem Festival of the Sacrifice.

Dar Al-Harb: "House of War," refers to non-Moslem lands which faithful Moslems are committed to regard as destined for Moslem rule either by conquest or peaceful conversion.

Dar Al-Islam: "House of Islam," refers to all lands in which Islam is or has been the dominant faith. *See* **Dar Al-Harb.**

Dhimmi: *See* **Ahl Ud-Dimma**.

Divan: Government bureau or chancery.

Dragoman: A multi-lingual translator. Such persons assumed disproportionately important roles at consulates dependent on their skills.

Druse: An Arabic speaking people who seceded from mainstream Islam to establish their own faith. Only an inner circle of initiates are fully informed of its principles. They maintain that they are descended from Jethro, the father-in-law of Moses.

Effendi: An Arab land-holding aristocrat.

Extraterritoriality: Describes the right of foreign diplomats to treat the property of embassies, legations, or consulates as though they were actually within the territorial limits of their homeland, rather than a part of the host country.

Eyalet: An administrative territorial division of the Ottoman Empire, presided over by a Musheer, and usually including numerous sanjaks or pashaliks. Pashas in each sanjak were answerable to the musheer, who in turn was subject to the wali holding administrative responsibility for two or more eyalets.

Fellahin: Arab peasants.

Firman: An imperial Ottoman decree issued by a sultan.

Frank: A term commonly used in the Near East to refer to all Europeans.

Ghiaour: An offensive Turkish epithet used to describe infidel foreigners.

Halukah: A "share" in community charitable funds apportioned to Jews registered with a Kollel for full time Jewish religious study. Funds for the Halukah were collected in the European community which was the ancestral home of the members of the Kollel. *See* **Kollel**.

Haskalah: Hebrew word meaning "Enlightenment." It may refer to the general eighteenth and nineteenth century European intellectual movement, so called. It is most commonly used to refer to Jewish attempts to become more fully assimilated into the general society, and the rejection of Jewish practices which might impede that process.

Howari: Locally recruited Arab military conscripts. *See* **Bashi-Bazouk.**

Hurva: Hebrew word for a ruin. Refers specifically to the oldest Ashkenazic Synagogue in Jerusalem which was begun in 1700, but which lay in an incomplete state for the next century and a half. It was destroyed again in 1948 following the Jordanian conquest of the Jewish Quarter of Jerusalem.

Islam: From Arabic "submission"; the appropriate name for the religion founded upon Mohammed's teachings set forth in the Koran.

Judenstaat, Der: Book published in 1896 by Theodor Herzl, describing the idealized Jewish State which he conceived would be created by political Zionism.

Kaaba: Islam's holiest shrine, located at Mecca. An observant Moslem must strive to make a pilgrimage there.

Kais: A confederation of Palestinian Arab clans claiming a common origin in the Arabian Peninsula, prior to the Arab conquest of Palestine in the seventh century. *See* **Yeminis.**

Kawass: Originally a bowman. By the nineteenth century, Kawassin were uniformed Moslem guards carrying a stout staff as a symbolic weapon, who were legally authorized to serve as guards for consuls and other non-Moslem notables. As only a Moslem could strike a Moslem with impunity, the presence of a Kawass was a symbolic assurance of the safety of persons authorized by the Turks to employ such guards.

Kollel: A corporate body through which funds are disbursed permitting married men to devote full time to Jewish religious studies. *See* **Halukah.**

Koran: Moslem scriptures representing divine revelation, received by Mohammed.

Kotel Ha-Maaravi: Hebrew term meaning Western Wall, referring to the portions of the outer retaining wall of the Temple Mount, still standing. Known for short as the "Kotel," Judaism's holiest shrine was formerly called the "Wailing Wall."

Ladino: An antique Hispanic language spoken by descendents of Jews expelled from Spain and Portugal in the fifteenth century. It is written in Hebrew letters, and contains many non-Spanish words, reflecting the local language used in North Africa, the Near East, or the Balkans where it was the primary tongue spoken by Jews.

Lebensraum: Literally "living space," a term defining the territories which a nation or people have described as essential to security or well being.

Makhkameh: The Moslem Supreme Court in a given district.

Mamelukes: Refers to the descendents of a body guard, composed of slaves, established by the heirs of Saladin in Egypt. The Mamelukes ultimately rebelled and created their own dynasty which continued as a factor in Egyptian government until the nineteenth century.

Maronites: Members of a Roman Catholic communion, centered in the Lebanon, who recognize the Pope and accept Roman Catholic theology, but who are allowed some unique practices. Among these are the use of Old Syriac in the celebration of the Mass, and the right of the lower orders of the secular clergy to marry.

Mechitza: A physical barrier separating men and women at Jewish religious services.

Medjlis: A council.

Meshullach: Hebrew word for emissary, referring usually to a Jewish charity collector sent abroad to raise funds for a Kollel or a Palestinian religious institution.

Mufti: A supreme local Moslem religious authority. He is competent to deliver a Fatwa or binding, formal legal opinion within the *Sharia* (Arabic for "path") or Moslem/Islamic religious law.

Musheer: A Turkish administrator having authority over the governors of all the sanjaks within his eyalet. On rare occasion, the title was given to the pasha of a single sanjak if the individual, as a consequence of familial distinction or service to the empire, had earned that honor.

Mutsellin: A subordinate Turkish official appointed by the Pasha of a sanjak to administer the affairs of a specific geographic area within the sanjak.

Pasha: Turkish title denoting "lord." Refers to the governors of sanjaks and other high Turkish officials.

Pashalik: A term usually used interchangeably with sanjak.

Peoples of the Book: *See* **Ahl Ud-Dimma.**

Rayah: Originally a term describing all Turkish subjects, it had come by the nineteenth century to refer to non-Moslem subjects, exclusively.

Rishon l'Zion: Hebrew for the "First in Zion"; the title borne by the Sephardic Chief Rabbi or Chacham Bashi in Palestine.

Sanjak: A Turkish provincial administrative unit under a pasha. The term pashalik is usually synonymous with it. Geographically contiguous sanjaks formed an eyalet under a musheer to whom the local governors or pashas were responsible.

Sepharad: Hebrew for Spain; the term Sephardim refers to all Jews descended from those expelled from the Iberian Peninsula in the fifteenth century. In a broad sense, all North African, Levantine and Oriental Jews are commonly called Sephardim whether or not, in fact, descended from true Sephardim. This differentiates them from the largely central and eastern European Ashkenazim and their descendants around the world.

Seraglio: The household and official entourage of a Turkish governor or higher official.

Shiite Moslems: A large minority movement in Islam which ascribes continuing religious authority to descendants of Ali, son-in-law of Mohammed.

Shochet: A Jew trained in the techniques required to slaughter kosher animals, ensuring instantaneous unconsciousness for the animal, and a maximum discharge of blood, inasmuch as observant Jews may not ingest blood. The stringent training of shochetim makes meat prepared by them acceptable to Moslems as well.

Sublime Porte: The sovereign entity of the Ottoman Empire was styled Bab Ali, literally the High Gate (*Bab*) of the palace where the sultan administered justice. Hence the French term, which translates the Turkish term, became the standard reference to the sultan's government.

Sunni Moslems: The dominant religious faction within Islam. Most Turks and a majority of Palestinian Arabs are Sunni and recognize only the first four caliphs who followed Mohammed as having a role in transmitting divine revelation. In this, Sunni Islam differs from the Shiites.

Sura: A Chapter in the Koran.

Talmud: Comprising Mishna, Gemara and later commentaries, the Talmud is the authoritative body of law binding upon Jews.

Tanzimat: The Reform Movement codified in the Hatti Sherif de Gulhané issued by Sultan Abdul Medjid at the instance of Grand Vizier Reshid Pasha in 1839.

Wakf: Moslem religious corporation which administers all property endowed for religious purposes.

Yeminis: A confederation of Palestinian Arab clans claiming a common origin in the southern Arabian Peninsula, prior to the Arab conquest of Palestine in the Seventh Century. Kais and Yemini clans were often at war with one another.

Yiddish: An antique Germanic tongue spoken by Jews whose ancestors moved eastward from Germany in the thirteenth and later centuries. It is written in Hebrew letters, and contains words used in the Gentile communities wherein Yiddish speaking Jews resided.

Yishuv: A Hebrew word denoting residential settlement. The term Old Yishuv refers to the primarily religious and nonnationalist Jewish community of Palestine prior to 1881. The term New Yishuv refers to the nationalist Zionist immigration to Palestine which began in 1881.

Zionism: A movement designed to normalize the status of world Jewry by creating a Jewish state in which Jews would fulfill all the functions of a complete society, constituting a majority of the population. The earliest organizations which actually acted on this program date from 1881–82. Political Zionism as a world movement dates from Theodor Herzl's publication of *Der Judenstaat* in 1896.

Bibliography

The list of works that follows is limited to those works which played an important role in the preparation of this book. Many classic works that were consulted made no significant contribution, and they have therefore been omitted. To render it easier for the reader to locate the full citation of a work, this bibliography has been divided into five clear-cut categories: Archival Sources; Printed Primary Sources; Secondary Sources; Journal Literature Exclusively in Hebrew; and Newspapers and Periodicals, 1838–1880. The arbitrary and often irrational separation of various types of secondary sources has been avoided. All works in this list are alphabetized within their categories under the titles that identify them in the notes. The works are listed under abbreviated titles when cited in this manner in the notes.

ARCHIVAL SOURCES

British Consulate, R.G.N. 123–1: This collection of odd files from the British Consulate in Jerusalem 1838–1914 is housed at the Israel State Archives in Jerusalem. Citations in this work from that collection always bear the Record Group Number 123–1 plus the file number assigned to the particular set of

documents by the Israel Archives. This Record Group occupies 1.3 meters of shelving at the Israel Archives.

German Consulate, R.G.N. 67: This collection of odd files from
the German Consulate in Jerusalem 1839–1939 is housed at
the Israel State Archives in Jerusalem. Citations in this work
from that collection always bear the Record Group number
67, plus the file number assigned to the particular dossier by
the Israel Archives. This Record Group occupies fifty-three
meters of shelving at the Israel Archives.

H.H.U.S.A.: Haus-Hof und Staatsarchiv, Vienna. Selected microfilms from the Austrian State Archives. These are in the
writer's possession.

P.R.O., F.O. microfilm: Public Record Office, London, Foreign
Office. All Public Record Office documents for the years
1846–64 cited in this work are drawn from the microfilm
collection housed at The Central Archives for the History of
the Jewish People in the Sprinzak Building on the Hebrew
University campus in Jerusalem.

U.S.N.A. S.D.C.: The United States National Archives, State
Department Correspondence is now completely microfilmed
through the year 1906. All enclosures, including trivia such
as newspaper clippings and printed matter, are faithfully
reproduced along with the straight runs of correspondence.
As all such diplomatic and consular correspondence is now
available for sale to the general public, this writer has simpli-
fied the citation method used in this study, giving only the
information that a scholar would need to obtain any National
Archives microfilm. This basic information consists of the
microcopy number for the general series in question and
the specific roll number within that series. This study has
involved examination of the United States correspondence
with consuls in Alexandria, Beirut, Jerusalem, and Smyrna,
and with United States ministers in Constantinople, Paris,
and London.

Vatican, Propaganda Fide: All citations from this collection are found in volumes titled Relazione Intorno Al Patriarcato, MSS at the Vatican Archives in Vatican City. This material on microfilm was obtained for the writer through the good offices of Bruce Kupelnick of the Harvard University Law School Fund.

PRINTED PRIMARY SOURCES

Adler, Cyrus, and Margalith, Aaron M. *With Firmness in the Right; American Diplomatic Action Affecting Jews 1840–1945*. New York: The American Jewish Committee, 1946. *Almanach de Gotha*, 1838–1880.

Barclay, James Turner. *The City of the Great King: or Jerusalem As It Was, As It Is, and As It Is To Be*. New York: Arno Press, 1977. Reprinted from the 1858 edition.

Bartlett, William H. *Jerusalem Revisited*. Jerusalem: Ariel Publishing Co., 1976. Reprinted from the edition of 1855.

——. *Walks About the City and Environs of Jerusalem; Summer 1842*. Jerusalem: Canaan Publishing House, 1974. Reprinted from the edition of 1844.

Bonar, Andrew Alexander and Robert Murray M'Cheyne. *Narrative of a Mission of Inquiry to the Jews from the Church of Scotland in 1839*. Philadelphia: Presbyterian Board of Publication, 1843.

Bourne, Kenneth. *The Foreign Policy of Victorian England, 1830–1902*. London: Oxford University Press, 1970.

Braude, Benjamin and Bernard Lewis, eds. *Christians and Jews in the Ottoman Empire; the Functioning of a Plural Society* (in 2 vols.). New York and London: Holmes and Meier Publishers, 1982.

Brandel-Syrier, Mia, ed. *The Religious Duties of Islam as Taught and Explained by Abu Baker Effendi*. Leiden: E.J. Brill, 1971.

Browne, John Ross. *Yusef, or the Journey of the Frangi: A Crusade in the East*. New York: Arno Press, 1977. Reprinted from the 1853 edition.

Churchill, Charles Henry. *The Druzes and the Maronites under the Turkish Rule from 1840 to 1860.* London: Arno Reprint, 1862.

Connell, Brian. *Regina v Palmerston; the Correspondence between Queen Victoria and her Foreign and Prime Minister 1837–1865.* London: Evans Bros., 1962.

Cox, Samuel Sullivan. *Orient Sunbeams, or From the Porte to the Pyramids by Way of Palestine.* New York: Arno Press, 1977. Reprinted from the 1882 edition.

Dorr, David F. *A Colored Man Round the World, by a Quadroon.* Cleveland, Ohio: Printed for the author, 1858.

Dugdale, Edgar T.S. *German Diplomatic Documents, 1871–1914* (in 4 vols.). New York: Barnes & Noble, 1969.

Ezekiel, Jacob. "Persecutions of the Jews in 1840." *Publications of the American Jewish Historical Society* 8 (1900):141–45.

Finn, Elizabeth Anne. *Reminiscences of Mrs. Finn, Member of the Royal Asiatic Society.* London: Marshall, Morgan and Scott, 3929.

Finn, James. *Stirring Times, or Records from Jerusalem Consular Chronicles of 1853 to 1856.* London: C. Kegan Paul, 1878.

Guedalla, Philip, ed. *The Palmerston Papers, Gladstone and Palmerston, Being the Correspondence of Lord Palmerston with Mr. Gladstone 1851–1865.* New York and London: Harper and Bros., 1928.

Henderson, Gavin B. "Problems of Neutrality, 1854: Documents from the Hamburg Staatsarchiv." *Journal of Modern History* 10 (1938):232–42.

Hertz, Rabbi Joseph H. *The Pentateuch and Haftorahs: Hebrew Text, English Translation and Commentary, Genesis.* London: Oxford University Press, 1929.

Hurewitz, J.D. *Diplomacy in the Near and Middle East. A Documentary Record: 1535–1956* (in 2 vols.) New York: Octagon Books, 1972.

Hyamson. Albert Montefiore. *The British Consulate in Jerusalem in Relation to the Jews of Palestine 1838–1914* (in 2 vols.). New York: AMS Press, 1975.

Jacobs, Joseph. "The Damascus Affair and the Jews of America." *Publications of the American Jewish Historical Society* 10 (1902):119–28.

Jagow, Kurt, ed. *Letters of the Prince Consort 1831–1861.* New York: E.P. Dutton, 1938.

Knaplund, Paul, ed. *Gladstone-Gordon Correspondence, 1851–1896; Selections from the Private Correspondence of a British Prime Minister and a Colonial Governor.* Philadelphia: The American Philosophical Society, 1961.

Loewe, L., ed. *Diaries of Sir Moses and Lady Montefiore* (in 2 vols.). Chicago: Belford-Clarke, 1890.

Loftus, Lord Augustus. The Diplomatic Reminiscences of Lord Augustus Loftus, 1837–1862 (2 vols.). London: Cassell & Co., 1892.

Lynch, William Francis. *Narrative of the United States Expedition to the River Jordan and the Dead Sea.* Philadelphia: Lea & Blanchard, 1849.

Malmesbury, Earl of. *Memoirs of an Ex-Minister.* London: Longmans, Green, and Co., 1885.

Melville, Herman. *Journal of a Visit to Europe and the Levant, October11, 1856–May 5, 1857.* Princeton: Princeton University Press, 1955.

Neumann, Philipp. *The Diary of Philipp von Neumann, 1819–1850* (in 2 vols.). London: P. Allan, 1928.

Parton, James. "Our Israelitish Brethren." *Atlantic Monthly* 26 (October 1870): 386–403.

Ponsonby, Sir Frederick, ed. *Letters of the Empress Frederick.* London: Macmillan & Company, 1928.

Russell, William Howard. *Russell's Despatches from the Crimea 1854–1856.* New York: Hill and Wang, 1966.

Samuel, Edwin Lord. *A Lifetime in Jerusalem; the Memoirs of the Second Viscount Samuel.* Jerusalem: Israel Universities Press, 1970.

Théodoridès, Jean. "Alexandre de Humboldt observateur de la France de Louis Philippe (Rapports diplomatiques, iné/dits) 1835–1847." *Revue d'Histoire Diplomatique* 85 (1971):193–380.

Twain, Mark. *The Innocents Abroad*. New York: Harper & Brothers, 1911. A reissue from the first printing of 1869.

Webster, Sir Charles. *The Foreign Policy of Palmerston 1830–1841, Britain, the Liberal Movement and the Eastern Question* (in 2 vols.). New York: Humanities Press, 1969.

Wilson, Sir Charles W. *Jerusalem the Holy City*. Jerusalem: Ariel Publishing House, n.d. Reprinted from the original edition of 1880.

SECONDARY SOURCES

Ahmad, Fezog. "The Relations of Great Britain with the Young Turks Between the Years 1908–1914." *Middle Eastern Studies* 1 (1966): 302–29.

Alexander, Y. and M., and M.S. Chertoff, eds. *A Bibliography of Israel*. New York: Herzl Press, 1981.

Amann, Peter. "Prophet in Zion: The Saga of George J. Adams." *The New England Quarterly* 37 (1964): 477–500.

Anderson, M.S. *The Eastern Question, 1764–1923; A Study in International Relations*. London: MacMillan, 1966.

Antonius, George. *The Arab Awakening*. New York: Capricorn Books, 1946.

Atiya, Aziz S. *History of Eastern Christianity*. Notre Dame, Indiana: University of Notre Dame Press, 1968.

Aumann, Moshe. *Land Ownership in Palestine, 1880–1948*. Jerusalem: Israel Academic Committee on the Middle East, n.d.

Baer, Gabriel. "The Evolution of Private Landownership in Egypt and the Fertile Crescent." In *The Economic History of the Middle East 1800–1914*, edited by Charles Issawi. Chicago: University of Chicago Press, 1975, pp. 79–90.

Bailey, Frank Edgar. *British Policy and the Turkish Reform Movement: A Study in Anglo-Turkish Relations 1826–1853*. New York: Howard Fertig, 1970.

Barber, Noe. *The Sultans*. New York: Simon and Schuster, 1973.

Barker, John. *Syria and Egypt Under the Last Five Sultans of Turkey* (in 2 vols.). New York: Arno Press Reprint, 1973.

Baron, Salo W. *A Social and Religious History of the Jews* (in 12 vols.). New York: Columbia University Press, 1952–67.

———. "The Jewish Question in the Nineteenth Century." *Journal of Modern History* 10 (1938):58–65.

Beatty, Charles. *De Lesseps of Suez; The Man and His Times.* New York: Harper & Brothers, 1956.

Bell, Herbert C.F. *Lord Palmerston* (in 2 vols.). Hamden, Conn.: Archon Books, 1966.

Ben-Arieh, Yohoshua. "The Growth of Jerusalem in the Nineteenth Century." *Annals of the Association of American Geographers* 65 (1975) 252–69.

———. *The Rediscovery of the Holy Land in the Nineteenth Century* [Translation from the original Hebrew of *Eretz Yisrael ba-meah ha-19*]. Detroit: Wayne State University Press, 1979.

Ben-Eliezer, Shimon. *Destruction and Renewal; the Synagogues of the Jewish Quarter.* Jerusalem: Alpha Press, 1975.

Blau, Joseph L. "Pilgrims to Zion – Activists for *Zion*." *Jewish Social Studies* 36 (1974):95–105.

Blumberg, Arnold. "The British and Prussian Consuls in Jerusalem and the Strange Last Will of Rabbi Hershell." *Zionism: an International Journal of Social, Political, and Intellectual History* 1 (1980):1–8.

———. *The Diplomacy of the Mexican Empire, 1863–1867.* Philadelphia: American Philosophical Society, 1971.

———. "An Early Project for a Suez Canal: The Aborted Plan of 1847." *The Mariner's Mirror* 68 (1982): 317–23.

———. *A View From Jerusalem, 1849–1858; The Consular Diary of James and Elizabeth Anne Finn.* East Brunswick, N.J.: Fairleigh Dickinson University Press, 1980.

Buckle, George E. and W.F. Monypenny. *The Life of Benjamin Disraeli, Earl of Beaconsfield* (6 vols.). New York: MacMillan, 1920.

Bury, J.B. *A History of the Eastern Roman Empire from the Fall of Irene to the Accession of Basil I (A.D. 802–A.D. 867).* New York: Russell & Russell, Inc., 1965.

Byrne, Leo Gerald. *The Great Ambassador.* Columbus, Oh.: Ohio State University Press, 1964.

Cameron, Rondo. *France and the Economic Development of Europe 1800–1914.* Chicago: Rand McNally, 1965.

Case, Lynn M. *Edouard Thouvenel et la Diplomatie du Second Empire.* Translated to French by Guillaume de Bertier de Sauvigny. Paris: Editions A. Pedone, 1976. Cohen, Amnon. *Palestine in the 18th Century; Patterns of Government and Administration.* Jerusalem: Magnes Press, 1973.

Cohen, Hayyim J. *The Jews of the Middle East, 1860–1972.* New York: John Wiley, 1973.

Corti, Egon Caesar Count. *Maximilian and Charlotte of Mexico* (2 vols.). New York: Alfred A. Knopf, 1928.

Costello, C. "Nineteenth Century Irish Explorers in the Levant." *Irish Geography* 7 (1974): 88–96.

Dash, Joan. *Summoned to Jerusalem; The Life of Henrietta Szold.* New York: Harper & Row, 1979.

Davison, Roderic. "Nationalism as an Ottoman Problem and the Ottoman Response." In *Nationalism in a Non-National State; The Dissolution of the Ottoman Empire*, edited by William Haddad and William Ochsenwald. Columbus: Ohio State University Press, 1977.

Dubnov, Simon. *History of the Jews* (5 vols.). Translated from Russian by Moshe Spiegel. New York & London: Thomas Yoseloff, 1973. *Encyclopedia Judaica.* Jerusalem: Keter Publishing House, 1971.

Eversley, Lord George and Sir Valentine Chirol. *The Turkish Empire From 1288 to 1924.* New York: Howard Fertig, 1969.

Finnie, David H. *Pioneers East, The Early American Experience in the Middle East.* Cambridge: Harvard University Press. 1967.

Fishbane, Simcha. "The Founding of Kollel America Tifereth

Yerushalayim." *American Jewish Historical Quarterly* 64 (1974): 120–36.

Fox, Frank. "Quaker, Shaker, Rabbi: Warder Cresson, The Story of a Philadelphia Mystic." *The Pennsylvania Magazine of History and Biography* (April 1971): 146–94.

Friedjung, Heinrich. *The Struggle for Supremacy in Germany.* London: MacMillan, 1935.

Goguel, Maurice. *The Primitive Church.* Translated from French by H.C. Snape. London: George Allen & Unwin, 1963.

Gooch, Brison D. *The Origins of the Crimean War.* Lexington, Mass.: D.C. Heath, 1969. Goodman, Paul. *Moses Montefiore.* Philadelphia: Jewish Publication Society of America, 1943.

Gough, Michael. *The Early Christians.* New York: Frederick A. Praeger, 1966.

Graetz, Heinrich. *History of the Jews* (in 6 vols.). Philadelphia: Jewish Publication Society, 1891–98.

Haddad, William W. "Nationalism in the Ottoman Empire." In *Nationalism in a Non-National Stale; the Dissolution of the Ottoman Empire,* edited by William Haddad and William Ochsenwald. Columbus: Ohio State University Press, 1977.

Heyd, Uriel. *Foundations of Turkish Nationalism; The Life and Teachings of Ziya Gökalp.* London: Harvill Press, 1950.

Hitti, Philip K. *History of the Arabs from the Earliest Times to the Present.* London: MacMillan, 1958.

———. *The Origins of the Druze People and Religion.* New York: Columbia University Press, 1928.

Holt. P.M. *Egypt and the Fertile Crescent 1516–1922.* Ithaca, N.Y.: Cornell University Press, 1969.

Hopwood, Derek. *The Russian Presence in Syria and Palestine 1843–1914; Church and Politics in the Near East.* Oxford: Clarendon Press, 1969.

Hoskins. Halford L. *British Routes to India.* New York: Octagon Press, 1928.

Hourani, Albert. *The Emergence of the Modern Middle East.* Berkeley: University of California Press, 1981.

Ingle, Harold N. *Nesselrode and the Russian Rapprochement with Britain, 1836–1844.* Berkeley: University of California Press, 1976.

Issawi, Charles, ed. *The Economic History of the Middle East 1800–1914.* Chicago: University of Chicago Press, 1975.

Jaszi, Oscar. *The Dissolution of the Habsburg Monarchy.* Chicago: University of Chicago Press, 1964.

Jelavich. Barbara. *The Habsburg Empire in European Affairs, 1814–1918.* Chicago: Rand McNally, 1969.

———. *The Ottoman Empire, the Great Powers, and the Straits Questions 1870–1887.* Bloomington: Indiana University Press, 1973.

Jenkins, Romilly. *Byzantium, the Imperial Centuries A.D. 610–1071.* New York: Random House, 1966.

Katz. Samuel. *Battleground – Fact and Fantasy in Palestine.* New York: Bantam Books, 1973.

Kellner, Jacob. *For Zion's Sake; World Jewry's Efforts to Relieve Distress in the Yishuv, 1869–1882.* Jerusalem: Yad Ben Zvi, 1976.

Kelly, J.B. *Britain and the Persian Gulf, 1795–1880.* Oxford: Clarendon Press, 1968.

Kitson-Clark, George S.R. *Churchmen and the Condition of England 1832–1885.* London: Methuen, 1973.

Kidd, B.J. *The Church of Eastern Christendom from A.D. 451 to the Present Time.* New York: Burt Franklin, 1973.

———. *A History of the Church to A.D. 461.* 3 vols. Oxford: Clarendon Press, 1922.

Kochan, Lionel. "The Life and Times of Sir Moses Montefiore." *History Today* 23 (January 1973): 46–53.

Landes, David. "Palestine Before the Zionists." *Commentary* 61 (February 1976):47–56.

Lewis, Bernard. *The Emergence of Modern Turkey.* London and New York: Oxford University Press, 1961.

Lobanov-Rostovsky, A. *Russia and Europe, 1825–1879.* Ann Arbor, Mich.: George Wahr, 1954.

MacDonald, Duncan B. *Development of Muslim Theology.*

Jurisprudence and Constitutional Theory. New York: Russell & Russell, 1965.

Mange, Alyce Edythe. *The Near Eastern Policy of the Emperor Napoleon III.* Westport, Conn.: Greenwood Press, 1975.

Ma'oz, Moshe. *Ottoman Reform in Syria and Palestine 1840–1861: The Impact of the Tanzimat on Politics and Society.* Oxford: Clarendon Press, 1968.

Mardin, Serif. *The Genesis of Young Ottoman Thought: A Study in the Modernization of Turkish Political Ideas.* Princeton, N.J.: Princeton University Press, 1962.

Margolis, Max L., and Alexander Marx. *A History of the Jewish People.* Philadelphia: Jewish Publication Society, 1927.

Marlowe, John. *A History of Modern Egypt and Anglo-Egyptian Relations, 1800–1956.* Hamden, Conn.: Archon Books, 1965.

Marmorstein, Emile. "European Jews in Muslim Palestine" *Middle Eastern Studies* 11 (1975):74–87.

Marston, Thomas E. *Britain's Imperial Role in the Red Sea Area 1800–1870.* Hamden, Conn.: The Shoe String Press, 1961.

Mattingly, Garrett. *Renaissance Diplomacy.* Baltimore: Penguin Books, 1964.

Mazar, Benjamin. *The Mountain of the Lord: Excavating in Jerusalem.* Garden City, N.Y.: Doubleday, 1975.

Miller, William. *The Ottoman Empire and its Successors 1801–1927.* New York: Octagon Books, 1966.

"Misgav Ladach, at 120, Takes a Look Ahead." *The Jerusalem Post,* November 3, 1975.

Morganstern, Arie. *The Pekidim and Amarcalim of Amsterdam and the Jewish Community in Palestine, 1810–1840.* Jerusalem: Hebrew University Unpublished Doctoral Dissertation, 1981.

Mosse, W.E. "Russia and the Levant, 1856–1862: Grand Duke Constantine Nicolaevich and the Russian Steam Navigation Company." *Journal of Modern History* 26 (1954): 39–48.

———. *The Rise and Fall of the Crimean System.* New York: Macmillan, 1963.

Nicolson, Harold. *The Evolution of Diplomacy.* New York: Collier Books, 1966.

Ollendorf, F. "Jerusalem's Russian Compound." *The Jerusalem Post,* December 24, 1975.

Ostrogorsky, George. *History of the Byzantine State.* Translated from German by Joan Hussey. New Brunswick, N.J.: Rutgers University Press, 1969.

Pares, Sir Bernard. *A History of Russia.* New York: Alfred A. Knopf, 1946.

Patai, Raphael. *The Arab Mind.* New York: Charles Scribner's Sons, 1976.

Peters, Joan. *From Time Immemorial; The Origins of the Arab-Jewish Conflict Over Palestine.* New York: Harper & Row, 1984.

Puryear, Vernon J. *England, Russia and the Straits Question.* Berkeley: University of California Press, 1931.

———. *France and the Levant, From the Bourbon Restoration to the Peace of Kutiah.* Berkeley: University of California Press, 1941.

Redlich, Joseph. *Emperor Francis Joseph of Austria; A Biography.* New York: MacMillan, 1929.

Robinson, Howard. *Carrying British Mails Overseas.* New York: New York University Press, 1964.

Rodkey, Frederick Stanley. "Lord Palmerston and the Rejuvenation of Turkey, 1830–1839." *Journal of Modern History* 1 (1929): 570–93.

———. "Lord Palmerston and the Rejuvenation of Turkey, 1830–1841." *Journal of Modern History* 2 (1930):193–225.

———. "Reshid Pasha's Memorandum of August 12, 1839." *Journal of Modern History* 2 (1930):251–57.

———. "The Attempts of Briggs and Company to Guide British Policy in the Levant in the Interest of Mehmet Ali Pasha, 1821–1841." *Journal of Modern History* 5 (1933):324–51.

Roth, Cecil. *A History of the Marranos.* Philadelphia: Jewish Publication Society, 1947.

Saab, Hassan. *The Arab Federalists of the Ottoman Empire.* Amsterdam: Djambatan Press, 1958.

Sachar, Howard M. *The Course of Modern Jewish History.* New York: World Publishing, 1958.

Samuel, Maurice. *Harvest in the Desert.* Philadelphia: Jewish Publication Society, 1945.

Schölch, Alexander. "European Penetration and the Economic Development of Palestine, 1856–1862." In *Studies in the Economic and Social History of Palestine in the Nineteenth and Twentieth Centuries,* edited by Roger Owen. Carbondale and Edwardsville: Southern Illinois University Press, 1982.

Schroeder, Paul W. *Austria, Great Britain and the Crimean War; The Destruction of the European Concert.* Ithaca and London: Cornell University Press, 1972.

Scult, Mel. "English Missions to the Jews – Conversion in the Age of Emancipation." *Jewish Social Studies* 35 (1973):3–17.

Serpell, David R. "American Consular Activities in Egypt, 1849–1863." *Journal of Modern History* 5 (1938):344–63.

Shotwell, James T. *Turkey at the Straits.* Freeport, N.Y.: Books for Libraries Press, 1971.

Sontag, Raymond James. *European Diplomatic History, 1871–1932.* New York: Appleton-Century-Crofts, 1961.

Spillman, General Georges. "150 Ans de Relations Franco-Libanaises." *Revue Historique des Armées* 3 (1976):32–54.

Taylor, A.J.P. *The Habsburg Monarchy 1809–1918.* New York: Harper & Row, 1965.

Temperley, Harold William. *England and the Near East: the Crimea* (Vol. II). Hamden, Conn.: Archon Books, 1964.

Theissen, Gerd. *Sociology of Early Palestinian Christianity.* Translated from German by John Bowden. Philadelphia: Fortress Press, 1978.

Thomas, Daniel H. "Princess Lieven's Last Diplomatic Confrontation." *The International History Review* 5 (1983): 550–60.

Thomas, J. and T. Baldwin. *Lippincott's Pronouncing Gazetteer.* Philadelphia: J.B. Lippincott, 1866.

Tibawi, Abdul Latif. *British Interests in Palestine 1800–1901; A Study of Religious and Educational Enterprises.* London: Oxford University Press, 1961.

Vilnay, Zev. *The Guide to Israel.* Jerusalem: Hamakor Press, 1972.

Vryonis, Speros. *The Decline of Medieval Hellenism and the Process of Islamization from the Eleventh through the Fifteenth Century.* Berkeley: University of California Press, 1971.

Warner, Philip. *The Crimean War; A Reappraisal.* New York: Taplinger, 1973.

Warringer, Doreen. "Land Tenure in the Fertile Crescent." In *The Economic History of the Middle East 1800–1914,* edited by Charles Issawi. Chicago: University of Chicago Press, 1975, pp. 71–78.

Webster, Sir Charles. *The Foreign Policy of Palmerston 1830–1841, Britain, the Liberal Movement and the Eastern Question* (in 2 vols.). New York: Humanities Press, 1969.

Zenner, W.P. and Gutmann, D. "Aquili Agha: The Strongman in the Ethnic Relations of the Ottoman Galilee." *Comparative Studies of Social History* 14 (1972): 169–92.

JOURNAL LITERATURE EXCLUSIVELY IN HEBREW

All of the articles listed below are in the Hebrew language publication *Cathedra,* which deals exclusively with Palestinian/Israeli history. Language barriers prevent them from being available to all scholars, but as their subject matter is germane to this work, they merit placement in this bibliography. A phonetic rendition of the Hebrew title is given, followed by an English translation, the volume, year, and page numbers.

Avitzur, Shmuel. "Terumatha shel Petach-Tiqva Lakeduma Hatiklaei Ve-Hat'asiatei shel Ha-Aretz B'shalavim HaRishonim Lakiuma (1878–1918)." ['The Contribution of Early Petach

Tiqva to the Agricultural and Industrial Development of the Land of Israel (1878–1918)"]. 10 (1979):129–41.

Barnai, Yaakov. "Meamda shel 'Harabanuth Ha-k'lalath" B'Yerushalayim B'tekufa Ha-Ottomanith." ["The Status of the 'General Rabbinate' in Jerusalem in the Ottoman Period"]. 13 (1979):47–70.

Bartal, Israel. "Yehudei Mizrach-Europa V'eretz Yisrael (1777–1881) Ha-aliyoth U'mivneh Ha-Yishuv Ha-ashkenazi." ["Jews of Eastern Europe and the Land of Israel (1777–1881); the Immigration and Building of the Ashkenazic Community"]. 16 (1980):3–12.

———. "Yishuv Yashan Ve'yishuv Chadash-Hadimui Ve'hamitziuth." ["The Old and the New Yishuv – Image and Reality"]. 2 (1976):3–19.

Bartur, Ron. "Parshioth Nivcharoth B'yachsei Haconsulia Ha-Americanith B'Yerushalayim im Ha-Kehilla Ha-Yehudith B'Meah 19, 1856–1906." ["Episodes in the Relations of the American Consulate in Jerusalem with the Jewish Community in the 19th Century (1856–1906)"]. 5 (1977):109–43.

Eliav, Mordechai. "Chevlai B'raishith shel Petach-Tiqva." ["The Birth Pains of Petach Tiqva"]. 9 (1978):3–25.

———. "Ha-consulia Haustrith B'Yerushalayim V'Hayishuv Hayehudi." ["The Austrian Consulate in Jerusalem and the Jewish Community"]. 18 (1981):73–110.

Freidin, Israel. N'siunoth Harishonim L'hakmath Beth-Cholim B'Tiveria B'Meah 19." ["First Attempts to Establish a Hospital in Tiberias in the 19th Century"]. 22 (1982):91-112.

———. "'Bikur Cholim Perushim' B'Yerushalayim M'Chevra L'Beth Cholim." ["'Bikur Cholim Perushim' in Jerusalem – from Society to Hospital"]. 27 (1983):117–140.

Friedman, Isaiah. "M'shtar Ha-capitulazioth Vayechsa shel Turchia LaAliya V'laha-tayeshuvoth 1856–1897." ["The Effect of the System of Capitulations on the Attitudes of the Turkish Government Towards Immigration and Settlement 1856–1897"]. 28 (1983):47–62.

Halevi, Shoshana. "Pardes Montefiori." ["The Montefiore Orange Grove"]. 2 (1976):153–67.

Israeli, Amihud. "Letoledoth Ha-zeitim V'hashemen Ba-Galil U'vebekaath-Beth Kerem B'tekufa Ha-Ottomanith U-vetekufath Ha-mandat." ["On the History of Olives and Olive Oil in the Galilee and the Beth-Hakerem Valley in Ottoman and Mandatory Times"]. 15 (1980):95–106.

Kaniel, Yehoshua. "Iggereth Ha-Rav Kalischer el Eliezer Raab." A Letter from Rabbi Kalischer to Eliezer Raab"]. 16 (1980): 153–60.

Karagila, Zvi. "L'koreoth Hachaluka B'Eretz-Yisrael." ["Sources on Chaluka in the Land of Israel"]. 20 (1981):56–76.

Kark, Ruth. "Ha-kehilla Ha-Yehudith B'Yaffo B'sof Ha'tekufath Ha'Sultan Ha'Ottomani." ["The Jewish Community in Jaffa at the End of the Ottoman Regime"]. 16 (1980):13–24.

———. "Pe'iloth Iri'ith Yerushalayim B'sof Ha-tekufa Ha-Ottomanith." ["Activities of the Jerusalem Municipality at the End of the Ottoman Period"]. 6 (1977):74–94.

Karmon, Yehuda. "Ha-moroth B'nof Ha'iruni shel Yerushalayim Be'Meah 19." ["Changes in the Urban Landscape of Jerusalem in the 19th Century"]. 6 (1977):38–73.

Katz, Shaul. "'Ha-telem Ha-rishon' – Ideologia, Ha-teyeshuvoth Vchekelioth B'Petach-Tiqva, B'asor Ha-shanim Harishonoth Leka'umah." ["'The First Furrow' – Ideology, Settlement and Agriculture in Petach Tiqva in its First Decade"]. 23 (1982): 7–124.

Kovac, Zvi. "Ha-aliya M'Mizrach Europa L'Eretz Yisrael B'emtsa Ha-meah 19." ["The Immigration from Eastern Europe to the Land of Israel in the Mid-Nineteenth Century"]. 9 (1978):193–204.

Kressel, G. "'Masa'oth Shime'on' – Hasefer U'mechavero Meah Shanah L'hof'ath 'Masa'oth Shimeon.'" ["A Journey to the Holy Land – 1870' The Book and its Author"]. 14 (1980): 181–202.

Landman, Shimon. "Ha-aroth L'tsurath Beth-Ha-megurim Ha-

Yerushalmi Ha-Aravi Bemeah 19." ["Notes on the Structure of Nineteenth Century Arab Dwellings in Jerusalem"]. 25 (1982):177–82.

Parfitt, Theodore. "Ha-consulia Ha-tsarfatith Ve-ha-yishuv Ha-Yehudi B'Eretz Yisrael B'meah 19." ["The French Consulate and the Jewish Yishuv in the Land of Israel in the 19th Century"]. 5 (1977):146–61.

Ram, Hanna. "Ha-techeloth shel Avodath-Adama B'ydai Yehudim B'ayazur Yaffo." ["The Beginnings of Jewish Agriculture in the Jaffa Region"]. 6 (1977):20–37.

Sapir, Shaul. "Mekoroth Chevroth Ha-mission Ha-Anglicanith She'paolo B'Yerushalayim Uv'eretz Yisrael B'meah 19 v'ad Ha-milchameth Ha-olam Ha-rishona."' ["Sources Relating to the Anglican Missionary Societies active in Jerusalem and the Land of Israel in the Nineteenth Century and Until World War I"]. 19 (1981):155–70.

Schur, Nathan. "Ha-yechas Ha-mispri bain Batei-Av Lesach'col Ha-nefashoth B'irei Eretz-Yisrael B'tekufa Ha-Ottomanith." ["The Numerical Relationship Between the Number of Households and the Total Population in the Cities of the Land of Israel During the Ottoman Period"]. 17 (1980):102–106.

Simon, Rachel. "Ha-maavak al Ha-m'komoth Ha-kedoshim L'notsroth B'Eretz Yisrael B'tekufa Ha-Ottomanith, 1516–1853" ['The Struggle for the Christian Holy Places in the Land of Israel in the Ottoman Period, 1516–1853"). 17 (1980):107–26.

Tennenbaum, Mark. "Ha-Consulia Ha-Britith B'Yerushalayim, 1858–1890." ["The British Consulate in Jerusalem 1858–1890."] 5 (1977):83–108.

Thalmann, Naftali. "Mosedoth Germanith V'ha-chevroth M'checker She'hukmo B'meah 19 Lecheker Eretz Yisrael V'limuda." ["German Exploration Associations and Institutes in the Nineteenth Century Land of Israel"]. 19 (1981):171–80.

NEWSPAPERS AND PERIODICALS, 1838–80

American Whig Review (New York), 1850–52.

Atlantic Monthly, 1857–80.
Baltimore American & Commercial Advertiser, 1849–58.
Blackwood's Magazine, 1849–58.
DeBows Review, 1849–58.
Edinburgh Review, 1849–58.
Harper's Magazine, 1850–80.
Harper's Weekly; A Journal of Civilization, 1857–60.
Historical Magazine (Boston), 1857–58.
Living Age, 1849–58.
New York Times, 1851–80.
North American Review, 1849–58.
Quarterly Review (London), 1849–58.
The Southern Quarterly Review (New Orleans), 1849–58.
The Times (London), 1838–1880.

Index

Ben Yehuda, Eliezer, 188

Ben Zakkai, *See* Yohanan Ben Zakkai

Berat, issuance of a, 154

Berlin, city of, 65, 85, 103, 109, 111–113, 166; Congress and Treaty of, 174, 175

Bernstorff, Albert, Count von (Prussian ambassador to Great Britain), 113

Beth Din, 142, 159, 169

Bethlehem, city of: Christian churches in, 60, 83, 90; population of, 28, 41

Bidwell, John, 62

Bikur Cholim Hospital, 147

Birthday celebrations of sovereigns, 72, 73, 98

Bishop of Jerusalem, Anglican. *See* Anglican Church

Bishop of Jerusalem, Russian Orthodox, 128

Bismarck, Count (later Prince) Otto von, 172–174, 183, 184

Black Sea, 32, 129, 172

Bonds, Russian government, 93

Bordochan (Bordaki), Rabbi Isaiah, 136

Botta, Paul-Emile (French consul), 94, 95, 106, 110, 190

Brabant, Leopold Louis Philippe Maria Victoria, Duke of (later Leopold II, King of the Belgians), 99

Brabant, Maria Amelia, Duchess of (later Queen of the Belgians), 99

Bracco, Latin Patriarch Vincent, 191

Buchanan, James (minister to Great Britain and president of the United States), 155

Bulgar Revolt, 174

Bunsen, Chevalier Christian Charles, Baron, 66

Byzantine Empire, 37, 38, 58

C

Cable, oceanic, 164, 165

Caboga-Cerva, Bernhard Count von (Austrian consul), 170, 190

Cadi, office of, 42, 51, 72, 77, 78, 97, 98, 139

Cairo, city of: as capital of Egypt, 33; foreign consuls at, 71, 80

Caliph ul-Islam, Moslem religious title, 69, 117

Cambridge University, Jesus College of, 102

Campbell, Patrick, 63

Canning, Sir Stratford. *See* Redcliffe

Cannon salutes, significance of, 72, 73, 98, 100, 102, 120

Canterbury, Archbishop of, 66, 67

Capitulations, 38, 182

Casa Nuova, Roman Catholic pilgrim hospice, 99

Catafago, Y.B., 79

Catherine the Great, Empress of Russia, 39, 53, 60, 127

Catherwood, F., 44

Cemeteries, 121, 134, 142

Census, 41, 138, 146

Chacham Bashi. *See* Rishon l'Zion

Chalcedon, Council of, 57, 88

Charcoal, importation of, 77

Charles V of Habsburg, Holy Roman Emperor, King of Spain, 38

Chasseaud, Jasper, 79, 80, 82; Augustus, Edwin, and George Washington Chasseaud, 82

Index

Index

Pizzamano, Count Josef de
(Austrian consul), 71, 95, 99,
100, 106, 110, 111, 125, 190
Pobedonovstyev, Constantine
(Procurator of the Holy Synod
of the Russian Orthodox
Church), 188
Polish Revolt of 1863, 154
Ponsonby, John, Baron (later
Viscount), 63
Pope, Roman Catholic, 58, 59, 88, 130
Postal service, 26
Prellezo e Isla, Mariano (consul of
Spain), 193
Prisons, 80, 134
Procopios II, Greek Orthodox
Patriarch, 191
Procurator of the Russian Holy
Synod, 127, 188
Prokesch-Osten, Baron Anton
von (Austrian Internunzio to
Turkey), 115
Property Ownership by non-
Moslems, 16, 44, 117
Proselytization of Moslems by
Christians forbidden, 61
Protégés, Status of Consular, 75, 78,
132, 135, 136, 138–141, 147, 148,
157, 158, 162, 181, 182
Protestant churches, 60, 61, 63–66
Prussia. See Germany

Q
Quarantine, Turkish sanitary
regulations for port, 73, 74

R
Rabbinate, Ashkenazic, 134, 160, 171
Rabbinate, Sephardic. See Rishon
l'Zion

Rachel (Biblical matriarch), 178
Railroads, 54
Ramés y Villanueva, Salvador
(consul of Spain), 193
Ramla, town of, 74
Rayahs, 45, 52, 64, 65, 74, 78, 79, 89,
116, 119, 126, 127, 138, 139, 147,
148, 154, 157, 182, 186,
Rebekah (Biblical matriarch), 44
Redcliffe, Lord Stratford de: efforts
to establish an Anglican church
at Jerusalem, 65; and firman of
Hatti-Humayun, 116–118; and
his influence at Constantinople,
91, 112, 118, 122, 126, 146; role in
Crimean War, 115
Reouf Pasha, governor of Jerusalem
and of Palestine, 192
Reshid Pasha, wali or governor-
general at Damascus, 170
Reshid Pasha, Grand Vizier, 70
Rhodes, Albert (United States
consul), 193
Rishon l'Zion, Office of, 51, 52, 55,
133, 134, 167, 168, 170, 171, 192.
See also Sephardim
Road construction in Palestine, 23
Rogers, Edward Thomas (British
consular chancellor at
Jerusalem, later vice consul at
Haifa), 107
Roman Catholicism, 38, 39, 59, 60,
63, 65, 75, 83, 87, 88
Rome, city of, 57, 58
Rose, Colonel Hugh Henry, First
Baron Strathnairn, 67, 136, 137
Rosen, Dr. Georg (Prussian consul),
91, 95, 105, 106, 108–114, 126, 131,
157, 158, 169, 170, 191
Rosen, Mrs. Georg, 95